Minoan Kingship and the Solar Goddess

Minoan Kingship and the Solar Goddess

A Near Eastern *Koine*

NANNO MARINATOS

UNIVERSITY OF ILLINOIS PRESS
Urbana, Chicago, and Springfield

Manufactured in the United States of America
C 6 5 4 3 2
∞ This book is printed on acid-free paper.

Library of Congress Cataloging-in-Publication Data
Marinatos, Nanno.
Minoan kingship and the solar goddess : a near Eastern *Koine* /
Nanno Marinatos.
p. cm.
Includes bibliographical references and index.
ISBN 978-0-252-03392-6 (cloth : alk. paper)
1. Minoans—Religion. 2. Minoans.
I. Title.
BL793.C7M335 2009
299'.1—dc22 2008029475

For Stylianos Alexiou and Othmar Keel,
who understand the ancient world

Contents

Preface ix

1. Introduction 1
2. The King and Queen in Art 12
3. The King and Queen as High Priests 32
4. Thrones of Gods—Thrones of Kings 50
5. The House of God 66
6. Who Sees the Gods Face to Face? 78
7. Minoan Prophecy and Royal Power 86
8. The Cosmic Mountain as a Frontier 103
9. The Double Axe, the Ankh, and the Ox Head 114
10. The Rosette, Half-Rosette, and "Incurved Altar" 131
11. Minoan Afterlife Beliefs 140
12. The Solar Goddess of Kingship 151
13. The Storm God 167
14. Translating the Gods of the Religious *Koine* 186
15. Conclusions: A Tribute to Sir Arthur Evans 193

Notes 197

Bibliography 225

Figures and Credits 247

Index 255

Preface

When I started writing this book, I thought that a few additions to *Minoan Religion* (1993) in the light of new evidence would suffice to produce a revised version. I was wrong. After the first few months, I realized that corrections and additions were not sufficient for a book written in the 1990s. My own view on Minoan society and religion had developed and even changed substantially on several points over the years. What was needed, I realized, was not a revision but a new frame of interpretation. My increasing familiarity with Egyptology and Near Eastern literature and history opened my eyes to aspects to which I was oblivious before, but my increasing familiarity with the scholarship of the past was equally effective in this. As I read and reread the four volumes of Evans's *Palace of Minos,* I was struck by the tremendous achievement of a single man who analyzed (and to a great extent deciphered) everything about the Minoans known at his time and tried to create a coherent history out of material remains without the aid of texts. In addition he put it into the context of Egypt and (to a lesser degree) the Near East. His view about the extent of the Minoan sphere of influence in the Aegean (which was made more extreme through his controversy with Alan Wace) has been confirmed by the excavations of Spyridon Marinatos at Thera. Evans even predicted the Minoan presence in the Egyptian Delta, which is now conclusively proven by the excavations of Manfred Bietak at Tell el Dab'a, Egypt.

And yet, Aegean studies are moving faster and faster away from the path opened by Evans, with the result that some of his most basic insights are in danger of being lost in the fog of the past. One of his contentions was that the history of Minoan civilization is tightly interwoven with the history of kingship. Evans began his *Palace of Minos* with the emergence of the palatial epoch and ended it with the fall of the last king of Knossos. Modern scholarship is less interested in a historically interconnected world dominated by kings; it is more excited about theoretical anthropological models derived from the study of tribal societies. In this book I am returning to the path laid by Evans.

I would like to express my indebtedness to my colleagues and friends whose ideas have helped shape mine. Walter Burkert alerted Classical scholars to the idea of a cultural *koine*. But I also owe much to Othmar Keel, for he was the one to introduce me to the visual *koine* of Near Eastern/biblical times. Keel's contribution is invaluable. He created a conceptual apparatus through which Near Eastern iconography and biblical texts became meaningfully interrelated. To him and Stylianos Alexiou this book is humbly dedicated.

I also owe a lot to Keel's collaborators and students in Fribourg, Bern, and Zürich, especially Thomas Staubli, Sylvia Schroer, and Christoph Uehlinger.

I thank my friends in Crete at the Herakleion Museum who showed me their finds and shared their thoughts. In particular, I would like to mention Nota Dimopoulou and George Rethemiotakis.

In the field of Minoan studies, Ingo Pini has set the highest standards imaginable through the publication of the Minoan and Mycenaean rings. The present work would not have been possible without the *Corpus der minoischen und mykenischen Siegel* in Marburg, Germany.

To my friends in the discipline of the history of religions who have read various versions of the manuscript, I am deeply indebted. In alphabetical order they are: Paul Griffiths, Dimitris Kyrtatas, Einar Thomassen, and Nicolas Wyatt. I thank Kenneth Lapatin and Thomas Staubli for invaluable suggestions during the final stages of the book.

Vassiliki Pliatsika, Bill Regier, and Sebastian Anderson have edited the manuscript. To their acuity, advice, and patience I owe a great deal.

Errors have certainly remained, and I take full responsibility.

Minoan Kingship and the Solar Goddess

1

Introduction

"Throughout its course Minoan civilization continued to absorb elements from the Asiatic side . . ."
—Sir Arthur Evans (1921)

"Der kretisch-mykenische Kulturkreis gehört durchaus zur anatolisch-nordsyrischen Kulturgemeinschaft."
—Helmut Theodor Bossert (1944)

In the pre–World War II era it was not unusual for people to regard Crete as part of the larger Near Eastern world. This has gradually changed: in the field of Aegean studies an invisible border separates East from West. Minoan Crete has become a department of Greek culture and archaeology; Near Eastern departments, on the other hand, do not deal much with what lies west of Asia Minor. Maps of the Near East do not include Crete, whereas maps of the Aegean do not include the Near East. One of my tasks in this work is to resituate palatial Crete on a mental map that includes the Near East, specifically, Anatolia, Syria, the Levant, and Egypt. Such an undertaking re-creates, I think, what a hypothetical, second-millennium king residing in Ugarit would have taken for granted. As I see it, there is no doubt: Crete was included in the conceptual and political geography of the Near East.

Although modern popular writers associate Crete with Minos and the labyrinth, neither word is mentioned in our ancient Near Eastern sources.[1] For the inhabitants of the Syro-Palestinian coast and Egypt alike the name of the island was Kaphtor or Kaptaru, and its inhabitants were called Keftiu.[2] The island was perceived as being at the western periphery of the world, in the midst of the sea.

Most of the references to Kaphtor (Ugaritic *kptr*) are in Egyptian, Ugaritic, and biblical sources.[3] In Ugaritic myths, Crete is the kingdom of the craftsman god Kothar-and-hasis, and Kaphtor (*kptr)* is referred to as "the seat of his dwelling."[4] "Shapsh, . . . carry my voice to Kothar-and-Hasis in Crete (*kptr*)," we read in an Ugaritic prayer.[5]

This last information comes as a surprise: who is this Ugaritic god with a double name and why is he associated with Crete? It is often stressed that he was a god of crafts. It is less known that he was also a pilot of the sun goddess Shapsh(u), ferrying her back to the netherworld.[6] That a deity of transition to the beyond had his residence in Crete is not without significance and suggests that Ugaritic peoples perceived the island as the land of the setting sun in the far west. To this effect, a passage in an Egyptian papyrus, "as far as the Keftiu," lends its support.[7] Crete was thus considered to be close to the edges of the civilized world in the west, a land close to the gods and the setting sun (see Fig. 1.1). (In the minds of the Greeks of later times similar roles were allotted to the long-lived Ethiopians and the fictional Phaecians, who also lived close to the gods in the periphery of the universe). This much is known about the mythical position of Crete in the Egyptian and Ugaritic mind.

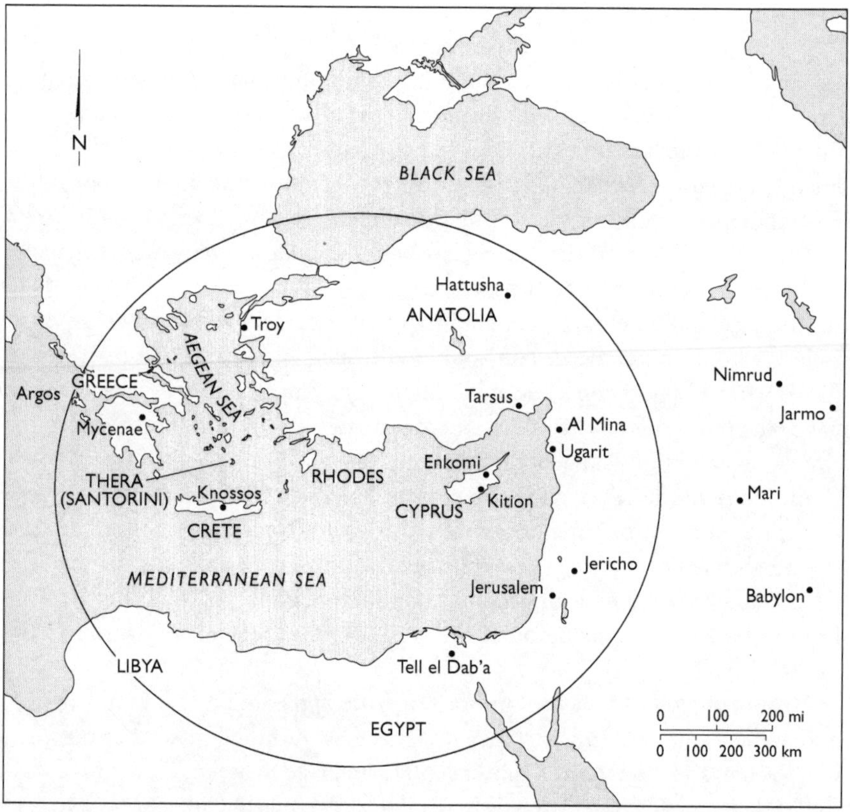

Fig. 1.1. East Mediterranean; Crete on the western periphery.

Chronology

The period covered in this book is that of the New Palaces, c. 1650–1390 BCE.[8] This era was designated by Sir Arthur Evans as the golden period of the Minoan kingdom, a period of peace and prosperity that he named *Pax Minoica.* It coincides with the late Hyksos dynasties and the beginning of the Eighteenth Dynasty in Egypt, and with the time of the Shaft Graves at Mycenae. It ends with the destruction of Knossos during the reign of Pharaoh Amenophis III.[9]

However, assigning absolute dates to this period is difficult, especially because the synchronization of the Aegean with Egypt and the Near East is a thorny and as yet unresolved matter. Much publicity is given today to dating methods based on natural science, which are deemed more accurate than archaeology. According to these methods, the New Palace period is given much higher dates than the ones arrived at by Evans. His synchronization scheme, revised by Peter Warren and Vroney Hankey (see Table 1), has much to recommend it, however, whereas natural science methods have not proven to be either totally accurate or completely uncontroversial.[10] Natural scientists work with hypotheses (as do scholars in the humanities), and their methods and tools may conflict among themselves.

The adoption of high or low chronology does not change the substance of my arguments because the political and economic factors that shaped kingship in Egypt and the Near East were the same in the seventeenth and sixteenth centuries, but the interregional relationships proposed in this book work best with the lower chronology given by Evans.[11]

Table 1.1. Minoan Kingdom Absolute Dates and Historical Eras

3650–3000 BCE	EM I	Pre-Palatial Period
2900–2300 BCE	EM II	
2300–2160 BCE	EM III	
2160–1979 BCE	MM IA	
1979–1700/1650 BCE	MM IB–MM IIIA	Old Palace Period
1650– BCE	MM IIIB	New Palace Period
	LM I	Eruption of the Volcano c. 1500
1425–1390 BCE	LM II	Fall of Knossos
1390–1370 BCE	LM IIIA1	

Source: Approximate dates are drawn from Warren and Hankey 1989.

A Historical Sketch

If we adopt the low chronology of Evans, the Minoan kingdom reached its peak between the seventeenth and early fourteenth centuries BCE (with a high point between 1550 and 1450). As stated previously, this was the period of the late Hyksos dynasties and the Eighteenth Dynasty in Egypt, a time period when the Mitanni and Egyptian empires competed for Syro-Palestine. The chief international language from the fifteenth century on was a form of Akkadian. William Moran speaks of a "cuneiform culture," a written language that enabled kings and their vassals to communicate.[12] In addition to a common written language, we may also speak of a common culture and ideology. Marc Van de Mieroop suggests that the royal families ruling the large kingdoms of Egypt and the Near East acted as if they were one great family and the whole world were a village; he even speaks of the "club of the great powers."[13] Van de Mieroop knows that Mycenaean Greece was part of this group, but he cannot say much about it because of the lack of available written historical sources.[14] Crete is absent from his account, and naturally so because there are no readable texts to go by.

Yet Evans saw clearly the role of Crete in precisely such an international milieu. He posited that Knossos was a huge metropolis, composed of as many as eighty-two thousand inhabitants. "The position of Knossos must have been unrivalled even in the East side of the Mediterranean basin. No fenced city surely, on the Syrian coast, shut in by walls . . . had either the expanse or its population."[15] "Never again," he writes, "till the Roman Governors put a final stop to the internecine feuds of the Greek cities did Crete enjoy throughout its length and breadth such uniform prosperity. . . . There is much in all this that recalls to mind the general well being fostered by the *Pax Romana* in the best days of the Empire."[16]

Evans's vision of the Minoan kingdom is historically very plausible.[17] We may easily conceive it as a member of the "club of great powers," and if so, it must have shared in the religious, ideological, and cultural *koine* of the period. Crete had to offer what every Near Eastern king might want: a powerful navy. Sadly, we have no written evidence about the specific nature of the political relations of the Keftiu (Minoans) with the great kings (*Grosskönige*) of Egypt, the Mitanni, the Hittites, and the less powerful kings of Cyprus and Ugarit. But it is tempting to suggest that an alliance with the Minoan naval force was much sought after by the monarchs of the Eastern empires.[18] By the time of Tuthmosis III (fourteenth century BCE) the Minoan kings were surely vassals of the pharaoh, and this is why they are depicted as tribute bearers in the tombs of Rekmire, Senmut, and others.[19] Vassalage, however, does not necessarily mean enslavement, but rather a type of hierarchical relationship in the nature of the alliance. The pharaoh or some other world ruler, such as the Hittite king (*Grosskönig*), would be acknowledged as a ruler of the *cosmos* and the principal policymaker of the region, but he would not necessarily exact taxes from Crete. Because he could not administrate the empire without dependable allies, namely other kings who followed his general policy, he might require only loyalty in matters of world affairs.[20] The Cretan navy would have been invaluable to any world ruler of Asia or Egypt who desired safe trade and control of the seas. Similar models of world dominion in the Near East with dependence on Aegean fleets are attested later, in the sixth century BCE, when the great kings Croesus of Lydia, Amasis of Egypt, and the Persians cultivated relationships with the Greek tyrants to seek the aid of their navy.[21]

It was not only the great powers that interacted with Minoan culture, however. Areas of secondary political prestige interspersed with city-state kingdoms (such as Ugarit) are important for this study as well, especially Cyprus, Syria, and the Levant. Syria, in particular, must feature prominently in the discussion, because it was the great junction of civilizations. "This is where all the roads met, Greek, Hittite, Hurrian, Mesopotamian, and Egyptian," Martin West writes about Syria in the first millennium.[22]

Although Crete played a role in world affairs, letters from Keftiu (Minoan) kings are absent from the Amarna archives in Egypt. The reason is that Knossos had apparently fallen by the time of the reign of Amenhotep III.[23] The destruction seems to have been caused, or at least triggered, by indigenous developments: a series of earthquakes, according to Evans.[24]

The occurrence of earthquakes is not the complete explanation for the demise of kingship in Crete, however.[25] It is difficult to fathom why the royal house failed to recuperate from this disaster and why Knossos was not repaired on a grand scale. To aid our understanding of this situation, we must backtrack and take into account another major natural disaster that occurred in the Aegean: the eruption of the volcano of Thera. Volcanologists have recently concluded that this was one of the major eruptions in the history of the planet.[26] To be sure, this event had taken place many decades before the final fall of Knossos; yet it is hard to believe that it had virtually no effect on the subsequent fate of Minoan Crete, as has been argued by many scholars.[27] On the contrary, it is reasonable to postulate that the eruption must have changed the social landscape in a significant way.

One short-term effect must have been the destruction of the naval force, which as we have seen, played a major role in securing the position of Crete in world affairs. Another immediate challenge would have been the management of the crisis: getting rid of the dead bodies in the debris, coping with poisoned wells, taking care of homeless and wounded people, dealing with hunger and restlessness. The long-term effect is evident in the archaeological record: all the secondary palaces in key positions on the island disappeared and only Knossos was rebuilt. A more centralized and perhaps more rigid organization replaced the older one.

Knossos survived for several decades. Then, as we have seen, earthquakes struck again: "The end was sudden, and the evidence once more points to an earthquake as the cause, followed by a widespread conflagration and, doubtless, ensuing pillage of the ruins left. But on this occasion the catastrophe was final," writes Evans.[28] It must be the case that the earthquakes struck an already weakened state that was perhaps too monolithic by its centralization to respond to natural disasters and too weak to adapt to a changing world.

Evans made several important observations. The first is that the last dynasty of Knossos was more theocratic than its predecessors, and that it was more closely modeled on Near Eastern structures: "The increased vogue of certain religious symbols and the growth of sacerdotalism, which characterizes the latest palatial phase at Knossos, seems to have been largely due to influences, both Egyptian and Oriental."[29] This observation suggests a tighter connection with Egypt, perhaps a more strict vassalage. This idea of Evans is supported by the depiction of Minoans in Egyptian tombs at about the time of Tuthmosis III and by the presence of Minoan paintings at Tell el Dab'a dating to the time of Hatshepsut or early Tuthmosis III.[30]

The second observation of Evans is that the dynasty was more militaristic and aggressive than its predecessors. He concluded that the Minoan kings conquered the mainland and eventually transferred the seat of power there.[31] If we take these two observations seriously, we may arrive at a possible scenario regarding the changed political position of Crete in the international milieu in the decades before the final fall of Knossos. We shall return to this scenario after considering another important point.

Although Evans knew that the last dynasts of Knossos used a new administrative language written in the script Linear B, he did not know that it was Greek: the decipherment of the language did not take place until 1952, after Evans's death. In any case, he would not have wanted to believe that the mainlanders had conquered Crete during this last stage of Minoan kingship.[32] Today it is taken for granted that this is just what happened: the Greek-speaking Mycenaeans took over Knossos, established their language and culture, and ruled Crete by conquest. Evans was wrong according to the standard view today.[33]

I propose a modified hypothesis. I propose a dynastic fusion between Knossos and Mycenae, perhaps through marriages, resulting in a common Minoan-Mycenaean administrative language, a common religion, and a common foreign policy during the last era of kingship on Crete. I also envisage a tighter alliance with Egypt, which the Egyptians regarded as vassalage.

In any case, the ethnic identity of the last dynast of Knossos matters little for the assessment of the history of the institution of kingship on Crete. Whatever his cultural origin may have been, the last king of Knossos could not cope with the disaster caused by the earthquakes of c. 1390. Knossos was destroyed and became a site for squatters. "In the 'Whirlgig of time,' it was ordained that the resting place of the old Priest Kings should not be re-occupied by new comers," wrote Evans.[34]

The real reason for the fall of Knossos must remain obscure at the present. The adoption of a broad interregional perspective, however, may throw light on this puzzle. Perhaps the answer to why Minoan kingship came to an end will emerge in the future from the other side of the Aegean.

A Lens

If we are to appreciate the Minoans as a world power, we must understand the international code of communication between royal courts. We must try to construct a lens through which we can decipher and eventually read Minoan images as part of the visual *koine* of the broader region. This is the best we can do because of the sad lack of readable texts.

What is visual decipherment? A linguistic definition, as suggested by John Chadwick, may provide a useful analogy: "Cryptography is a science of deduction and controlled experiment; hypotheses are formed, tested and often discarded."[35] To test their hypotheses, linguists rely on bilingual or trilingual texts.

Images, as well, are a kind of script with codes that may be broken by cryptographic methods. For this to happen, however, we need multicultural visual data from both sides of the Aegean; no system is decipherable by reference to itself only. The visual signs need to be ordered in sense-making patterns, their morphology needs to be observed, and the syntax (the combination of the signs) needs to be compared and analyzed. A hypothesis can then be formed. A lens is constructed, and the reading provided by this lens is tested against the evidence.

The traditional lens has been Greek mythology. It is often taken for granted that Minoan culture reflects Greek myths. But this hypothesis (like all others) may need reexamination. There is much that the Greek myth hypothesis does not explain; here we may detect the biggest weakness of Evans's lens for reading Minoan religion. The projection of Greek myth onto the past does not satisfactorily explain Minoan deities as we see them in art (see Chapters 12–14). My hypothesis is that Minoan society and religion may better be understood with the help of data derived from Egypt, Syria, the Levant, Anatolia, and, to a lesser extent, Mesopotamia. Each of these cultures has, of course, distinct characteristics, but there is also a lot in common that may be termed a *koine*.[36] This broader regional *koine* will be the lens through which I will decipher images of kingship and the gods of Minoan Crete.

That such a religious and cultural *koine* existed between historical Greece and the Near East has now been proven beyond reasonable doubt by Walter Burkert and Martin West.[37] Burkert goes so far as to claim that Greek culture cannot be properly appreciated if we do not take into account what transpired culturally between the two sides of the Aegean: "Let us try to see what was there before Hellenism, and not only celebrate singular achievements but spell out the results of interaction and dialogue in a continuing East Mediterranean *koine*."[38]

The Bias of the Material: Minoan and Mycenaean Gold Rings

In this work, one of my main sources, but by no means the only one, is gold rings. They represent a biased material for the following reasons.

Access to gold was not easy in the second millennium BCE. This can be inferred clearly from the royal correspondence found at Amarna, the capital of the Egyptian empire in the fourteenth century BCE. In the letters exchanged between the Egyptian pharaoh and his "brothers" (allies or vassals) the issue is often gold. Indeed, it was so coveted that the writers of the letters employed various forms of flattery and pleaded to achieve their purposes. The Mitanni ruler Tushratta, for example, asks his "brother" to grant him more gold than was granted his father.[39] He even writes directly to Queen Teje, wife of Amenhotep III and mother of Amenhotep IV, to ask her to mediate on his behalf.[40]

Rulers are explicit about why they need it: they want to embellish their palaces or temples and increase their prestige. King Assur-uballit of Assyria writes, "Gold in your country is dirt; one simply gathers it up. Why are you so sparing of it? I am engaged in building a new palace. Send me as much gold as is needed for its adornment."[41]

Complaints about the quality of the gold sent are also evident in some of the letters that the pharaoh received. "You have sent me as my greeting gift, the only thing in six years, thirty pounds of gold that looked like silver."[42] This is the grievance of a Babylonian king to his Egyptian "brother."[43] Another king, Burr-Buriash, writes to the pharaoh: "As for your messenger whom you sent to me. The 20 minas of gold that were brought here were not all there. When they put it into the kiln, not 5 minas of gold were apparent."[44]

The concern that so many kings express about the quantity and quality of gold they want from Egypt has led Van de Mieroop to suggest that this raw material was an Egyptian monopoly in the second part of the second millennium. For the first millennium, we have Biblical texts: King Solomon asks the king of Tyre for gold (1 Kings 11:14 and 2 Chronicles 8:18).

The limited access to and the need for this precious metal throws light on how we understand the iconography of the Minoan rings. If the kings of Crete were dependent on Egypt for gold, they surely did not part easily with it. The subjects of the Minoan monarchs were dependent on the palace for access to gold as their own means of self-glorification. Consequently, it may be inferred that a king gave a gold ring only to a trusted and loyal emissary. If this is the case, the iconography of the rings is palace-controlled. This leads to the further thought that iconography reflects what the royal family wants to promote about itself and its relationship to the gods. For this reason, the Minoan rings are biased material.

"Historiography," writes Nicolas Wyatt, "has always been a public and collective genre, expressing the sense of cohesion and common tradition of a community; it has traditionally served the interests of the ruling class, which has historically had the power to suppress alternative stories of the community's past, and so has its primary roots in royal propaganda . . . it is thus ideological in purpose."[45] The same claim can be made for the rings of Minoan Crete: they are documents of royal ideology, not personal biographies or artistic experiments of a flourishing local bourgeois class.[46]

It is tempting to speculate on the role of the ring bearers in Minoan Crete.[47] I envisage them as high-level officials in the service of the royal house. I consider the rings to be *insignia dignitatis* of these officials; their iconography, however, does not reflect the specific identity of the ring bearer, but rather that of the king and queen to whom the ring bearer wants to relate. Such a view is congruent with what Near Eastern experts say about cylinder seals.[48] Often we find that the king and the gods are the principal protagonists on the cylinders and that the seal bearer is a servant of god and king alike.[49]

I suggest that the Mycenaean ring bearers had a similar role to the Minoan ones as emissaries of the king. The gems of this culture have the same iconography as the Minoan ones, and many of the Mycenaean rings must be of Minoan manufacture anyway, in some cases heirlooms. There is no real iconographical criterion for distinguishing Minoan from Mycenaean; therefore, I consider specimens from both the island and the mainland as equally valid sources for my analysis of kingship.[50]

Despite their different ethnic origins, Minoan and Mycenaean peoples seem to have converged totally in the sphere of royal ideology even before they merged, as I have suggested. The term *Minoan-Mycenaean,* which today is often viewed as imprecise, is still extremely useful and may need to be revived. It explains well the ideological unity of Minoan and Mycenaean iconography on the level of royal ideology.

How to Understand Mythology

In many respects, this work differs significantly from my *Minoan Religion,* published in 1993, in which the dominant methodology was the classification of the images into types and the creation of social categories (such as rites of passage). I thought then that we could understand Minoan religion with the help of anthropology. My classification criteria have proved to be somewhat useful, but they yielded limited results. I argued then that female deities are represented as nurturers and as one with nature, whereas male gods are represented as powerful and combative towards animals. The results of the present study confirm these early thoughts but go far beyond them because a narrative content has been added. This progress was made possible only by the adoption of the lens of a Near Eastern *koine*. In *Minoan Religion*, I saw the pattern but did not have the lens to read the narrative. I have changed my mind on certain issues, such as the use of the term *high priestess*, which (as I now know) has little social meaning in a theocracy. I then used the term *epiphany* in the same way as Fr. Matz (ecstatic revelation), but I offer a new view here, which has a social angle and places the royal couple in the center of the experience.[51]

The biggest pay-off of the adoption of a Near Eastern prism has been the deciphering of the central symbol of Minoan religion: the double axe. In 1993 I wrote, "We do not know what symbolic significance the double axe had for the Minoans. It is paradoxical that it is held by females rather than a male weather god. It obviously denotes power, but more we cannot say."[52] Applying a Near Eastern lens to Minoan iconography has enabled a new reading of the Minoan syntax as regards the double axe and symbols related to it. I have come to realize that they represent a cosmological system closely linked to the institution of kingship, which traditionally has an investment in world dominion.

Written Sources and Royal Libraries

The Minoans probably had literature written in the as yet undeciphered Linear A script. The fact that the only records that have survived were written on clay tablets or were inscribed on stone vessels may well be an accident of history because leather and papyrus do not survive. We must not assume that clay was the only, or even the main, medium on which writing was recorded. In fact, such a hypothesis is highly unlikely. It is far more probable that the main body of literature in Minoan Crete and Mycenaean Greece was written on leather or papyrus, for which linear scripts (as opposed to cuneiform) are particularly well suited.[53] Because such materials do not survive, this almost certainly means that we will never be able to retrieve the literature of the Minoans.

What are the chances that Minoan literature existed in written form? I think that they are high. All kingdoms (small or large) of the region around Crete had libraries. Why would Crete be an exception? Ugarit, which was more modest than Knossos, was especially multilingual and rich: tablets in Ugaritic, Akkadian, and Cypro-Minoan, among other languages, were found even in its houses.[54] It is therefore a historically plausible (indeed an unavoidable) postulate that Minoan palaces contained libraries and literature. If that were the case, it would be easy to understand why and how myths spread: exchange of written documents across the Aegean sea would have greatly facilitated the diffusion of the conceptual and religious *koine* of myths and symbols.

There is, of course, little chance that a Minoan library will ever be discovered. Fortunately, as has already been mentioned, images also tell a story. The task of reading Minoan culture through visual data is undertaken in the ensuing chapters.

2

The King and Queen in Art

Evans's vision of a priest king in Minoan palatial Crete is consistent with the traditions of the Ancient Orient. The king is the chief priest and presides in all major state festivals, as we can tell from Egyptian, Hittite, Ugaritic, Mesopotamian, and Syrian sources. He is the only legitimate intermediary between the human and the divine worlds, and it would be unthinkable for Near Eastern specialists to write an account of festivals without references to the king.[1] If kings existed in Minoan Crete in the second millennium BCE, then the concept of priest king is self-evident, indeed inevitable. The king is the high priest *ex officio.*

Yet, Evans's notion of sacral kingship, which was once acceptable,[2] has been subject to much criticism recently and characterized as an outdated Victorian model. It is considered a reflection of British kingship on the one hand and nineteenth-century anthropology on the other.[3] Instead, scholars prefer to postulate chiefdoms based on social models that would be hardly at home in the mid second millennium BCE.

It must be admitted that there are some problems with Evans's view of *papa re,* as he called his Minoan king.[4] It was partially constructed with king Minos of Greek myth in mind, and it was one of Evans's weaknesses that he relied on Greek mythology for reconstructing society in Minoan Crete. He, of course, followed the interpretative models of his time, believing that legends are remembrances of things past. With the impact of structuralism and semiotics, we have learned to read stories in a different way, as systems of social codes that reflect the mindset of the time of their creation rather than the truths of the past.[5] If this prism is adopted, we can see clearly that the legend of king Minos is a mirror of Athenian social realities, not of Bronze Age Cretan institutions. Minos is constructed as an opponent to the Athenians and as the archetypal bad tyrant (this much is acknowledged by Evans). By associating Minos with the palace of Knossos, the great British scholar created a set of associations for the general public that are as unwarranted as they are false. Many may not even realize that *Minoan* is a term coined by Evans, and that we do not really know what the people of Crete called themselves in the Bronze Age. A reasonable guess is that they called themselves *Kephtiu,* because this is how they were known in the Near East (see Chapter 1).

But Evans was far wiser than he appears to his critics. He did not construct his *papa re* on the basis of Greek mythology alone but relied also on the Near Eastern evidence: "the legendary account of Minos, like another Moses or Hammurabi, receiving the law from the divinity itself on the sacred mountain, may well be taken to cover the actual existence of a code associated with the name of one of the old priest-kings of Crete."[6]

Alternative Regime Models

It is important to explore the possibility of regime models of government in Minoan Crete between the seventeenth and fourteenth centuries BCE before we examine the issue of kingship. Some recent suggestions are that the island was ruled by aristocratic elites, which included a chief, a *primus inter pares;* sometimes the term *peer polity* is used.[7] Such models, plausible as they are from the anthropological point of view, are quite implausible for the sixteenth and fifteenth centuries BCE, a period of large empires and smaller kingdoms interconnected by a system of vassalage. Crete was part of a broad cultural domain that today we call the Aegean, although Evans called it Minoan with some justification, I think. For archaeological evidence fully supports the notion that Crete was a major political power in the Aegean. Cretan artifacts have been found throughout the islands and the coast of Asia Minor, especially in the sixteenth and fifteenth centuries BCE. It has been argued that this may imply nothing more than trade.[8] If so, it is hard to explain why tools of trade reflect Cretan standards, weights, and measures, and why the administrative language was written in the Minoan script Linear A. As well, trade does not adequately explain why Minoan religious symbols were used throughout the Aegean, and why they were eventually adopted by Mycenaean kings on the mainland.[9] The most economic explanation for the phenomenon of this homogenization is to postulate a major kingdom (dare we call it an empire?) centered at Knossos. Without a major king it is hard to imagine how piracy was eliminated and how effective international policy abroad was conducted.

Evans's kingship model still has followers today. Olivier Pelon and Massimo Cultraro have both argued the case on archaeological and iconographical grounds.[10] Philip Betancourt has made the case succinctly by reviewing the architectural and administrative data: "The evidence indicates that Cretan palaces had strong direction and the most likely situation requires a central political leader, which we would call king. No other system can adequately explain the scale of the evidence for social and economic advancement over a period of several centuries within a peaceful landscape."[11]

Detecting the Ruler in the Iconography

But where are these kings in Minoan art and how are they represented? Aegean specialists have a problem here because clear representations of the king seem to be absent. The "missing ruler iconography" has thrown doubt on the very existence of kingship, not to mention sacral kingship as Evans envisioned it.[12] First, we ought to consider the nature of our material and the accidents of historical preservation as regards what is missing. The closest we get to monumental representations are relief wall paintings, of which few have remained, but this is certainly due to chance. If we consider the few relief paintings that we do have, the Prince of the Lilies found at Knossos may be interpreted as a king (this figure will be discussed subsequently). It is perfectly possible to detect the king in Minoan art by using the same criteria as are used by Egyptian and Near Eastern art historians: crown, size, dress, *insignia dignitatis*, earrings, and chariot.

The Plumed Crown

Evans found a relief painting of a figure wearing a plumed crown topped with a lily/papyrus combination (Fig. 2.1). The crown made such an impression on him as a symbol of kingship that he used it as an emblem for his *Palace of Minos*, stamped on the cover in gold. This crown is worn by males and females alike in Minoan art (most frequently c. 1400 BCE), and it was adopted also by Mycenaean officials.

Before we discuss the crown of the Knossos figure, we may look at a ring impression from Knossos where a figure wears a similar one (Fig. 2.2). He is a muscular male, flanked by two massive dogs; this heraldic arrangement suggests that he is a god. He seems to be wearing a plumed crown, although the sealing is not well preserved on the top and the discernment of details is not possible.[13]

The plumed crown is also worn by sphinxes.[14] One example is an ivory mirror handle from a tomb near Knossos. It dates to the fourteenth century BCE and shows a sphinx wearing a plumed papyrus headdress (Fig. 2.3).[15]

So far we have seen that only divine figures and sphinxes wear this crown. It is perhaps important to digress and take a look at Syrian and Egyptian art. It is fully agreed that in Egypt the sphinx is a deified form of the pharaoh. This idea was not confined to Egypt alone. On Syrian seals with Egyptianizing features, sphinxes are likewise associated with the king.[16]

A good example of such royal association occurs on an Egyptianizing Syrian

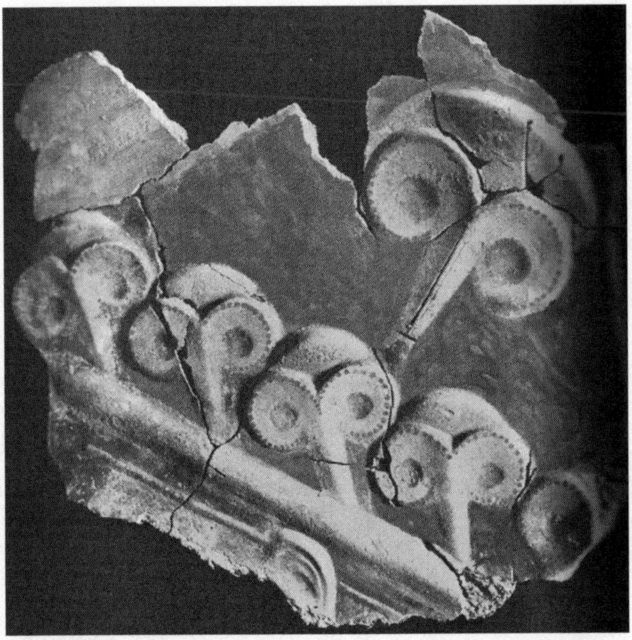

Fig. 2.1. Minoan plumed crown. Detail from Knossos fresco known as "Prince of Lilies."

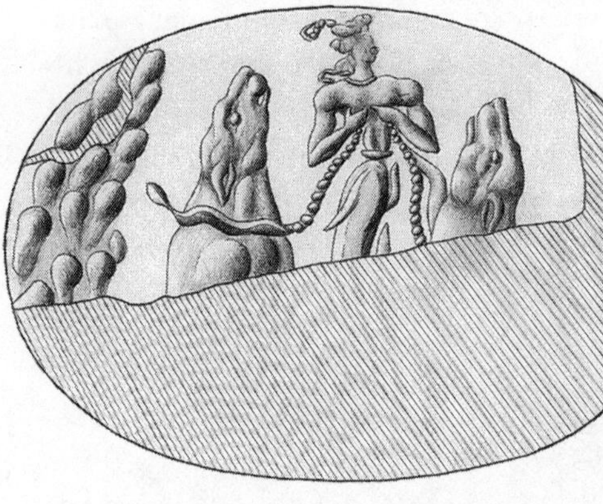

Fig. 2.2. God wearing plumed crown and flanked by beasts. Ring impression from Knossos.

Fig. 2.3. Sphinx wearing plumed crown. Ivory mirror handle from cemetery, Zafer Papoura, at Knossos.

seal dating to the Middle Bronze Age II B (1700–1600 BCE). Here, two sphinxes wear the royal atef crowns and flank winged sun discs (Fig. 2.4).[17]

I suggest that in Crete as well the sphinx has the same royal connotations linking kingship and the solar deity. The issue of what sphinxes mean cannot be pursued further here; suffice it to state that the plumed crown may be a mark of royalty when worn by humans. This hypothesis will be subsequently tested.

On a clay coffin from Hagia Triada (c. 1400 BCE), a woman with a plumed crown is shown twice, once on each side. She wears a long robe and a crown but note that the papyrus/lily plumed crown is attested securely only on one side. This woman cannot be a goddess because she is officiating in sacrificial acts (Fig. 2.5). Can she be a priestess? This title does not provide the answer to our question because "high priestess" does not designate a profession: in the second millennium BCE the high priestess is always the queen *ex officio*.

Consequently, this woman is the queen. The further inference is that the plumed crown designates three categories: gods, sphinxes, and royalty. There is a further inference: these categories are visually and conceptually linked.

We now may finally return to the examination of the identity of the figure with the lily crown on the relief fresco from the South Propylon of the palace of Knossos.[18] It is incompletely preserved, but Evans and his artists, E. Gilliéron *père* and *fils*, made impressive reconstructions. (A replica made by Gilliéron *fils* still decorates the South Propylon of the palace of Knossos). Because the fragments are few and because there are no secure joins, the restoration has been contested. What remains besides the crown are the limbs and torso of a male figure with a lily necklace and a colorful codpiece. The skin is painted in a light reddish color, not the dark red that usually (it is believed) designates males; yet the costume and musculature leave no doubt as to the male anatomy. His

Fig. 2.4. Sphinxes wearing royal *atef* crown. Syrian seal.

Fig. 2.5. Officiating queen with plumed crown. Sarcophagus of Hagia Triada.

head has not been preserved, but Evans and the Gilliérons assumed that it was turned to the left so that the crown could be fitted on it. Wolf-Dietrich Niemeier recombined the fragments and suggested that the figure is a god facing to the right, and that the crown ought to be ascribed to a sphinx; however, no traces of such a sphinx were found (Fig. 2.6).[19]

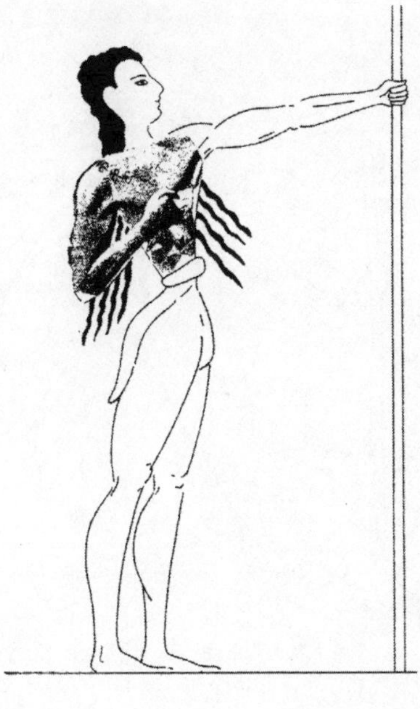

Fig. 2.6. "Prince of the Lilies" reconstructed as god. Fresco from Knossos, W-D. Niemeier's restoration.

Recently, Maria Shaw has found detailed evidence to support Evans's original reconstruction, noting that the lilies on the crown match exactly the lilies around the neck of the figure.[20] Evans's reconstruction therefore remains the most likely one and I present here the restoration executed by Gilliéron *fils* (Fig. 2.7). That the figure resembles the representation of a Hittite king (or prince) carved on a rock (Fig. 2.8), may be taken as an indirect confirmation that Evans and the Gilliérons were on the right track.

I conclude that the plumed crown is one of the most important visual criteria for identifying sacred kings and queens in Creto-Mycenaean art. The Knossian figure is a king, depicted in a prominent place at the South Propylon of the palace of Knossos, exactly where we would expect him to be. That the restoration of Evans has been so readily abandoned is astounding. It is the most economical reconstruction of all hitherto proposed because it makes coherent sense of all the existing fragments: the crown, the lily, the butterfly, and the limbs of a rigorous male. We shall meet the lily again in connection with the double axe (Chapter 9). One question remains: is the figure perhaps a god?[21] We need not decide between god or king at this point because the ambiguity may be deliberate suggesting the very notion that Evans promoted, namely, sacred kingship.

Fig. 2.7."Prince of the Lilies" reconstructed as king. Fresco from Knossos, E. Gilliéron and A. Evans's restoration.

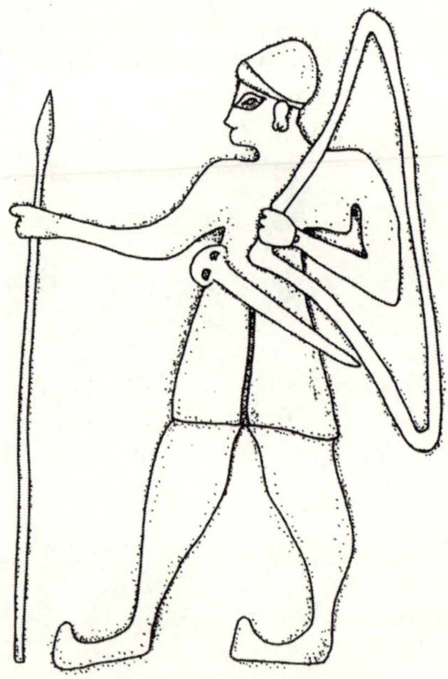

Fig. 2.8. Hittite king (or prince). Carved on the Anti-Taurus Mountains (Ala Dag).

The Long Syrian Mantle with the Seam (*Wulstsaummantel*)

Apart from the crown, there is another feature that may distinguish the Minoan king from ordinary people: a long fringed mantle with bulging seams worn obliquely over the shoulder. Precisely such a garment is worn by royal (or divine) figures in Mesopotamian, Syrian, Anatolian, and Levantine art. In a study of Syro-Palestinian seals, Sylvia Schroer has shown that the long robe with the fringe designates rulers or deified kings.[22] On a Syro-Palestinian seal of the nineteenth to eighteenth century BCE, for example, the ruler is represented with a long robe and a curved *lictus* standing in front of an altar (Fig. 2.9).[23] We find similarly dressed rulers on a Hittite silver vessel (Fig. 2.10), a statue from Qatna in Syria (Fig. 2.11), and a Middle Bronze Age scarab seal from Jericho (Fig. 2.12).[24] In all cases, the mantle in question designates gods *or* rulers, and this is the case throughout the second half of the second millennium.

We now return to the Minoan seals, where we see the same type of figures with longed fringed robes. They each carry an *insignium dignitatis,* an axe of the Syrian type, a mace, or a bow, or they are accompanied by a dolphin (Fig. 2.13).[25] There is no doubt that these are emblems of power; for this reason, it is difficult to see why the figures have been traditionally identified as priests rather than kings.[26] Somewhat surprisingly, one scholar has even suggested that they are middle administrators.[27] The dress would have been instantly recognizable as a *royal robe* by a second millennium viewer, whereas the mace, the bow, and

Fig. 2.9. Ruler with fringed mantle and curved *lictus* scepter in front of offering table and ankh. Old Syrian seal.

Fig. 2.10. Hittite king. Silver vessel.

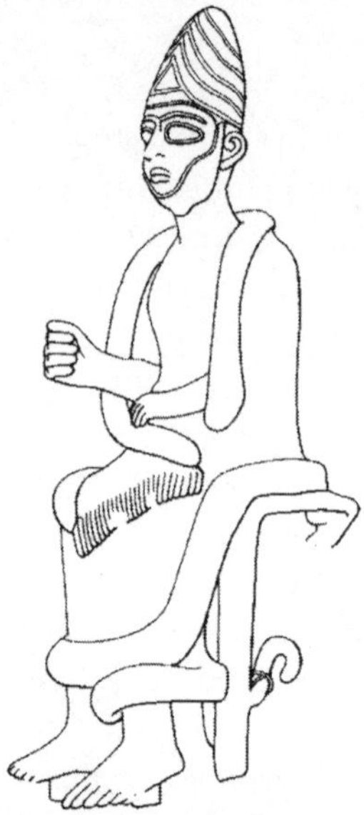

Fig. 2.11. Syrian god.
Statuette from Qatna, Syria.

Fig. 2.12. Ruler.
Scarab seal from Jericho.

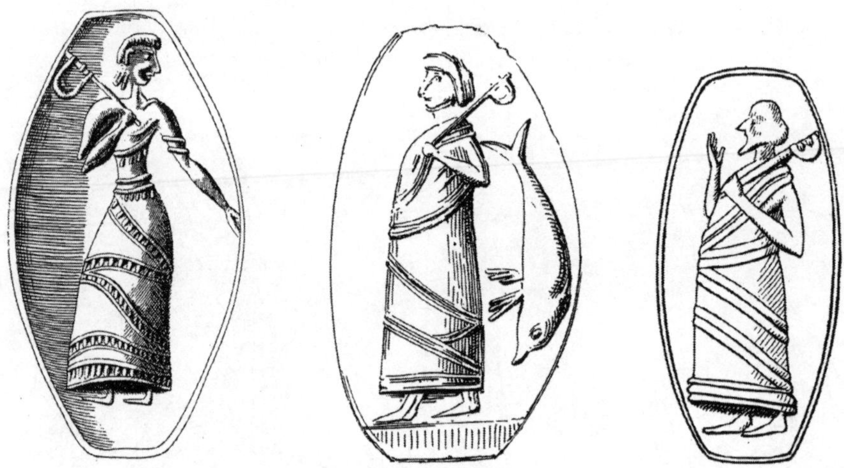

Fig. 2.13. Kings wearing long mantle and holding oval axe. Seals from Knossos.

axe would have been recognized as symbols of secular (and not sacerdotal) power. Oval axes are never used in sacrifice in Minoan art. Real specimens of axes such as held by the man in Figure 2.13 have been found on both sides of the Aegean in royal tombs, for example, at Syrian Ebla and at Vapheio on the Peloponnese. It is to be concluded, then, that these are royal insignia.[28]

If the fringed mantle is a sign of royalty in Mesopotamia, Syria, and Palestine, why should Crete be an exception? I conclude that if we apply a Near Eastern lens of interpretation to Minoan art, the long fringed mantle, coupled with insignia of power, identifies the king.

There is an additional important argument to associate the men with the long fringed mantle with divine kingship. On two seals, one from Vapheio and the other now in Geneva, the long-robed figures hold griffins on a leash (Figs. 2.14a and 2.14b).[29] This leaves no doubt that they are either gods or kings and that the iconography conflates divine and royal identity.

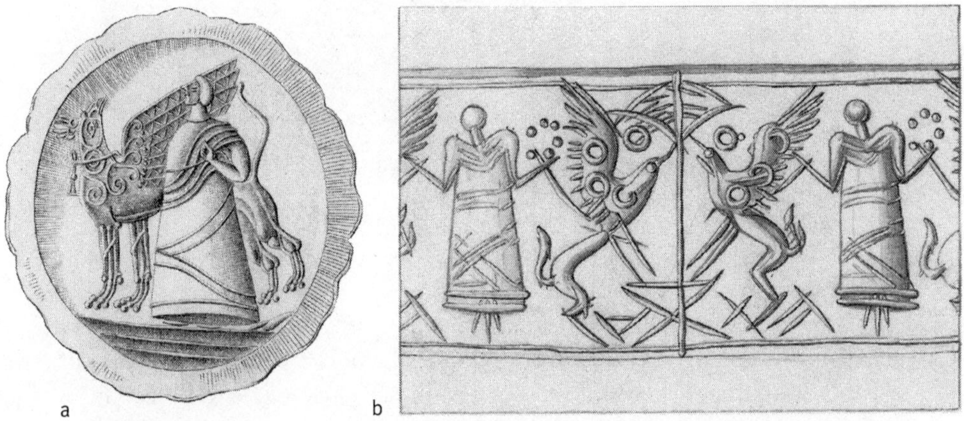

a b

Fig. 2.14. Gods or rulers with griffins. (a) Seal from Vapheio, Lakonia. (b) Cylinder seal.

The Dress with the Scales

The king can be recognized by yet another type of garment. On a steatite vessel from Hagia Triada, the so-called Harvester's Vase (Fig. 2.15), the subject is a procession of lively youths carrying pitchforks after a harvest. Some youths are singing, others are rattling the sistrum, and one has fallen. Yet one man, singled out by size and dress, is the undoubted leader of the procession. His garment consists of scales and ends in a fringe. Scholars have debated whether it is a metal cuirass or some other type of ritual dress; in any case, it is an unusual garment.[30] The leader is normally described as a priest; Evans, who thought of him as such, added that he was in an orgiastic singing state and described him as "a rustic Coryphaeus," borrowing the terminology from Greek tragedy. Evans and others who followed him were mistaken.[31] The leader of the procession is distinguished from his followers not just by size and dress, but also by his hairstyle, which matches exactly that of the men with the long fringed mantle on the seals shown in Figures 2.13 and 2.14). A village chief

Fig. 2.15. King with scale-garment, leading the harvest procession. "Harvesters' Vase" from Hagia Triada.

would not have been emblematized in such a way.[32] Dressed in a sacral dress, this man embodies both divine and secular authority acting as a leader of the harvest procession, similar to the Egyptian pharaoh involved in the feast of *opet.* "Throughout the Near East," writes Othmar Keel, "cultic responsibilities devolve upon the king."[33]

Portrait Seals

On some Minoan and Mycenaean seals are found men's heads with short hair, a forelock, and a beard; they have been excavated both at Knossos and in the royal graves of Mycenae (Fig. 2.16a).[34] The traditional interpretation is that these heads belong to priests.[35] As argued already, however, the term "high priest" does not denote a profession in theocratic kingships but a cult title of the king. I shall consequently argue that these typified portraits are royal ones. What supports this hypothesis is that the bearded heads have equivalents in the masks of the Mycenaean Shaft Graves as well as on the seals reviewed above (Figs. 2.13 and 2.16a-b). If we accept that the bearded masks represent kings, why must the portraits on the seals represent priests and not kings?

On two occasions, the bearded head is juxtaposed to another head that is smaller and not bearded, evidently representing a youth (Fig. 2.17).[36] This juxtaposition may best be explained if the heads represent father and son, namely two generations. Such an interpretation fits perfectly the template of kingship for which there exist Egyptian parallels.[37] The king promotes not just himself but also his successor and son.

a

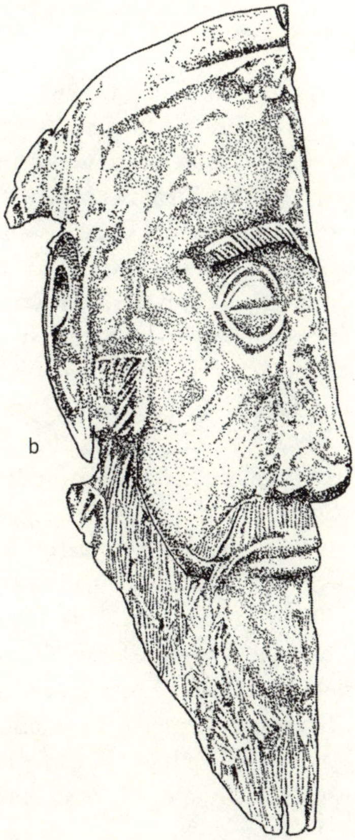

b

Fig. 2.16. Portraits of kings. (a) Seal impression from Knossos. (b) Gold mask/portrait from Mycenaean Shaft Grave, Grave Circle A.

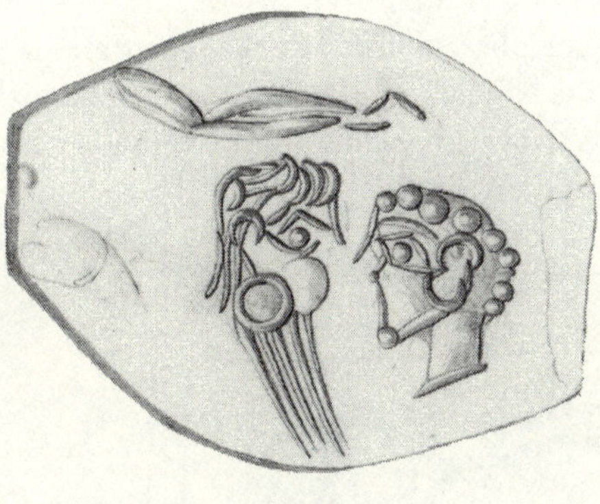

Fig. 2.17. King and prince, both wearing earrings. Stone seal.

A final note concerns the earrings shown on the man and youth in Figure 2.17, which are obviously marks of distinction. On a mural from Thera, a hoop earring is worn by a man with a plume on his head who stands in front of a palm.[38] The painting is currently being restored, and it seems that this man is associated with a griffin, a shrine, and a seated goddess. Thus, the painting from Thera confirms the hypothesis that figures wearing earrings and plumes on their heads are most likely rulers. A final confirmation is that hoop earrings also characterize Hittite kings (note, for example, that the Hittite king in Figure 2.10 wears such an earring).

The Chariot

Another way of identifying the king is by the presence of a chariot. The first visual occurrence of chariots in the Aegean coincides with the peak of kingship at *both* Mycenae and Knossos and with the Eighteenth Dynasty in Egypt.[39] This period is designated as MMIIIB/LMI for Crete and LHI for the mainland, and, because the terminology is somewhat puzzling to the nonspecialist, it must be explained that it is based on strata and ceramic sequence. If we look at contemporary Egypt and the Near East, we shall find that this is a period when strong world empires assert themselves: Egyptian, Mitanni, and eventually Hittite.

The chariot with the pharaoh appears on scarab seals in Egypt and Syro-Palestine early in the Eighteenth Dynasty but *not before* (Fig. 2.18).[40] If the charioteer is always the king in Egypt and Syro-Palestine, there is an *a priori* likelihood that the motif had a similar meaning in Minoan and Mycenaean art of the same period. Consequently, the concurrent appearance of the chariot on Crete and Mycenae enables us to detect an emblem of royal power and synchronize Crete with its neighboring kingdoms.

The visual formula king+chariot is most evident on the Shaft Grave *stelai* from Mycenae. There, the king rides alone without a charioteer. This detail should be noted because in Egyptian art as well the pharaoh rides alone. Sometimes the Mycenaean king, like the pharaoh of the Nineteenth Dynasty, is accompanied by a lion, which hunts its own prey (Fig. 2.19). This is surely the royal lion, which is not itself hunted but is an alter ego of the king.[41]

Fig. 2.18. Pharaoh in his chariot. Egyptianizing seal from Southern Palestine.

On Crete we have ring impressions that show a single charioteer riding his vehicle. The simultaneous appearance of war chariot iconography in the Minoan and Mycenaean worlds, Syria, Palestine, and Egypt must give us pause for thought. Few scholars would deny that the Mycenaean charioteer is a royal figure, but the fact that the same iconography appears in Crete has not drawn particular attention and the figures have not been identified as kings (Fig. 2.20).[42] There is, however, even more evidence to support the argument that the chariot is a royal vehicle in Minoan Crete. From the same time as the chariot sealings comes a ring imprint on which the vehicle is drawn by griffins. The passenger is, thus, undoubtedly a god (Fig. 2.21). The similarity of the iconography suggests that the charioteer is not an ordinary mortal but a king.

We now turn to a mural from Knossos depicting a chariot scene and dating to around 1400, a century or so later than the rings (Fig. 2.22).[43] A figure with a long robe is shown within a chariot, driving his vehicle. Behind the chariot is a bull, which leaves no doubt that the scene represents a festival.[44] If we use some of the criteria we have established, long fringed mantle and chariot, we can identify him as a king leading a bull to sacrifice in his function as high priest. Even the whip he holds in his right hand recalls the whip held by the pharaoh (compare to Fig. 2.18).

Fig. 2.19. King hunting in his chariot. Stele from Mycenaean Shaft Grave, Grave V.

Fig. 2.20. King in his chariot. Composite drawing made of ring imprints from Hagia Triada, Sklavokampos, and Akrotiri.

Fig. 2.21. God riding griffin-drawn chariot. Ring impression from Knossos.

Fig. 2.22. Processional scene showing king in chariot, leading bull to sacrifice. Mural from palace of Knossos.

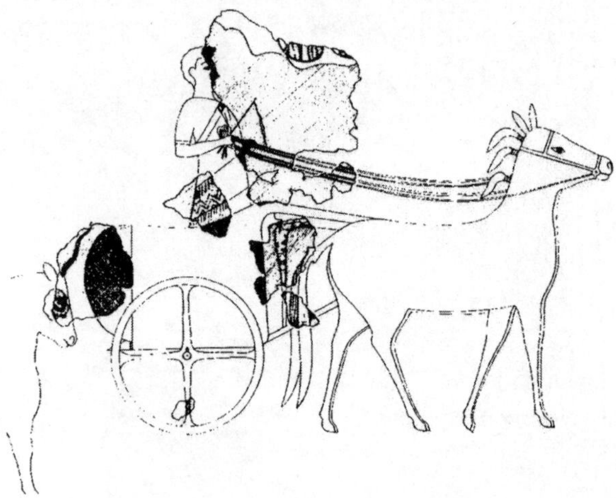

The Rosette: A Solar and Royal Symbol

There is yet another way to identify royal personages: the rosette or half-rosette design. A garment decorated with half-rosettes in its hem is attested on two frescoes found at the palaces of Knossos and Pylos. At Knossos, the mural was part of a large processional composition along the north-south axis of the West Corridor of the palace. The procession converged around a figure, the hem of whose dress is decorated with half-rosettes (Fig. 2.23a). Only the white feet of the figures are preserved in both paintings. They have, therefore, been identified as females. Let us assume that they are, indeed, women, although I am not as sure as other scholars that white always identifies females, I focus here on the royal identity rather than the gender of the figures in question.[45] A case can be made that the Knossos figure is the queen because the exact same design occurs in the throne room at Knossos (Fig. 2.23b). This means that there was a deliberate visual echo between the garment of the procession figure and the enthroned goddess in the throne room at Knossos (about which mention shall be made again in Chapter 4).[46] The Pylos figure is also royal if we follow this logic.[47]

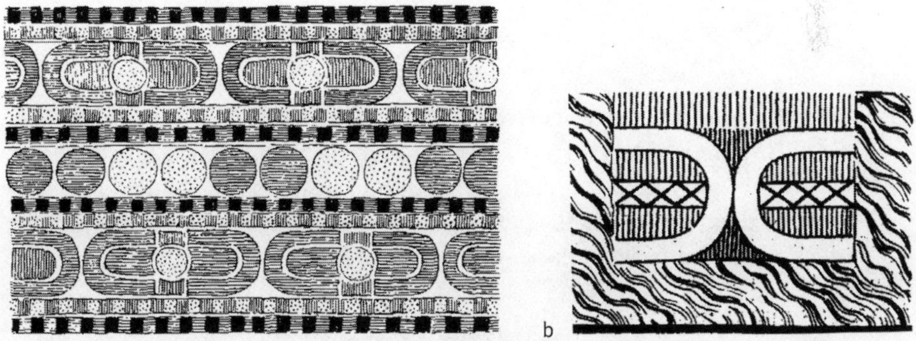

a b

Fig. 2.23. Half-rosette pattern. (a) From dress of female (goddess or queen) in Corridor of Processions from palace of Knossos. (b) From throne room at Knossos.

The rosette is also a central symbol on murals and stone friezes on the façade of the palace of Knossos.[48] There it takes the more naturalistic form of a stylized flower with a central core and petals (Fig. 2.24).[49]

Evans noted the importance of the rosette as a palatial emblem, but its meaning eluded him.[50] The subject of meaning will be addressed in Chapter 10; here we simply note that it is another visual emblem of kingship.

One more comparison will be useful to elucidate the rosette as a palatial emblem. A gold ring found in Tiryns and dating to the fourteenth century BCE depicts a goddess seated on a throne receiving tribute from her lion-demon

Fig. 2.24. Rosette motif. Façade mural from palace of Knossos.

servants (Fig. 2.25). Above her is the solar disc, the moon crescent, and shooting stars. Below the goddess is a frieze of split rosettes. The rosette frieze on this ring links the rosette with the enthroned mistress of heavens and shows that it is a royal and divine symbol at the same time. The palaces of Knossos and Mycenae were probably considered the earthly counterparts of the divine dwelling.

Fig. 2.25. Enthroned goddess served by lion-headed demons with sun and moon above and rosette frieze below. Gold ring from Tiryns.

The rosette persists as a royal insignium through the ages in the Aegean and the Near East. My first example is an armlet that belonged to a Mycenaean king buried in Shaft Grave IV in the second part of the sixteenth century BCE. It is stunningly decorated with a single rosette (Fig. 2.26a).[51] The second example is a relief of king Assurnassipal of Nimrud dating to the ninth century BCE (Fig. 2.26b).[52] Despite the time difference, the same type of bracelet marks the king.

a

b

Fig. 2.26. Rosette bracelets. (a) From Mycenaean Shaft Grave (sixteenth century BCE) (b) On relief showing King Assurnassipal of Nimrud (ninth century BCE).

Conclusions: King and God

Can Minoan royalty be distinguished in art? It has been argued here that yes, it can. In fact, there exist not one but several features through which king and queen can be identified: crown, dress, adornment, and even relative size. In the process, it has also been noted, however, that although the king and queen are distinguishable from other humans, it is less easy to differentiate them from gods. This ambiguity is valid also for Near Eastern seal iconography. Dominique Collon writes: "It is probable that deities were represented as wearing much the same type of dress as mortals, and high borne ladies probably wore clothes like those which the Syrian goddess is represented as wearing, with only the headdress to mark the difference." However, notes Collon, the tall oval headdress is not an absolutely secure criterion for distinguishing kings from gods because, in some cases, it lacks the horns that unambiguously determine gods. Collon concludes that "some figures must remain in doubt."[53]

We move to thirteenth century Hittite Anatolia. In Figure 2.27 we see the Hittite king and his tutelary sun god, both from the rock sanctuary of Yazilikaya. In both examples, the figures wear the long robe: king and god are dressed exactly alike.

a

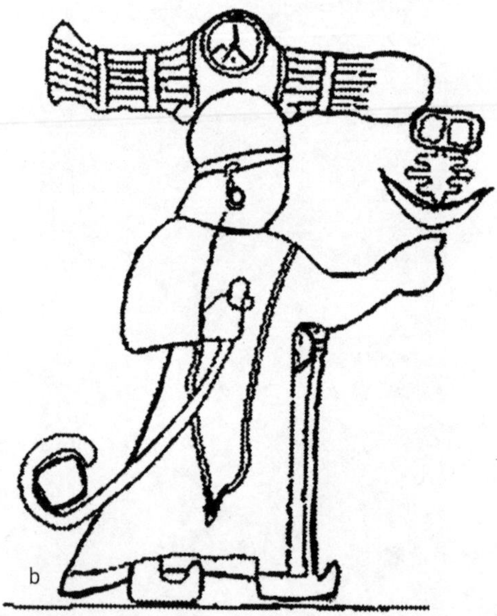
b

Fig. 2.27. (a) Hittite king and (b) Sun god. From rock sanctuary at Yazilikaya.

There can thus be no question: in Syro-Anatolia the images of god and king are molded by the same template. The identification (if it comes at all) is through inscribed titles or the horn-crown that gods wear. Is "ruler iconography" really missing in Minoan Crete, then, or have we been unable to recognize it?[54] If ambiguity does exist, is it deliberate so as to make kings and gods mirror each other? The king can thus be viewed as akin to the gods.[55]

One observation needs to be added, namely, that the enthroned king, a common iconographical type in the Near East, is admittedly lacking in Creto-Mycenaean art. But this does not constitute proof for the absence of kingship, because this peculiarity also applies to Minoan male gods who are *never* shown enthroned (Chapter 13). It must be noted that official art is often paradigmatic: the king follows the visual iconography of his patron god. Thus, the question of the missing enthroned king leads to the further question of the missing enthroned god. This issue will be addressed in Chapter 13. At any rate, in no way is the missing iconography of enthronement an argument against the existence of kingship.

3

The King and Queen as High Priests

"It seems certain that we must recognize in Minos the bearer of a divine title . . . But this divine element in Minos has a special significance in view of a series of analogies supplied by the great centers of the geographically connected Anatolian regions."

—Sir Arthur Evans

Evans was correct that the Minoan king was at the same time a high priest and that the institution of kingship in Crete was similar to other theocracies in the "great centres" of the sophisticated palatial civilizations of the Near East. At these places, the king was the *only* legitimate intermediary between the human and divine worlds, and, for this reason, division between secular and religious office was meaningless. Note that the same applies to the queen: the stronger the theocracy, the more exalted the role of the queen because she is not only the wife of the king, but also the mother of the heir to the throne. But Evans did not follow his reasoning through. He spoke of sacerdotal figures, although, as we will see, the high-priesthood cannot be distinguished in iconography from kingship.

This is not to deny that colleges of priests existed in Crete, as they did also in the Near East and Egypt. In Mycenaean Greece the Linear B tablets attest to the office of *i-je-re-u,* namely priest.[1] Nor is it to deny that priests had power (they could even manipulate the king himself during certain periods of history).[2] What is doubted here is that the chief priest of any priestly college would be represented repeatedly in art *instead of the king.* Yet what we have been asked to believe about Minoan society is that no images of the king exist, whereas sacerdotal figures abound. What a discrepancy this is with Near Eastern Ugaritic and Hittite sacrificial texts, which stress only the role of the king in offering ceremonies![3]

We return now to the Minoan portrait heads on seals examined in the previous chapter, where it was suggested that they are heads of rulers rather than priests. The same bearded portraits are associated with animal heads. This makes sense: if the king is also the high priest, he would naturally be associated visually with sacrificial animals (Fig. 3.1).[4]

One important dimension of the royal high priesthood was economy: the king was the main provider of sacrificial animals in all the major public ceremonies. Art and texts show that feasting was part of the message of opulence that royal self-presentation sought to convey: the greater the king, the greater the spectacle. In Egyptian texts and images of the second millennium, we get vivid descriptions of state festivals in which musicians, dancers, and acrobats are involved. Even a whole flotilla of ships sailed in the Nile.[5] The multiplicity and variety of offerings is another means of display. At the time of Ramses II, the provisions to the temple were of the grandest scale recorded in inscriptions: 11,400 loaves and cakes; 358 jugs of beer; and a myriad of miscellaneous offerings of meat and incense.[6] Ugaritic tablets from the thirteenth and eleventh centuries BCE provide evidence for dozens of offerings of rams and other animals.[7] If the king could

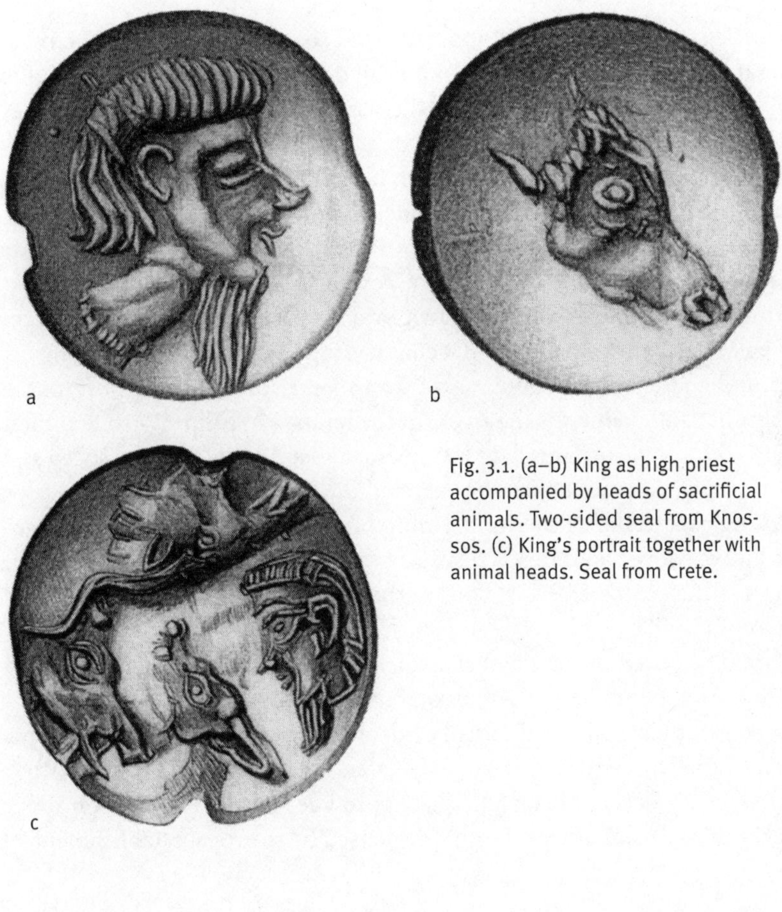

Fig. 3.1. (a–b) King as high priest accompanied by heads of sacrificial animals. Two-sided seal from Knossos. (c) King's portrait together with animal heads. Seal from Crete.

show that he could supply the gods with abundant offerings, he could also feed the populace adequately, sending the message to locals and foreigners alike that he had a rich kingdom. Consider the following Ugaritic text:

SACRIFICES FOR THE GODS OF MOUNT SAPUNU

For Ilu (El) a bull and a ram
For Dagan a bull and a ram
For Balu of Sapunu a bull and a ram
Also for Balu a bull and a ram . . .
For Arsu wa Sanuma a ram
For Kotaru a ram
For Yarihu a ram,
For Attary a ram . . .
For the Assembly of the Gods a ram
For Yamu a ram
For the Kimmary a ram, two bulls, two birds,
a cow: as a burnt offering. (RS 24.643)[8]

In this Ugaritic list, the gods are many and so are the offerings. The royal palace safeguards its kingdom by pleasing all deities and establishing its cultic role in a wide territory. There are detailed specifications as to which species and what quantity of each animal is to be offered, what type of bloodless offerings each deity will receive, and which libations will be poured where. The festival is a rather complex affair with rules that need to be followed precisely. The observance of detail is the duty of the priests; the king has only to provide and perform.

An interesting parallel may be drawn by a Linear B tablet from the Mycenaean palace of Pylos, where the Mycenaean king (*wanax*) provides a long list of gods and goddesses with gold vases.[9] Consider, also, a biblical text from the Iron Age that still maintains the flavor of theocratic kingship. When Solomon dedicated the temple of Yahweh in Jerusalem, he sacrificed "so many sheep and oxen that they could not be numbered or counted" (2 Chronicles 5:7).

The king as a leader of sacrifices riding his chariot and followed by a sacrificial bull is shown on a fresco from Knossos (Fig 2.22). Similar images can be found in the palace of Pylos, both in the vestibule of the palace and in the throne room itself.[10]

It should be noted that the archaeological picture in the New Palace Period of Crete fully supports the hypothesis of the king as a chief sacrificial priest. Minoan palaces have provided a lot of evidence of feasting; most notable in this respect is the newly excavated palace of Galatas.[11] Also, the Linear B tablets from the Mycenaean palaces of Pylos and Thebes provide relevant information about sacrificial animals and other offerings dispensed by the royal establishment.[12]

Entrance and Exit Rites into Sacrality

There is no question, then, that the king was the center of the well-being of his people and that he acted as an intermediary between the divine and human worlds. The issue to be addressed next, however, is of a different nature. How was sacrality conceived? Was it an ontological state of being or was it a simple role, a mere duty like all the others? It is argued here that it was indeed a state of being; the king and queen entered and exited it ceremonially.

It is best to start with conceptualizations that belong to the second millennium BCE and not to our own times. For this reason I shall look at a festival attested in an Ugaritic text. The two translations of this text by Nicolas Wyatt and Dennis Pardee differ somewhat, but there is agreement on the general course of events.[13]

The festival begins with an offering of grapes on the day of the new moon. The main responsibility falls on the king, who has complex duties lasting over a period of many days. He has to travel from one sanctuary to the other and make offerings to a wide variety of gods: Baal, Anat, El, Athirat, Reshep, and others. Animals of all kinds are to be offered: rams, birds, heifers, and bulls. Libations are poured into holes or depressions. Diverse types of vessels are used: jars, chalices, and cups.[14] Sometimes the libations are poured on the rooftops of sacred edifices.[15] Processions must be envisioned as part of the festival, because the king (and perhaps the entire royal family) traveled back and forth between palace and various sanctuaries. All this surpasses the imagination of the most fanciful of archaeologists, who could easily be accused of finding too much evidence for cult in excavated sites.

At the end of the text is the following stipulation: "when the sun sets, the king will be 'desacralized.'" This is Wyatt's translation.[16] Pardee renders the same phrase as "the [k]ing will be free (of further cultic obligations)."[17] The two differing translations show that there is as much difficulty with the concept as with its rendition into English. Whichever translation we choose, we still wonder: why must the king be "set free" or "desacralized"? This implies that he was in a special state from which he had to exit before he could return to normal life.

The next question is what did sacrality entail? Wyatt, whom I follow, thinks it is an ontological state. He notes that purification is obsessively repeated, "the king is to wash himself thoroughly," and so is the accompanying phrase "the king is desacralized or set free."[18] He concludes that each entry of the king into a state of ritual purity reaffirmed his ontological transformation at his installation.[19]

What I would like to add is that a physical transformation enforced the state of sacrality and made it visible to all, and that the signs of this transformation may be detected in Minoan art. But before we look at art, let us consider another document, this time from the Hittite kingdom of the thirteenth century BCE.

This text records in some detail the royal rituals during the festival of the Storm God. It begins with a procession led by the king and the queen, accompanied by a multitude of officials and entertainers who add pomp to the spectacular procession. As stated previously, the greater the king, the more splendid the spectacle. "Entertainers stand beside the king, hold their hands up and whirl around on the spot; they also recite psalmodies."[20] At some point, the king and the queen change clothes in a place called the *halentuwa* house: "The king and the queen put on their ritual dress in the *halentuwa* house."[21] It is not clear where this is, but it is most likely a sanctuary within the palace itself, as Theo van den Hout has argued.[22] Having new clothes, the royal couple now proceeds to the temple of the Storm God. The next event mentioned is the arrival of the king and queen at the gate, an event ritualized by a special performance of the entertainers: "The king arrives *at the gateway* and the dancers whirl around once."[23] Next, the couple enters what seems to be the inner sanctuary, where a cult statue stands. They prostrate themselves once before the god. Purification rites are mentioned several times. For example, "Two palace servants bring to the king (and) the queen water for washing their hands in a basin."[24] Later, we read: "Two palace servants bring to the king (and) the queen water for washing their hands in a golden basin."[25]

The Hittite account of the festival reinforces Wyatt's impression that repeated washing is a necessary affirmation of the state of royal sacrality through maintenance of purity. It also adds another piece of information to strengthen our hypothesis about the royal transformation, namely that the couple starts off the procession wearing one set of clothes but they enter the temple wearing a different garment. The change is thus visually demonstrable.

We find support in Egypt for this phenomenon: the pharaoh wore a variety of cultic robes depending on the deity to which he made the offering and the moment of the festival in which he conducted the sacrifices.[26] It might be useful to think of van Gennep's model of *Rites of Passage,* in which transformation is signaled by change of clothes.[27]

Is Sacrality Manifested in Images of Minoan Crete?

Minoan images make a contribution to the issue of the sacralization of the king because he and the queen wear three or four distinct types of garments (Fig 3.2).[28] The first type is the fringed long mantle with seams (Fig 3.2a), which has already been identified as a royal dress in Chapter 2 (see Figs. 2.13–2.14). The second type has metal scales and is worn by the king on the Hagia Triada "Harvesters' Vase" (Fig. 3.2b). The third is a hide skirt that is worn by king and queen alike on special sacrificial occasions (Fig. 3.2c). The fourth type is the typical

Fig. 3.2. Sacral garments of king. (a) Garment with metal scales. Stone "Harvesters' Vase" from Hagia Triada. (b) Fringed mantle with seams. Ring impression from Knossos. (c) Hide skirt. Hagia Triada sarcophagus.

Minoan costume: kilt for men, flounced skirt for women. This last example is not specific to royal personages.

What we observe is that the first type, the fringed, seamed dress (Fig. 3.2a), is a splendid heavy garment that resembles Elizabethan royal mantles and may be worn on any formal occasion to stress the king's exalted status. The other two types, however, have a peculiarity about them that single out the personage wearing them not as splendid and luxurious but as primitive. The peculiar nature of the scale dress, worn by the leader of the harvest procession (Fig. 2.15 and 3.2b), whom we have identified as a king, is worth stressing. Evans intuited this peculiarity and named the leader a "rustic."[29] Perhaps primitiveness is the very impression that sacrality seeks to convey. The hide dress certainly does *not* convey royal grandeur, but rustic simplicity (as Evans would say). It might be interesting to note that the Egyptian pharaoh wore a cultic dress with a bull's tail, and that this, too, is both primitive and yet sacral, because this bull-tail dress mirrors the dress of the gods (Fig. 3.3).

Fig. 3.3. Pharaoh Seti I (thirteenth century BCE) wearing a dress with a bull's tail (marked here in black).

The *sem* funerary priests wore a panther's skin, and this was occasionally put on by the king himself, as we see in Tutankhamun's tomb.[30] These peculiar animal dresses bring the king closer to nature and away from culture; perhaps they are meant to signify his exit from this world and entry into a liminal sphere that is closer to the gods. One could adduce parallels about royal liminality derived from anthropological material but it may be enough to stay within antiquity.[31] In Mesopotamia, there was a tradition of cultic nudity or at least of bare feet.[32] Such visual evidence is not lacking from the Near East either: Sumerian priests are shown with hide skirts. I conclude that through the hide dress and the metal stole the king and the queen manifested their physical transformation.

Minoan images emphasize also another important moment in the process of sacralization: the arrival of the royal couple at the gate of the sanctuary. We have discussed the importance of this moment in a Hittite text where we read that the entertainers whirled around the king when he and the queen arrived at the gate during the festival of the Storm God.[33] Two Minoan/Mycenaean rings are shown below in Figure 3.4, both of which depict processions of women arriving at the gate of a sanctuary. In Figure 3.4b, the central woman is evidently larger than the rest and her gesture shows that she is greeting a deity (for parallels see Chapter 6). She must be the queen. She is differentiated here not by dress but by size and gesture of the clinched fist.

Hittite and Ugaritic texts supply information about festivals that may seem tedious at first but which is very useful: how many animals of each type were sacrificed, how many libations were poured, how many times the king washed his hands, etc. Pictures, on the other hand, are synoptic, compressing several procedures into what is considered to be the crucial event of a long sequence. Minoan images project what is deemed important and omit the rest. They are thus a useful guide to the mentality of Minoan religion. In Minoan/Mycenaean images, the arrival of the procession with the queen at the gate of a sanctuary is a subject of several rings, an indication that arrival was considered an important moment in the festival. Indeed, it marks the time as well as location of the interaction between humans and deities.

Images have a further advantage: they may be deliberately ambiguous. The enthroned figure in Figure 3.5 (male or female?) may be divine or human. Whichever the case, the depiction recalls royal enthronement.[34] In this sense, the image reflects both the cultic actuality and the myth of kings. The selectivity of images is a useful supplement to the prescriptive sacrificial texts of the Near East. If Minoan Crete belongs to the broader horizon of the cultural continuum that we call the Ancient Near East, it is hoped that the Minoan evidence from rings will be a useful guide to Near Eastern experts as well.

The Sacrificing King and Queen on the Hagia Triada Sarcophagus

We now apply the previously established criteria to a set of coherently related scenes painted on a clay coffin found in a tomb in Hagia Triada in southern Crete and dating to around 1400 BCE.[35] It is painted on all its four sides with six different scenes that I believe constitute the narrative of a festival. The sarcophagus has been much discussed because it provides us with the most complete visual record of sacrificial offerings in Minoan times.[36] A full description would be superfluous here; instead, I focus on the priesthood of the king and the queen, asking the very questions that have been occupying us thus far. Can we detect the royal couple in their capacity as high priests? Is there evidence of their transformation into a state of sacrality? To whom are they offering? Surprisingly enough, the Hagia Triada sarcophagus has never been considered as a source of documentation for royal priesthood. The scenes are tabulated here to create a synoptic presentation of the main ritual events (Fig 3.6).

a

b

Fig. 3.4. Processions arriving at gate of sanctuary. Gold rings from Mycenaean mainland.

Fig. 3.5. Enthroned figure of unspecified gender, perhaps king wearing long seamed mantle. Gold ring from Mycenae.

Fig. 3.6. Summary of ritual offerings on two long sides of sarcophagus of Hagia Triada. (a) Sacrifice of bull. (b) Libation poured into container between two double axes. (c) Libation at gate of house of god in front of double axe. (d) Offerings to dead personage.

Scene 1. Sacrifice of a bull or cow. The leader of the procession is a woman with a long dress. Her head is not preserved. She lays her hands above the animal, perhaps in prayer (Fig. 3.6a).

Scene 2. Bloodless offerings are made at an altar outside the gate of the house of god (the gate of the sanctuary is sometimes described as an altar, but this is erroneous). There is also a cult standard in the form of a double axe. The officiant is a woman wearing a hide skirt. She lays her hands above the bowl, perhaps in prayer (Fig. 3.6b).

Scene 3. A libation is performed between two double axes (aniconic cult standards) by a woman in a hide skirt. Behind her is a woman in a long robe and plumed hat who carries two buckets. A male lyre player in a long robe follows (Fig. 3.6c).

> *Scene 4.* Offerings are brought to a mummy-like figure (the dead) standing in front of a tomb. The leader of the procession is a man in a hide skirt (Fig. 3.6d).
>
> In summary: all four scenes on the two long sides represent offerings of various types, which are separated into bloody and bloodless. They take place either in front of double axes or a dead person. The ritual procedures are summarized visually on Figs. 3.6 a-d. They have been divided into two vertical columns reflecting the long sides.

We now turn to the chief priests of the offerings. The female, in three out of the four scenes, wears either the long regal robe with the plumed hat or an animal hide skirt. The male wears the hide dress only. What do we deduce from that? A first conclusion is that there must be an analogy between the male and female officiants: if one of them is royal, the others must be too, and vice versa.

The next step is to determine if any of the officiating women may be identified as a queen. This is a simple matter to confirm, because, as we determined in Chapter 2, the only human who may wear the plumed crown is the queen; otherwise only divinities and sphinxes have it. The woman with the plumed crown on the sarcophagus is traditionally identified as a priestess, but we have seen that this designation is inadequate because the queen *is* the high priestess *ex officio.*[37] Then a further question arises. If she is the queen, who is the woman with the animal hide skirt? It is difficult to believe that there is a high priestess that looks exactly like the queen and has a higher duty than she does. It would make sense to see her as the same person who is being depicted in two stages of action, in a cinema-like narrative. The women look exactly alike, and their progress in time and space is suggested by the different background colors of each sub-scene. There is precedent for such narrative techniques in Near Eastern art. The best examples come from the first millennium BCE: a Phoenician bowl found in a tomb at Praeneste shows the king several times in a series of adventures carved along the rim of the bowl.[38] An even better example is a base of a cult standard from the time of the Assyrian king Tukulti Ninurta (1243–1207 BCE) (Fig. 3.7). The king is shown twice in the same scene. In phase one he is standing; in phase two he is kneeling in front of the cult emblems of his god.[39] Other good examples are the hunt-reliefs of Ashurbanibal from his palace at Nineveh (c. 645 BCE), where the king is shown several times in adjacent scenes during the different stages of the hunt.[40]

Closer to the time period we are examining are the Egyptian cultic narratives of the festivals at Luxor, Medinet Habu, and Abydos during the Eighteenth and Nineteenth Dynasties in Egypt. The king is shown several times, dressed in different attires in successive scenes.[41] In Minoan art, a sequence of actions has been argued for the Vapheio cups.[42]

Fig. 3.7. Assyrian King Tukulti Ninurta I (1243–1207 BCE) shown in two stages of action. Base of cult standard.

Coming back to the Hagia Triada sarcophagus, it is argued here that the queen is shown twice: in her regal robe and in the sacral hide skirt. If so, then the male figure on the other side of the sarcophagus should, by analogy, be the king leading a procession of males to a mummy/dead standing in front of the tomb. The king stands out from the rest because his head is larger than that of the other figures following him.[43]

The queen's hide dress signifies her "sacrality," the degree of her involvement in the office of priesthood. In Figure 3.8 it becomes evident that only those wearing the hide garment are in close contact with the sanctuary. When the officiants are approaching in procession, they wear the long regal garment. When they are performing the actual offering, they are wearing a hide skirt. The dress thus signifies degree of involvement in the ritual.

Recall that in the Hittite festival of the Storm God, the king and the queen enter the sanctuary only when they have "put on their ritual dress."[44] With this change of garment they transform into high priests. If we read this procedure in the images of the Hagia Triada sarcophagus, we might deduce the following sequence of the events depicted:

Fig. 3.8. Queen and king wearing hide skirt and performing offerings. Hagia Triada sarcophagus (fourteenth century BCE).

1. The Minoan queen (as I have identified her) leads a procession that first arrives at a holy place. A bull or, rather, cow has been sacrificed, and two goats are waiting their turn. The queen places her hands on the bleeding animal and consecrates it, possibly uttering a prayer. This act shows that she is the sponsor of the sacrifices. The queen wears her regal attire (Fig. 3.6a).
2. The queen proceeds to the house of god and performs libations and other offerings outside the gate.[45] She is now wearing the hide skirt, because she is close to the house of god. She is also barefoot (Fig. 3.6b). Compare with the Ugaritic text in which it is stated that the king puts his sandals on after the sacrifice.[46]
3. In the first stage of action, the queen is dressed in a long robe as she brings the libation liquids. In the second stage of action, the queen performs the libation dressed in a hide skirt (Fig. 3.6c).
4. The king makes offerings to the dead, wearing the hide skirt (Fig. 3.6d).

This structure corresponds roughly to the sequence of events narrated in the Hittite account of the festival of the Storm God. There, too, the change of dress marks the entry of the royal couple into a sacral state. On the Minoan sarcophagus, the garment is of crucial importance to indicate the sacrality of the act. No doubt such garments had a special name in Minoan language. In Ugaritic, a type of sacred dress is designated as *ipd,* which may be etymologically related to the *ephod* of the Hebrew bible.[47]

The parallelism that has been detected between the Minoan, Egyptian, Ugaritic, and Hittite evidence does not imply that I am reading specific Near Eastern rituals into the Minoan painting or *vice versa.* Rather, it means that similarities about the structure and properties of these rituals are made manifest when texts and images from the same historical and geographical horizons are read together. Indeed, when combined, they may mutually shed light on each other.

There is another Hittite source that may be of help. It is a scene engraved on a silver vessel in the shape of a fist, dating to the fourteenth century (approximately contemporary to the sarcophagus) (Figs. 3.9a and b). It shows the Hittite king making a libation to the altar of the Storm God.[48] The altar is flanked by rosettes (for their significance see Chapter 10).[49] Note that the Minoan sarcophagus as well is framed by rosettes in its upper and lower borders (Fig. 3.8). If we compare the libating woman on the Minoan sarcophagus with the libating king on the Hittite vessel, the similarities in the syntax of the motifs on the scenes is evident. The syntactical analogy supports the hypothesis that the Minoan woman with the hide skirt is indeed the queen, because the two figures have equivalent positions in the two pictures. On both the Hittite and Minoan representations, they are followed by harp players. The imagery recalls the entertainers' group escorting the king and queen mentioned in the Hittite festival of the Storm God. Seeing the two together in Fig. 3.9, it becomes easier to understand the perspective of the Minoan viewer whose mental expectations would have been closer to those of the Hittites than to our own.

a

b

Fig. 3.9. Hittite and Minoan scenes from fourteenth century BCE. (a) Hittite silver cup. (b) Sarcophagus from Hagia Triada.

The King and His Ancestor

One question has not been answered yet. Who is the mummy/dead person depicted on the Hagia Triada sarcophagus (Fig 3.8)? He has been universally identified as the spirit of a dead man or a hero standing in front of his tomb.[50] The altar and the sacred tree in front of the tomb show that the latter has features that we may find in a sanctuary. I adopt Martin P. Nilsson's view that the mummy-like figure is a divinized king, because such a hypothesis finds striking support from both Ugaritic and Hittite texts, not to mention Egyptian evidence.

Let us consider the Hittite festival of the Storm God once more. When the king and queen have entered the sanctuary, one official named "the foreman of the cooks" pours out libations to a statue of a dead king: "Also for the statue of Hattusilis [Hattushili] he pours out a libation. The king prostrates himself; the worshipper of statues recites hymns, the *kitash* calls."[51] The inference is that a statue of a deified king coexisted with statues of gods in the same temple, and that the Hittite king honored both his ancestor and the gods.

Other Ugaritic texts yield more information about the cult of deified kings called *rpum*.[52] They are invoked and given the epithet "saviors," presumably because the king wants their help. This is reminiscent of the function of heroes in later Greek cult and (like the later Greek heroes) the *rpum* are described as making a journey to render their support to the new king.[53] Interestingly enough, the divine patron of these royal ancestors in the underworld is the sun and underworld goddess herself; we shall return to her role in Chapter 12.[54]

Were Minoan kings deified? The evidence is strong in favor of such a view. There is a royal "Temple Tomb" at Knossos and another at Isopata, both of which certainly suggest royal cult. All this has been argued cogently by Evans, who found concrete archaeological evidence for offerings in these tombs.[55]

The identification of the divinized king on the Minoan sarcophagus would explain the royal involvement in the ceremonies that have been described previously. A king must sacrifice to his predecessors: this is self-evident in a theocratic society.[56] But still, we need to look at the priestly roles of queens in the Near East, asking which deity they served.

Queens and Their Priestly Function in the Near East and Egypt

The queen is not just the wife of the king, but is a figure of authority herself. She is also the royal mother, who had a position of great consequence in the Egyptian, Hittite, and Ugaritic kingdoms, as indeed in most theocracies. Among the Hittites of the Old and New Kingdom (sixteenth through thirteenth centuries BCE) she had the cult title *tawannana*.[57] The latter had a certain independence from the king and could even rival his powers.[58] Having access to ritual and financial means, the *tawannana* was a force with which to be reckoned and even received her own cult after death.[59] One particular queen, who was a step-mother of King Hattushili, tried to bring his downfall by interpreting an eclipse of the sun: she predicted the downfall of her step-son, manipulating evidence in her capacity as prophetess.[60] For our purposes, it is interesting to note that the *tawannana* served as priestess of the sun goddess of the holy city of Arinna in the period of the New Empire, which coincides with the period of the Minoan sarcophagus.[61]

In Ugarit, the queen mother was the high priestess of Athirat, who is arguably also a sun goddess. The queen mother was very important, according to Wyatt, because it was through her line that future kings became established. Because fictional reality mirrors social conditions, we may postulate that mythical matrilineal succession reflected the official position of the queen mother.[62] The dowager queen was given the title *rbt* in Ugarit, which means "great lady."[63]

We now consider biblical evidence. A strong case can be made that Israelite queens were the high priestesses of Asherah, who may well be a sun goddess with the palm as her sacred tree.[64] One passage speaks of king Asa, who was loyal to Jahweh and removed the queen from the office: "Asa did what was right in the eyes of the Lord . . . he removed Maachah from being a queen mother because she had made an obscene image of Asherah" (1 Kings 15:13). The implication is that the dowager queen had the authority to set up new cult images of Asherah. Also, Jezebel, the wife of Ahab, must have been a high priestess of Asherah, judging by the fact that she hosted four hundred prophets of this goddess who ate at her table (1 Kings 18:19). There is further evidence reviewed by Wyatt that both of these queens and a third one, Solomon's mother Bathsheba, held the official position of *gebira*. This word means "the great one" and may correspond roughly to the Mycenaean title *po-ti-ni-ja* (mistress). These are titles shared by the queen and goddess alike.

The Egyptian queen and queen mother were the high priestesses of Hathor, a goddess with solar associations.[65] In her capacity as bearer of the solar disc, Hathor was a nurturer of both the sun and the king. The etymology of her name is "House of Horus" which need not refer to her womb as a mother but to her capacity as a protectress of the palace of the king.[66]

In summary, queens in Egypt, Syria, and Anatolia in the second half of the second millennium were high priestesses of the sun goddess. This pattern has not been noticed, perhaps because, under the influence of later Greek mythology, the sun is always assumed to have been male.[67] If the high priesthood of the sun goddess is an essential aspect of queenship, then the hypothesis that the Minoan queen might also be her priestess must be entertained; and if so, the double axe should be her cult symbol. How the sun goddess was related to the double axe and a dead king will be further explored in Chapters 9 through 12. One question must be answered now. Why do scenes with the king and queen decorate the coffin of a wealthy and eminent and yet not royal person?

It is not possible, I believe, to argue that the representations refer to a private funeral and that the dead spirit in front of the tomb is that of the deceased buried in the sarcophagus.[68] Such biographical information on a coffin would be highly unlikely in the ancient world; compare with the mythical iconography of Roman and Christian sarcophagi, for example. Consequently, the two sides of the Hagia Triada sarcophagus show a public festival, not a funeral. It is a festival both for the sun goddess (in her capacity as a celestial and underworld deity) and for the divinized king.[69] The dead interred in the sarcophagus would benefit from these rites because he or she would participate indirectly (through the paintings) in royal rituals of communal importance, much like an Egyptian noble of the Eighteenth Dynasty would participate in royal rituals included in the iconography of his tomb. During the Amarna period many officials included the king as the main protagonist in their tomb paintings.

The King's Duties and Anxieties

What does sacred kingship really mean? We have seen that it really implies two things. Firstly, the king (in fact the royal couple) was the high priest and only legitimate intermediary between people and the gods. Secondly, he was divinized after death. These categories should be kept distinct because they imply different degrees of sacrality. With few exceptions, the divinized dead king and not the living king received offerings.[70]

The king-priest was not like other people because he entered a special state of sacrality when coming into contact with the gods. It is clear that the royal couple could not live like this all the time, and that they had to exit the sacral state at sunset, as we infer from the Ugaritic texts cited previously.

The life of the king was not as glorious as it may seem at first. Hittite and Ugaritic texts show a certain preoccupation on the part of the royal administration with petty details of ritual performances. This no doubt explains why the prescriptive sacrificial texts from these kingdoms were kept in the archives of officials, although some were found in various parts of the site.[71] The records functioned as laws establishing precedent. We know (from Hittite texts) of oracles that were consulted about how many sheep should be sacrificed to which god, in what order, and when. If any part of the detailed rituals was not meticulously performed, there was fear that gods might be angry. If a festival was omitted, there was anxiety about possible dire consequences.[72] The king underwent constant purifications to be purged from curses and reconfirm his sacrality. Consider the prayer of the Hittite King Tudhaliya IV to the sun goddess of Arinna: "I sinned [towards the sun goddess of Arinna] my lady, and I offended the sun goddess of Arinna, my lady, and when I began to ask you for oracular guidance, it turned out that I omitted festivals due to you. If you, o sun goddess of Arinna, my lady, became angry with me . . . then reckon again with me to defeat my enemy."[73] The king subsequently promised to redress the evil and perform the prescribed festivals.

The anxious mind of royal administration is reflected on the extraordinary insistence on detail. It is to be suspected that the festival painted on the Hagia Triada sarcophagus must have been screened for accuracy as well: correct rendition of performance would have been considered essential for the desired result. The royal family was subject to a bureaucracy of ritual that must have placed a big constraint on their personal life and freedom. If a disaster occurred (plague, famine, or military defeat), the king could be accused of having done something wrong towards the gods, and he had to be purged from possible curses.[74] This situation is familiar from the Greek tragedy *Oedipus Rex* by Sophocles. The king, trying to avert a plague, consults the oracle of Delphi for advice: had he omitted something? It turned out that he was indeed responsible. But who controlled or oversaw the king? This is not a question that can be readily answered here, but one may suspect that the college of priests and diviners, who were the king's servants, could instigate rebellions, and that they could (and did) get out of control. Courtiers and diviners alike may have had power to influence common opinion, especially if they allied themselves with dissident members of the royal family. As noted previously, there were incidences when *tawannana(s)* (Hittite priestess queens) rebelled against the kings.[75] This type of situation could occur in the unlikely but not impossible event when the religious authority of the priestess queen clashed with the absolute authority of the king. The king was not inviolable.

Busy with frequent performances, travels to various sanctuaries, pouring of libations and reciting incantations, the king and his queen cannot have had too easy a life. The sunset, which set the royal personages free of their cultic obligations, as we read in the Ugaritic text, must have come as a huge relief.

4

Throones of Gods—Thrones of Kings

"A Minoan priest-king may have sat upon the throne at Knossos, the adopted Son on earth of the Great Mother of its island mysteries."
—Sir Arthur Evans

In the heart of the palace of Knossos and west of the central court, Evans found the oldest stone throne of the Aegean world, indeed the oldest in Europe, as tourist guides love to tell visitors of the Cretan palace (Fig. 4.1).[1] The throne room was part of a larger suite that included an anteroom, a throne room proper (both rooms were lined with benches), and an inner chamber with a ledge that seems to have been a chapel. The complex was evidently designed for ceremonies. The service and storage areas show that food was prepared and consumed there. Indeed, some thirty people could be accommodated in the benches of the throne room and its anteroom according to Evans's estimate.[2]

From the beginning, Evans had no doubt that this whole area was designed to serve a religious purpose.[3] The large cult vessels found broken in front of the throne were witnesses to the last moments of the life of the king in the palace.

How does evidence from the Near East help us understand the purpose and function of the throne room suite? We shall go back to the earlier half of the second millennium in the eighteenth century BCE and compare the Knossos throne suite (Fig. 4.2a) with its equivalent throne suite in the palace of Mari by the Euphrates (Fig. 4.2b). We find there the same architectural "vocabulary" (throne room + anteroom + sanctuary + service sections and storage). Yet, the similarities between the Mesopotamian and Minoan throne rooms cannot be explained by direct influence or imitation because the Mari palace antedated its Knossian equivalent by more than three centuries. We do not know what the palace of Knossos looked like in the eighteenth century BCE because it was overbuilt by the later edifice. However, the similarity of the architectural vocabulary between the Mesopotamian and Knossian palaces may be explained by a com-

Fig. 4.1. Throne room at Knossos.

mon tradition that was already in place on Crete during the period of the Old Palaces (nineteenth century BCE) and persisted more than four hundred years.

There is historical and textual evidence that suggests that king Zimrilim's palace at Mari was a model that was imitated by other kings in the Near East; also there is no doubt that Mari had contacts with the Cretans (Keftiu) during that period.[4] That a Knossian king of the eighteenth century might have wanted to imitate the best palace of his times stands to reason. There could also be an ideological connection: the murals of both the Mari and Knossos palaces demonstrate the same partnership of the king with his female patron deity. This association was a long-standing tradition of which the viewer has two partial glimpses of palaces frozen in time: one at Mari, the other at Knossos.

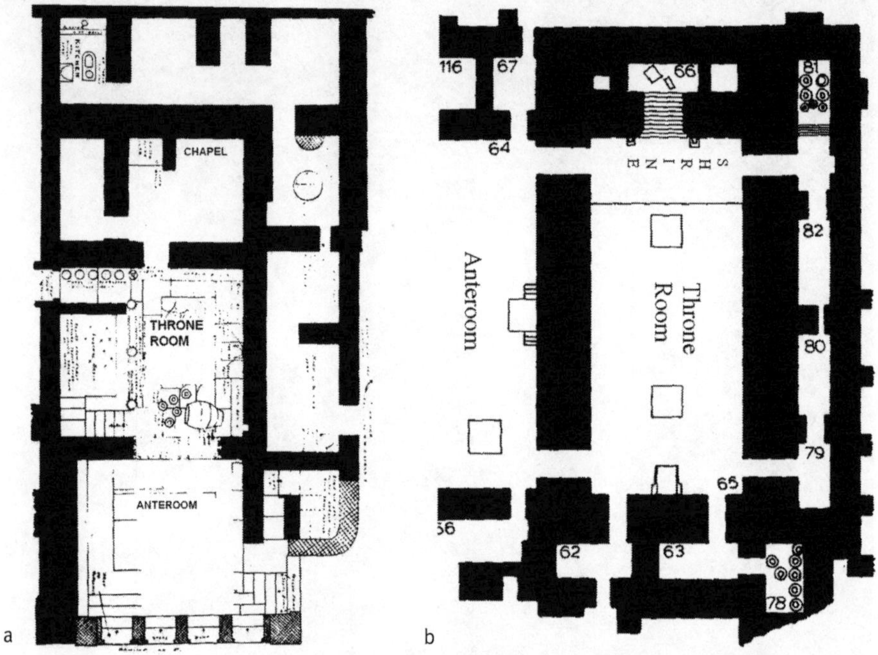

Fig. 4.2. Plans of throne room suites (not in scale) of (a) Knossos and (b) Mari.

Who Sat on the Throne?

Evans identified the stone throne as the seat of king Minos. He evidently applied the interpretative lens of Greek mythology in his attempt to associate a figure and a name with the throne. What better candidate than king Minos, whom Thucydides called the first great king to have organized a navy (Thuc. 1.4)? But one question has puzzled scholars since: how could this modest area be the audience hall of a king? In this respect the Mari throne room was more grandiose than its equivalent at Knossos.

A quite different solution was proposed by the German scholar Helga Reusch some thirty years later. She threw doubts on Evans's theory that a king sat on the throne, suggesting instead that the throne room was a sanctuary designed for a female divinity. She argued this principally on two grounds. First, she observed that the frieze on the lower side of the throne, consisting of a design known as a split rosette, was exactly the same as the Hittite hieroglyph (Luwian in origin) which is a determinative for *deity* (see also Chapter 10).[5] Second, Reusch noted the symmetrical arrangement of griffins flanking the throne. Griffins flank only divinities of the female gender, she stressed.[6] The logical inference was that the throne belonged to a goddess and that a priestess represented her corporeal epiphany ("*leibhafte Epiphanie*").[7] This implies some sort of performance or enactment by a selected priestess. This idea was developed some twenty years later by Robin Hägg, who combined the ideas of Reusch with those of Friedrich Matz and suggested a lively scenario of enacted epiphany performed by a priestess impersonating the goddess.[8] Wolf-Dietrich Niemeier followed with an architectural study of the entrances and exits and traced the route of the goddess impersonator from the service section to the throne itself.[9]

These scenaria are plausible, but what is missing for the enacted epiphany is a social setting. What was the status of the high priestess that performed the epiphany? How was she selected? Who witnessed the epiphany? What was the underlying ideology for such a performance, namely, who gained what? Who believed that she was a goddess and not an impersonator? Finally, are there any parallels from the ancient Orient for such an enactment?

The Hittite King and Queen and the Throne of God in a Hittite Festival

While I follow Reusch's argument in all its stages, I will come back to Evans's insight, which had the advantage of providing an answer to the question: "which social class profited from such a performance." Evans painted his king Minos with a palette that did not match perfectly the Minos of Greek myth. His figure was not just a dominant ruler of the seas but a priest king: "It seems certain that we must recognize in Minos the bearer of a divine title. . . . the priest not only represented the God, wore his dress and wielded his authority, but often also bore his name."[10]

Evans was perfectly correct. It has been stressed here repeatedly that in Near Eastern theocracies there is no high priest higher than the king, or priestess higher than the queen. The main protagonists of any major festival must have been the royal couple. Such a scenario of royal performance may be found among Hittite texts. The festival of the Storm God has already been briefly described in Chapter 3, and it has been mentioned there that the Hittite king and queen were the protagonists leading all the festivities. At some point they arrived at the temple of the war and Storm God and entered his inner sanctuary where a throne was situated: "The king takes his stand on the throne, but the queen enters the inner temple."[11]

There follows a list of offerings and libations cited already in Chapter 3. Next, some officials are driven out of the inner sanctuary, and then the king and queen take their seat on the throne. "Then they drive out the worshipper of statues, the liturgists, the *psalmodists* and the *kitash*. The king and the queen *sit down on the throne*."[12]

This is exactly the ritual play that could fit the Knossos throne room. The protagonists are either the king or the queen or both, and they take their seat on the throne of the deity situated in the sanctuary. Unfortunately it is not clear in the Hittite text if the enthronement is double, i.e. if there were two thrones or if the royal couple took turns. The next event is of some consequence for our interpretation of the enthronement: "Then the palace servant brings the pennant of a gold lance and the *kalmush*. He hands the pennant of the gold lance to the king, but the *kalmush* he places on the throne of the king."[13]

The passage shows that sacred objects were handled by the king, presumably the very weapons of the Storm God. There are more references to the gold lance and the *mukar* later in the text. Their exact significance is foggy, but it is nevertheless clear that handling divine paraphernalia was a privilege exclusively granted to the royal couple. It may be surmised that this activity signified a symbolic partnership of the king with his divine patrons.

Other details about the festival would be too cumbersome to relate, but even in this brief account one gets the definite impression that the ceremony is like a show with the royal couple as chief performers. The rites are never quite public because admission to the sanctuary requires selective screening. The thirty people envisaged by Evans sitting in the Knossos throne room, would have represented selected courtiers.

But is there any reason to adopt the Hittite scenario? The main reason is that it fits our Knossian evidence like a glove.[14] It explains why there is a sanctuary within the palace, and it elucidates the role of the royal couple in rituals of sacrality and enthronement within it (Chapter 3). It also gives plausible answers to some of the social questions posed above as regards the status of the "high priestess." There is a further issue, however, and it has to do with the gender of the person seated on the Knossos throne. We need not assume that because the throne belonged to a female deity, as Reusch rightly demonstrated, only the queen could sit on it. In the world of religious and mythical imagination, it is the king who is the main protégé of the chief goddess because he is her mythical son. The act of sitting on the throne of the goddess confirms his relationship to her. Does not the Egyptian pharaoh sit on the throne of Isis? And does not this goddess have the throne as an emblem of her identity? Does not Hathor, a goddess similar to Isis and the pharaoh's mythical mother, mean "house of Horus," that is, his palace?[15] The pharaoh and his fictive mothers Isis or Hathor are related through the symbols of kingship: throne and palace.[16] I propose that, after all, it was the king who sat on the throne of the goddess, establishing and demonstrating his relationship with her.

We now turn to details of the ceremony in Knossos, as it may be plausibly reconstructed on the basis of the Hittite account and the finds. Washing and anointing of the king can be inferred by the various vessels found on the floor at the time of its destruction because these vases (*alabastra*) were designed for holding oil and unguents.[17] The large stone basin displayed today in the room of the throne may have been used for purification rituals, as Evans originally thought, although it was not found *in situ*.[18] Indirect confirmation of such a scenario comes from the Ugaritic story of king Keret. We read there that he underwent ritual washing, put on make up (rouge), and then entered the sanctuary.[19]

The scenario that I suggest for Knossos is as follows: the king (or possibly also the queen or queen mother) changed clothes, washed thoroughly, and entered the anteroom and throne room using the back door of the throne room, which was flanked by griffins (Fig. 4.3).[20]

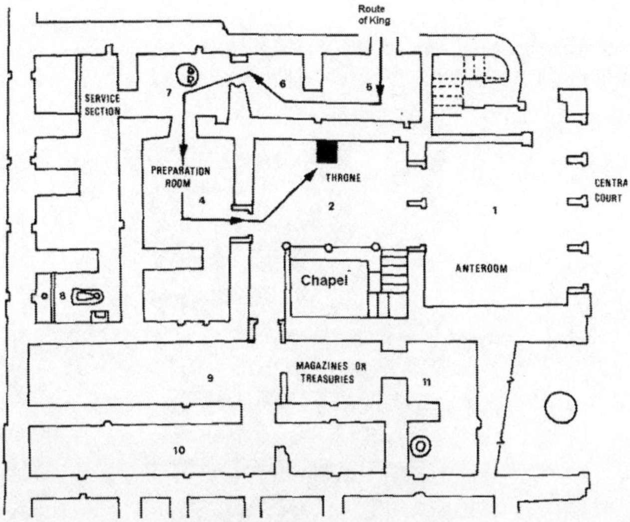

Fig. 4.3. Route of king or queen from inner suites of palace to throne room. Knossos.

Seals and rings illustrated in Figure 4.4 perhaps provide us with a glimpse of these rituals: personages (which I would interpret as members of the royal family) carry sacred objects similarly to the Hittite king and queen in the festival of the Storm God.[21] The female in Figure 4.4a could well be the queen.[22]

Once in the main room, the king was enthroned, and this event was witnessed by the seated courtiers on the benches. We know little about the activities in the anteroom where there was a second podium. On it, Evans reconstructed a wooden throne. Was it really a throne (perhaps for the queen) or was it designed for an aniconic emblem of the deity, such as a palm tree or a double axe? We cannot be certain; at any rate, Evans restored a wooden throne, which is still in good condition, sometimes occupied by the resident palace cat (Fig. 4.5).

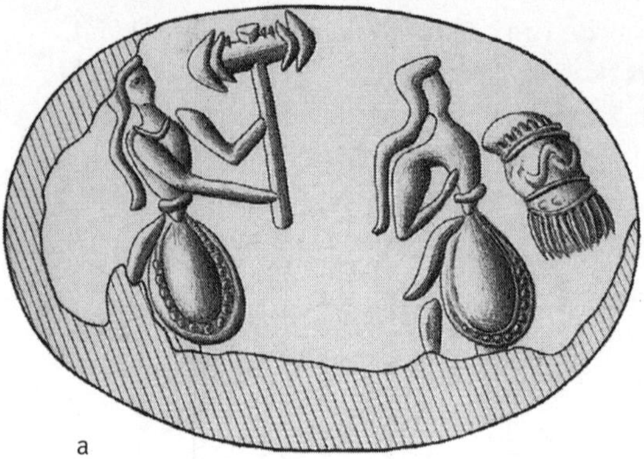

a

b

Fig. 4.4. Royal personages carrying a sacred garment and a double axe. (a) Ring impression from Zakros. (b) Seal from Knossos.

Fig. 4.5. Wooden throne (reconstructed by Evans) on original podium in the anteroom of throne room. Knossos.

In the religious festival posited here, the central court of the palace would serve as a public forum for the religious performance; the royal couple would be the main leaders while large audiences would be watching the spectacle.[23] The throne room suite was the principal sanctuary of the palace deity where the king and queen performed offerings and established their partnership with the patron deity of the palace. This is exactly the message also of the mural in the throne room of the palace of Mari. Offering ceremonies took place, such as those attested in the Hittite text. Such ceremonies account for the fact that a kitchen and a service section were situated nearby. Offerings were made also in the chapel (Lustral Basin) (see Fig. 4.3). The supplies were kept in storage jars, of which plenty were found in the area.[24] The mechanism of excluding some people while including others in a religious ritual is an important feature of theocratic systems.

Thrones within Temples in the Near East

The presence of thrones within sanctuaries is attested in Near Eastern texts.[25] A document from Mari mentions a throne offered to the god Dagan (eighteenth century BCE).[26] Another reports that a great throne was donated by King Zimrilim to the sun god Shamash, and this implies that the throne of the sun god was inside his temple.[27]

An Ugaritic text (twelfth century BCE) stipulates that on the twenty-sixth day of the calendar period "the king will wash himself clean." On that night "the throne is to be prepared."[28] Will the throne be prepared for the god or the king? Probably both: if the king needs to be washed, this means that he will have some involvement with the throne of the god.

In Egypt, the partnership of god and king is evident in almost all the manifestations of kingship, as Henri Frankfort has brilliantly demonstrated.[29] We need only be reminded here of a double statue, commissioned by the successor of Tutankhamun, King Horemheb, which represents the king sitting next to Horus (Fig. 4.6), fourteenth century BCE.[30] Othmar Keel has noted that this partnership closely reflects biblical Psalms: "the Lord says to my lord (king): Sit at my right hand" (Psalm 110:1).[31] Compare also with the Book of Chronicles: "Then Solomon sat on the throne of the lord" (1 Chron. 29:23). The ritual enthronement of the king (or also of the queen) signifies a bond between the royal couple and the patron deity of kingship whose sanctuary was located in the heart of the palace.

Mountain Thrones and Palms: The Sacred Landscape

We now discuss the divinity to whom the sanctuary and the throne belonged. The clue is given by the landscape that decorated the throne room proper.[32] It represents a paradise-field with reeds or lilies, palms, and possibly more plants

Fig. 4.6. Egyptian pharaoh seated next to Horus. Double statue from New Kingdom period.

that did not survive. Of the palms, one was preserved *in situ* to the right of the throne. For some reason it was omitted by Evans's restorer Emile Gilliéron when he reconstructed the mural of the throne room, but he included palms in the frontispiece of the last volume of *Palace of Minos.* Attention to the palms was also given by Mark Cameron.[33]

We start with the throne itself, the shape of which is worth noting. Its back has undulating contours that represent mountains in Minoan art (Fig. 4.8a). An exact parallel may be found on a stone vessel from the palace of Zakros, where a mountain top is flanked by goats (Fig. 4.8b).[34]

Mountains are the abodes of gods in the ancient world and are often conceived as their thrones: "the high mountain that you saw whose peak is like the throne of God," we read in the Book of Enoch.[35] When the mountain is coupled with the palm and griffin, we may suspect that the combination represents a sacred landscape and may even reveal something about the identity of the deity to whom the throne belonged. This question was raised already by Reusch. Her conclusion was that the throne belonged to a goddess, as we have seen above, and this is certainly correct. But which goddess is this? And does she have a relationship with the ruler?

Fig. 4.7. Palm landscape framing throne at Knossos.

a b

Fig. 4.8. Mountain contours. (a) On back of throne at Knossos. (b) Mountain top flanked by goats, depicted on stone vessel from palace of Zakros.

Let us now go back to the palace of Mari of the eighteenth century BCE, which may have furnished the prototype of the original Cretan palace in the earlier half of the second millennium. The painting of its throne room depicts the king facing the goddess Ishtar (Fig. 4.9). Both goddess and king are situated in a landscape framed by palms and griffins, as well as other creatures.[36] The landscape of Ishtar is similar to that of the divinity in the Knossos throne room, and this supports Reusch's conclusion that a female deity was the owner of the throne. Note, however, that the king is also present on the Mari painting, and that *he* is the protagonist: Ishtar hands him the insignia of his reign.

We cannot rely on Mari alone, of course, but must look at more examples from the Near East that are closer in time and space to the New Palace period of Crete. For a rich supply of evidence we turn to Syro-Palestinian seals, which date to the Middle Bronze Age and later, coinciding roughly with the end of the Old Palace and the beginning of the New Palace period on Crete. These seals supply us with a rich vocabulary of concepts formed under Egyptian and Mesopotamian influence, but which retain a Syrian idiom. They are the best documents of the religious *koine* in the East Mediterranean from the Old Palace period of Crete onwards. What is the role of the palm and the griffin on these seals?

The first observation is that both griffin and palm are associated with the sun in Syrian glyptic. The palm is often linked with a winged rosette disc, a

Fig. 4.9. Throne room mural showing king and goddess Ishtar. Fresco from palace of Mari (eighteenth century BCE).

Levantine idiom of the Egyptian winged sun disc.[37] We may draw the further inference, which is of some consequence, that there existed stylized, human-made, wooden cult standards imitating the palm. This would explain why the solar disc (also part of the object) was attached on top.

Examples may be found on Syrian seals (Fig. 4.10). An example of two palm-trunk standards (one of the sun and one of the moon) is shown on the Syrian seal in Figure 4.10a). Only the solar standard is flanked by griffins.[38] Another seal shows a palm standard with a winged sun above it (Fig. 4.10b). It stands between the figure of a bearded ruler and a goddess.[39]

a

b

Fig. 4.10. Palm standards on Syrian seals topped by sun and moon emblems.

There are many more cases but these few will suffice to show that the palm was regarded as a tree of a solar deity. Beatrice Teissier says: "The association of the sun with the palm was both an Egyptian and Mesopotamian concept but Syrian imagery was derived from the latter. In Egypt the palm was considered to be one of the seats of Re at his rising."[40]

An important observation is that the griffin is also a solar bird in Levantine iconography. I cite Teissier again, who summarizes the history of the motif and its migration from Egypt to the Levant: "In Egypt it is first attested in the Middle Kingdom, but it was developed during the New Kingdom when the griffin is frequently portrayed with a solar disc on its head. In the Late period, he can appear sitting on a lotus within a sun disc. . . . In Levantine iconography the griffin's associations with the tree usually include a direct link with solar mythology."[41]

The contention that griffins are associated with the sun is supported by Ugaritic seals on which the mythical creatures flank a solar disc (Fig. 4.11). In light of the above, I suggest that both palm trees and griffins had solar connotations in Minoan art, and griffins are sacred to the sun deity, as a ring impression from Knossos shows (Fig. 4. 12).[42]

Fig. 4.11. Griffins flanking solar disc. Ugaritic seal.

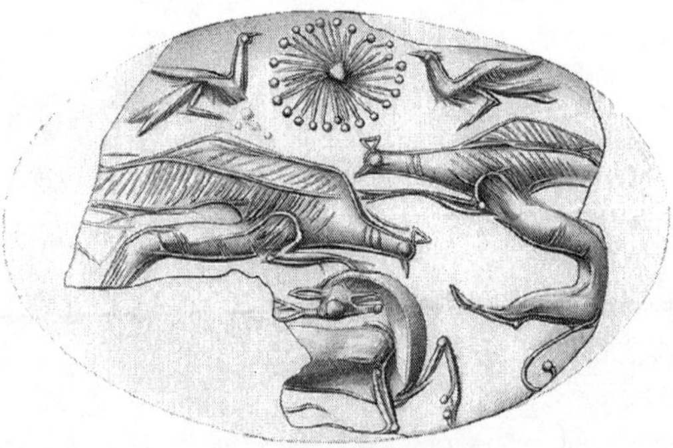

Fig. 4.12. Griffins attacking prey below solar disc. Ring impression from Crete (fifteenth century BCE).

This means that the deity of the throne room at Knossos may be identified as a solar goddess. This hypothesis will be pursued further and substantiated with more evidence in Chapters 10 and 12.

A final observation on Syrian/Levantine visual evidence is that the solar palm tree is combined with the figure of the ruler, and there is little doubt that the solar goddess is the patroness of the king.[43] (See Figs. 4.9 and 4.10b.)

We now test the hypothesis on our Minoan material. I argued some years ago that the palm was a sacred tree in Minoan religion, and I made a distinction between the naturalistic and the stylized palm, which I now recognize to be a cult standard: "the naturalistic representations, in which the palm is part of a landscape, are quite different from the symbolic religious ones, in which the tree is very stylized. It is important to emphasize that the stylization of the tree is not due to convention alone. The tree is a meaningful sign."[44] I did not understand then that the stylized palm was a human-made cult standard akin to the biblical *asherah.* The meaning of *asherah* and its relation to Jahweh is a contested issue in the Hebrew Bible. Suffice it to say here that it is a *cult object* in the shape of a palm tree and not a mere name of the female goddess of Ancient Israel.[45] The evidence from Minoan Crete is very congruent with this hypothesis and elucidates further the function of the palm cult standard. The most telling representation comes from a seal now in the Fogg Art Museum, Harvard University. It shows a Minoan goddess standing atop a stylized palm that stands on an incurved podium (Fig 4.13; see also Chapter 10).[46]

Here we have all the elements that we observed in the Syro-Palestinian *koine.* A palm goddess, a palm standard, and the flanking griffins. The Syrian lens works as an interpretative tool for Minoan religion because it enables a richer reading of the throne room landscape.

And what about the ruler? Is there any evidence that the syntactic formula palm+solar cult is connected with kingship in Minoan Crete? Indeed there is such evidence. On a seal from Naxos we see a ruler with the plumed hat which has been identified in Chapter 2 as the king's distinctive mark (Fig. 4.14). The king extends his arm in a gesture of authority. In front of him is a table of offer-

Fig. 4.13. Palm standard with goddess on top. Seal from Mycenae.

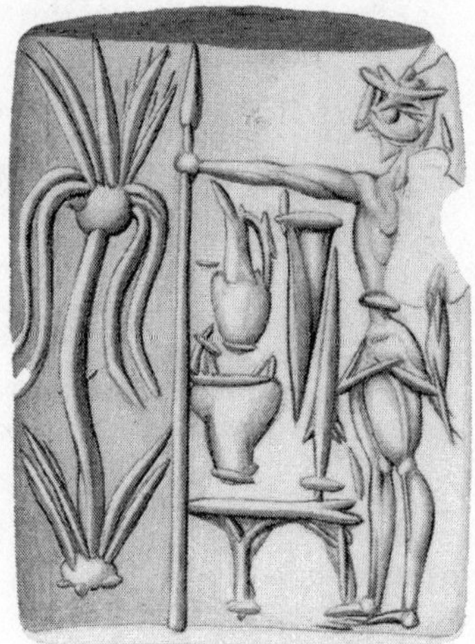

Fig. 4.14. Ruler making offerings to solar palm. Seal from Naxos.

ings and cult equipment such as a rhyton, a ewer, and a receptacle for liquids.[47] The king makes the offerings but the recipient must be the goddess of the palm tree (the Minoan equivalent to *asherah);* no other deity is visible. The seal from Naxos confirms the ruler's involvement with the palm tree.

Some further evidence that shows the assimilation of the palm to the patron goddess of the king comes from a ring from Mycenae that depicts two sphinxes flanking a stylized palm (Fig. 4.15a). This ring may be compared to a Syrian seal of a slightly earlier period (Fig. 4.15b). The similarity of the visual syntax shows that a *koine* was operative on both sides of the Aegean.

a

b

Fig. 4.15. Palms flanked by sphinxes. (a) Gold ring from Mycenae. (b) Egyptianizing Syro-Palestinian seal.

Conclusion

All this leads to some major conclusions. One is that the throne room of Knossos fits the model of divine kingship perfectly. Only in a theocratic society can we imagine that divinities reside within the palace sharing their residence with royalty. It has been stressed repeatedly that the notion that a high priestess sat on the throne is not quite adequate as a social model. First, a high priestess cannot be any other person than the queen or queen mother in a palatial society. Second, the queen cannot impersonate the goddess and make offerings to her at the same time: this would be illogical. Third, we must not assume that the main cult officiant had to be of the same sex as the deity. The scenario that I have suggested here is that the king sat on the throne of the goddess to establish his relationship with her as her earthly representative and son, just as the pharaoh sat on the lap of Isis (Chapter 10).

Another conclusion is that the goddess who resided in the palace was not primarily a fertility deity but *a solar goddess*. This has been argued on the basis of two iconographical motifs, griffin and palm, both of which are related to solar worship in Syria-Palestine, Egypt, and Anatolia. We shall add the rosette to this conspectus in Chapter 10. This suggestion modifies the theory of the fertility goddess, but does not negate it completely because solar deities are responsible for life, plant growth, and all the regeneration and blessings that the sun can bestow. A solar goddess would explain why Minoan wall paintings abound in motifs of lush vegetation, birds, monkeys, and ungulates. They celebrate nature as the sun's gift to men.

Lucy Goodison has also argued convincingly for a solar cult in Crete, specifically in the throne room of Knossos, but on quite different grounds.[48] She suggested that the rays of the morning sun would penetrate the throne room through the open doors during a specific time of year. The sunrays would illuminate the throne, and the sunlight would be a kind of epiphany.[49] This scenario would fit well with Ugaritic and Hittite evidence, because we read that many rituals begin at sunrise. Also the Jerusalem temple was oriented towards the east so that the sunlight would penetrate it at sunrise.

In the Ancient Orient sun deities (male or female) are the principal patrons of kings; it is arguable that the absence of kingship from Greece and its abolition in Israel explain the marginalization of sun worship in these cultures. Elsewhere the sun is always a primary deity, and although Egyptian Re and Horus and Babylonian Shamash are male, the Hittites had a supreme female sun deity, the goddess of Arinna or Hepat, and they adopted the sun disk as the emblem of royalty. In Ugarit the sun goddesses Shapshu and Athirat played a major role in the narratives of royal ideology.[50] If we include Minoan Crete within the cultural horizon of the Near East, a solar goddess who would protect the king is hardly an anomaly, but the very deity we might expect, and a perfect fit for the template of kingship: the king sat on the lap of the goddess, as it were.

Says a Hittite queen: "O sun deity . . . [i.e., a goddess], have benevolent eyes and look upon the king and queen with benevolent eyes and keep them alive."[51]

5

The House of God

"The cumulative results of the exploration of the great building at Knossos have served more and more to bring out the fact that it was inter-penetrated with religious elements."

—Sir Arthur Evans

Although gods live on tops of mountains, rivers, or caves, in the depths of the sea, or even in the underworld, they also visit earthly dwellings built for them by men. The edifices that host the cult image or aniconic emblems of the deity are "houses of god."

Minoan Crete presents us with a seeming paradox. Temples, which typify most palatial societies from Mesopotamia to Asia Minor and Egypt, seem to be missing.[1] There exist palaces and house-shrines in towns, and yet no separate temples have been found.[2] One scholar was led by this anomaly to suggest that religious activity was, for the most part, confined to "house cults."[3] Had this been the case, there would have been a complete dissociation of the ruling class from leadership in religious cults, a scenario which is not only highly unlikely, but virtually impossible to imagine in the ancient world.

The first step towards solving the problem of the missing temples is to adjust our terminology. The term *temple* carries with it associations of a specific architectural plan projected backwards to the second millennium BCE from first-millennium Greek and Near Eastern temples with cellas. In general, archaeologists in the Near East have sometimes difficulties in distinguishing between altar, "high place" shrine, and temple.[4] I suggest that as a starting premise for our discussion we replace "temple" with "house of god," remembering that in ancient terms the temple is called the "house of god" (*bêt Elohim*). In this way we will not be restricted to a particular architectural typology or size.

My concern here, however, will not be architecture but iconography. Through the images we may come closer to the way the Minoans themselves conceptualized their sacred buildings. The best example of a sacred building is one represented on a stone ritual vessel found at the palace of Zakros (Fig. 5.1).[5] It is a solitary structure located on a mountain. Goats roam there freely, birds fly about, but there is no human to be seen: the building is located in the wilderness.[6] Its center is dominated by a large gate and flanked by two smaller niches or windows. The significance of the gates will be addressed later; for the moment let us note that pairs of ⊔ surmount the side portals or windows. The central gate is topped by a lintel on which two pairs of goats are resting. The goats flank an object with undulating contours, which can be identified as a stylized mountain top.[7] Its shape is identical with the back of the throne of Knossos (fig. 4.8). This similarity is the key to interpreting the image: the mountain is the throne of the Knossos goddess (identified in Chapter 4) protruding above the gate of the divine palace. That the mountain is a throne is a well-established *topos* in Near Eastern literature and the Hebrew Bible.[8]

Attempts have been made to search for buildings that would have served as the prototype of the structure represented on the Zakros rhyton, but this path cannot be very fruitful because art never reproduces a photographic version of actuality.[9] The image renders not any specific edifice of Minoan Crete, but an idealized prototype of what the house of god *ought to look like.* Although it contains elements of real architecture (⊔, isodomic blocks of masonry, pillars, gates), it transcends the particularities of location and form.[10] Its environment is a region beyond settled human habitation, populated only by wild animals. At the same time, however, the house of god is central in a cosmological sense. The mountain above the central gate is conceptualized as the throne of god, an *axis mundi* of the cosmos.

A three-dimensional clay model found in a sanctuary in East Crete will take us even further into the realm of symbolism. It has the form of two huge ⊔, one within the other (Fig. 5.2).[11] Again there is a gate in the center, flanked by two smaller portals and two more ⊔. The symbolic nature of the building is quite evident because the entire structure is conceived as a conglomerate of ⊔ and gates; no one would argue that this is real architecture. It will be shown in Chapter 8 that ⊔ means mountain, and that the house of god is conceived as one. The sacred building on the Zakros rhyton and the clay model (Figs. 5.1 and 5.2) have common features: gates and ⊔. We must therefore come to the conclusion that these two signs constitute the basic pictorial vocabulary of sacred architecture.

It is easy to understand why the gate is important: it is the boundary between the divine and human realms.[12] The Minoan system of tripartite gates reflects cosmological concepts defining the center and the periphery of the universe in the east and west.[13]

On some rings, a god or goddess is shown next to his or her respective dwelling, which includes ⊔. For example, on a ring impression from Knossos, the divine palace, several stories high, is surmounted by pairs of ⊔ with central

Fig. 5.1. House of god (or divine place). Stone rhyton from Zakros.

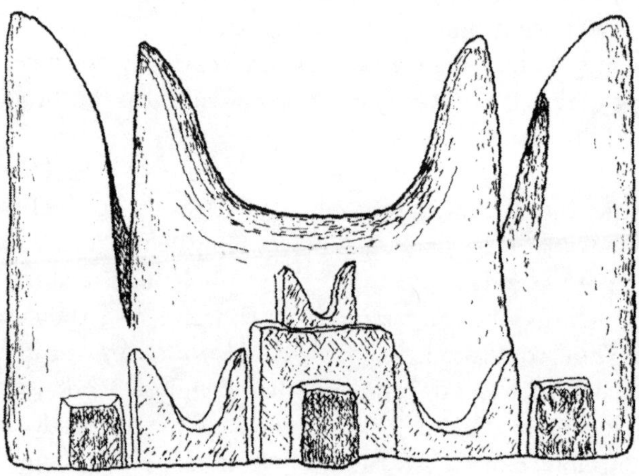

Fig. 5.2. Conceptualized house of god. Clay model from East Crete.

columns between them (Fig. 5.3).[14] A goddess with her back to this palace stands on her mountain and faces a male who salutes her. [15]

On a ring from Thebes a similar architectural vocabulary is employed to represent the divine palace. This time the goddess uses the edifice as her throne (Fig. 5.4). We find again ⊔ and a central column; in addition, we note to the very right an oval design, which may be interpreted as a half rosette.[16] Its significance will be fully appreciated in comparison with the similar motif that occurs on the buildings shown in Figures 5.6 and 5.8. In Figure 5.4 we also see the sun represented above the horizon line. The association of the sun and the semicircle of the split rosette has already been noted in the Tiryns ring (Fig. 2.25), and we shall return to its full interpretation in Chapter 10.

These images show that the house of god in art is definable by means of a specialized visual vocabulary drawn from a pool of cosmic symbols: ⊔, gates, central columns, and rosettes. This vocabulary overlaps and is partly drawn from the hieroglyphs of the Old Palace period and survives into later times (Chapters 8, 9, and 10). On a vase from Cyprus dating more than a century later than the Minoan rings, a goddess stands inside her divine dwelling, which is characterized by ⊔ (Fig. 5.5).[17]

There can be no doubt that this visual vocabulary translated also into actual architecture; the palace of Knossos as well as other palaces and edifices on the mainland and the island of Thera have yielded actual specimens of ⊔. In art, the palace of Knossos was characterized by all the features mentioned here.[18] Take, for example, a building represented on a recently published ring from a tomb at Poros, Crete (Fig. 5.6).[19] It is characterized by ⊔ and by a half rosette. The building on the Poros ring evokes the palace of Knossos, yet it does not represent a specific building but rather its mythical prototype located on the rocky terrain of a mountain.[20]

The Palace as the House of God in the Near East

The house of god and house of king were conceptually fused in the Near East. The palace of Mari, admired and envied by many magnates in the region, was discussed in the previous chapter.[21] We have seen that in its very heart it contained a shrine of Ishtar. This means that the palace of King Zimrilim was also the house of Ishtar: goddess and king shared a dwelling.

Textual testimony from Ugarit further elucidates the role of the palace as a dwelling place of deities, since the god Athtart is said to enter it: "when Athtart-of-the-steppe enters the king's palace."[22] Other deities also come to the royal house, such as the goddesses Shapshu-Pagri and the Tarrumannuma.[23] There is also mention of transfer of divine effigies from sanctuaries to palaces and back.[24] For these reasons, the palace is a place where sacrifices take place, and this means that it incorporates the functions of a sanctuary: "In the royal palace . . . sheep/goats in the HMN-sanctuary, a ram in the sanctuary, in the upper room, a ram in the HMN-sanctuary of Nikkal . . . and a singer shall sing the song, several times, before the king."[25] Among the Hittites, as well, the palace of the king housed chapels of the gods.[26]

We now return to Knossos. If gods had their chapels in the royal house, the

Fig. 5.3. House of god. Ring impression from Knossos.

Fig. 5.4. Minoan/Mycenaean goddess seated on her "palace." Ring from Thebes.

Fig. 5.5. House of god, dwelling with goddess inside. Vase from Cyprus.

Fig. 5.6. Woman votary (perhaps queen) in front of house of god or divine palace. Ring from Poros.

palace of Knossos was a house of divinities and primarily it housed the chief deity of Minoan religion, the solar goddess of kingship, as was observed in Chapter 4 (also see Chapter 12). This explains why statuettes of snake goddesses were found in the repositories of the west wing.[27] They were probably displayed in procession during festivals and sacrifices, and were stored away when not in use until they were finally disposed.[28] The archaeological context of the statuettes in the west wing consists of a mixture of sacrificial remnants (jars, charred bones) and divine images. These remains can be perfectly explained through the prism of the Ugaritic texts, where we read about sacrifices performed to gods in various parts of the palace.

Only in a theocracy do gods and their statues, or divine emblems, reside in the same place as the rulers. Theocratic regimes ensure, through religious ceremonies, unity between social classes and the royal couple.

The House of God with a Sacred Tree and/or Stone

So far we have seen that the palace is the house of god and ruler combined. Open air sanctuaries also existed in Crete, however, and this is perfectly compatible with Levantine and Anatolian evidence.[29]

From the point of view of iconography the tree sanctuaries constitute a different category from the divine palace, because their main feature is a tree or a rock. They do have a gate, but it is rarely embellished by symbols such as the rosette and the central column. As far as we understand, no anthropomorphic cult images were present in these sanctuaries.[30] As we will see here, Minoan sacred trees took their place constituting the focus of the cult.

The open-air sanctuaries as here defined (based on iconography) reflect very closely biblical descriptions. Menahem Haran defines open-air sanctuaries as being characterized by "an altar, a pillar, a sacred tree."[31] In Deuteronomy, sacred tree and sacred image are equivalent: "You shall not plant for yourself any tree, *as a wooden image*, near the altar which you build for yourself to the Lord your God" (Deut. 16:21, my emphasis). "You shall utterly destroy . . . all the places where the nations that you dispossess served their gods . . . under every green tree" (Deut. 12:2). Ahaz "built images of Baal and made sacrifices in high places on hills, and under every green tree" (2 Chron. 28:4).

The prohibition rules cited above from Deuteronomy and Chronicles were made by the followers of Jahweh in the Iron Age, and they reveal how important the sacred tree was in Canaanite and Ancient Israelite cult.[32] They further show that sacrifices were performed next to or under a sacred tree, which means that the latter was a focal point of the cult, taking the place of a cult statue, as I have argued elsewhere.[33]

Trees within sanctuaries are places of divine epiphany. In Genesis, God appears to Abraham under the oak tree of Mamre, an open-air sanctuary north of Hebron (Gen. 18:1).[34] In Judges, Gideon witnesses an epiphany of the lord's angel under a tree: "Now the angel of the lord came and sat under the terebinth tree which was at Oprah. . . . And the angel of the lord appeared to him, and said to him, 'the lord is with you, you mighty man of valor'" (Judges 6: 11).

The biblical passages are much later than our Minoan evidence, and a direct link between the Israelites and the Minoans is not posited here. Rather, what is argued is that both religious systems are part of a Near Eastern tradition (compare with a Tyrian coin, Fig. 7.1). If properly evaluated, this tradition may help us recreate the reality behind Minoan representations of open-air tree sanctuaries.

With this background established, we turn to a ring from Knossos (Fig. 5.7) where the sanctuary has a prominent gate, but it is not embellished by rosettes or other emblems that we have associated with the divine palace. The tree projecting above the gate reveals that this is an open-air sanctuary with a tree as its focus.[35] The resident god is himself present, shown as a small floating image rapidly descending from the sky. In front of him is a pole reaching up towards the sky. This object is identical to Egyptian flagpoles, as Stylianos Alexiou has noted.[36] Thus, the tree sanctuary is a place where the epiphany of a deity occurs to a votary. The building may be defined typologically as an open-air sanctuary, but conceptually it is a *house of god* just as the palace is.

Some sanctuaries are even simpler in their imagery, lacking any architecture and consisting only of a tree and a wooden structure (which is perhaps an altar). Often they are located in the wilderness. In Figure 5.8 rocks and a wild goat show that the sacred tree is in the open country or on a mountainside. In Figure 5.8 the man simply touches the tree, but in Figure 5.9 we see worshippers bringing offerings to the tree. This iconographical language shows that the tree takes the place of a cult statue; the tree is thus conceived as the deity's dwelling place.

The combination of two monuments, tree and rock, is embedded in Near Eastern religious tradition and goes back to the third millennium. An Akkadian seal from that time shows the god Shamash stepping on his sacred rock, next to his tree.[37] The seal has many similarities with the ring from Aidonia (Fig. 5.9); yet there can be no question of influence, because the two are a thousand years apart. What the parallelism shows is a continuity of religious conceptualization in the Near East—which must be distinguished from iconographical tradition—resulting in similar images.

The City of God

"He [the Lord] brought me, in visions of God, to the land of Israel, and set me down upon a very high mountain, on which there was a structure like a city to the south" (Ezekiel 40:2).

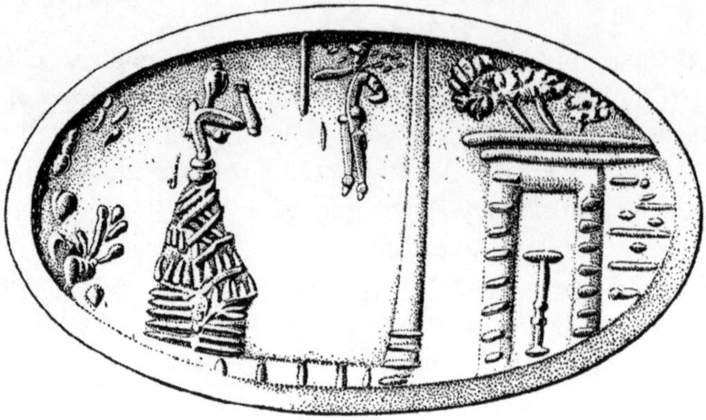

Fig. 5.7. Ritual actions in front of a tree. Ring from Knossos.

Fig. 5.8. Ring from Mycenae.

Fig. 5.9. Ring from Aidonia.

Gods possess not just temples but entire cities; this concept is well rooted in Ancient Mediterranean and Near Eastern tradition. Babylon (the city of El), Jerusalem (the city of Jahweh), Athens (the city of Athena), Memphis (the city of Ptah), Nineveh (the city of Ishtar)—these are just a few examples from the second and first millennia BCE. The city of god is often thought to be at the very center of the universe.[38]

The Minoans, too, evidently had sacred cities, as shown on a ring impression from Chania, western Crete. When the imprint was discovered, it was important news; never before was a male god shown in such glory (Fig. 5.10).[39] Literalist interpretations of the ring impression have been suggested. It was thought that the city is Chania itself, but the archaeological picture does not match the iconography; there is no hill at Chania. Scholars will look in vain for a town with the features represented on the image.

How can we interpret the city on the ring? Keeping in mind that an image is never an exact reproduction of reality, but is an interpretation thereof, we no-

Fig. 5.10. Epiphany of god above town. Ring impression from house at Chania.

tice that the focus of the scene is not so much the town itself but the god who looms large over it. He appears above the central gate, which is flanked by two more portals to the east and west. If I am correct, it is a city of god in the sense that it belongs to the deity and the three gates are references to the east, west, and center of the cosmos. Note that the east and west portals are crowned by half rosettes, a symbol that we have met repeatedly and that, as will be shown in Chapter 10, is a sign with cosmological overtones.[40]

The city of god mirrors the human city that belongs to the king; the god is like the ruler and the ruler is like a god.[41] Mythical and ideological manifestations converge on this representation.[42]

Creating Conceptual Categories: An Answer to the Riddle of the Missing Temples

So what is the answer to the riddle of missing temples in Crete? The conclusion of this discussion is that we need an additional typology of concepts to add to the already existing archaeological typology. Minoan specialists speak of "palace shrines," "house shrines," "public shrines," "bench shrines," "peak sanctuaries," "cave sanctuaries," and "spring sanctuaries." Only "temples" do not seem to exist. This, I would argue, is due to an inadequate definition of the term *temple.* Let us review the state of affairs as they are at present.

Important and necessary work towards classification of shrine typology has been made by M. P. Nilsson, N. Platon, G. Gesell for Minoan urban shrines and by B. Rutkowski, A. Peafield and V. Watrous for nature and mountain peak sanctuaries.[43] Colin Renfrew has made a major contribution on theory and cult as manifested in archaeological remains.[44] All of these scholars have created some order in our evidence by establishing categories without which there could have been no understanding of religious architecture at all. The categories, however, are descriptive of either topography (caves, mountains, springs, towns) or of the physical properties within a building (benches, pillars). This is problematic because the properties selected by archaeologists do not match the categories selected by the Minoans themselves in their iconographical representations. The divergence between our classification of the archaeological evidence and the typology manifested in Minoan imagery means simply this: second millennium Cretans did not conceptualize the house of god in the way we have done. On the other hand, the Minoan images match relatively well the conceptualizations of divine dwellings attested in Near Eastern literature, where the term used for temple (regardless of location and size) is "house of god," in biblical vocabulary *bêt elohim.*

I propose the following solutions:

1. That all the iconographical and architectural categories discussed here may be classified as "houses of god," namely the place where the god resides or visits;
2. That the Minoans distinguished between two types of sanctuaries: a palace, the characteristics of which is the tripartite façade and cosmic symbols, such as the half rosette and ; an open-air sanctuary, which has a single, rather than a tripartite gate, and which includes a tree or stone inside the sacred space;
3. That the house of god is not necessarily an independent structure, but a complex integrated within a larger building (a palace, mayor's house, or even a simpler house); in imagery, however, this sanctuary is still conceived as the house of god, so it follows the usual visual formula (Figs. 5.1–6);
4. That it is impossible to find exact correspondence between archaeological remains and iconography.

The solution to the mystery of the missing temples in Crete may require a simple adjustment of terms or, more precisely, a separation of archaeological from conceptual categories. At any rate, the house of god is clearly conceived as the palace of the ruler. This path has also led us to theocracy.

6

Who Sees the Gods Face to Face?

Christians are not too surprised by visions nor were people in the ancient world because they occurred relatively frequently. However, *why* visions were recorded and *by whom* is not self-evident. This is the question that will be considered in this chapter: who sees gods on Minoan gold rings and why?

We start with some theoretical considerations. In the theocratic systems of the ancient Orient, the privilege of seeing a god face to face was not allotted to everyone, at least as far as official art was concerned. It was the rare privilege of the king to look on the face of deities, a fact that he could advertise in his ideological artistic program. The Minoan rings are biased material, as has been suggested in Chapter 1, because they propagated royal ideology. Consequently, the epiphany scenes that they represent are in some way related to the palace. We might ask why the subject of epiphanies was chosen at all.

Although Evans and Nilsson both noticed that such scenes were relatively common on the rings, neither of them asked why. Their concern was the form of the deity and the method of invocation rather than the social identity of the visionaries.[1] The German scholar Friedrich Matz introduced a novel approach, which may be termed "art-historical anthropology." Epiphanic vision, he said, was an outstanding feature of Minoan religion because epiphany was shaped by the subjective perspective of the worshipper. A crucial key to understanding epiphany, according to Matz, was the small size of the deity in the sky, which implied an application of *distance perspective,* a feature otherwise rare in the ancient world. The peculiarity of Minoan epiphanic representations was due to the fact that the Minoans had no anthropomorphic cult statues of their gods. Consequently their deities were not conceived as stiff statuelike figures, but rather as naturalistic lifelike apparitions seen in the distance. In this, argued

Matz, the Minoans differed from the peoples of the Near East and Egypt who possessed cult images. The Minoan worshipper could actually "see" the god because he or she was in a state of ecstasy.[2]

Matz's view is brilliant, but it is based on the assumption that Minoan culture is different from, rather than similar to, its Near Eastern neighbors. Despite many sensitive readings of epiphany scenes in recent years, the Minoan phenomenon remains vague in the minds of scholars.[3] But if we look at the Near East, we shall find that the *syntax* of the epiphany scenes is not at all peculiar to Crete. The exploration of the syntax will lead us to review not just the social identity of the worshippers but the very message of the iconography.

The King Sees God Face to Face in Near Eastern Art

Seeing and greeting gods directly in the official art of the Near East and Egypt is a privilege reserved mostly for the king. Note that I am discussing the *direct* vision, rather than offering scenes in front of an altar.

One of the best-known monuments of the ancient Orient is the stele of the Babylonian king Hammurabi in the eighteenth century BCE, a ruler best known for his laws. It was inscribed in forty vertical columns and set up by the king in the temple of the chief deity, Marduk, in Babylon. Copies existed throughout the kingdom. On top of the stele is an image of Hammurabi standing in front of the sun god Shamash, whom the king greets by raising his hand, seemingly conversing with him (Fig. 6.1).[4]

The purpose of the iconography can only be properly assessed in connection with the inscribed laws below it. The fact that Hammurabi sees a god face to face singles him out from the rest of mankind. This fact is publicly advertised and acts as a ratification device for the laws below the image. The picture thus has a clear purpose as a legitimation device for the ruler's edicts.[5]

The epilogue of the text reads: "These are the laws of justice, which Hammurabi the able king has established. . . . That the strong may not oppress the weak, to give justice to the orphan and the widow; I have inscribed my precious words on my stele and established it in Babylon before my statue called King of Justice" (transl. J. Oates).[6]

A different type of iconography on a royal monument propagates the king's military victory. Naram Sin, king of Akkad, was a builder of a large empire in the third millennium BCE (c. 2300). He erected a two-meter-high stele on which he is represented as a god wearing the horned helmet that characterizes divinities. Trampling on his enemies, he walks up a mountain, at the top of which he witnesses the epiphany of two major stellar gods of the pantheon, the Sun and the Moon.[7] In this case, divine favor is not expressed by a vision of god but as a

Fig. 6.1. King Hammurabi of Babylon facing sun god Shamash. Diorite stele (eighteenth century BCE)

star epiphany. Still, it is the unique relationship of king and gods that is central to the understanding of the stele. The message is clear: the king's war activities are endorsed by the gods.

Much later in time, on a stone stele depicting king Nabonidus (555–539 BCE) and found in the ruins of the great mosque at Harran in northern Syria, a similar scene is depicted: Nabonidus faces three deities depicted as stellar bodies.[8] Like the Hammurabi stele (1792–50), this one propagates royal accomplishments.[9] One god in particular, the moon god, Sin, is the king's patron deity. It is Sin who entrusted the king with a specific task, and he reports it in the text: "At midnight he (Sin) made me have a dream and said (in the dream) as follows. 'Rebuild splendid Elhul, the temple of Sin at Harran and I will hand over to you all the countries.'"[10].

The dream epiphany is referred to very briefly in the text; the greatest emphasis is placed on Nabonidus's accomplishments as a king: how he managed to overcome rebellious cities, unite the kingdom, and execute Sin's command to build a new temple at Elhul. He is promised success in war and domination over neighboring countries. The epiphany is therefore not as significant in its own right as it is proof that Nabonidus is a protégé of the gods.

Closer to Minoan art in time and space are seals from Syro-Palestine (eighteenth to fifteenth centuries BCE). We meet the king and his patron deity there as well. Consider a Syrian seal on which the king greets a Hathor-type deity, evidently his patron goddess (Fig. 6.2).[11] The ankh signifies that the king is blessed by his goddess. Recall also Figures 4.10a and b, in which the ruler faces his pa-

Fig. 6.2. Ruler greeting goddess. Syro-Palestinian seal.

tron goddess in the vicinity of a palm tree topped by a solar-winged rosette disc. These are only some of the many examples of seals that exhibit an iconography similar to that of large-scale royal monuments. Being instruments of royal ideology, the scenes of the seals suggest that mainly kings see gods face to face.[12]

The images reviewed here cover a large span of time, from the second to the first millennium BCE. This wide chronological gamut shows that a common visual syntax was utilized in the Near East to demonstrate that the epiphany of deities had a special significance in official art, namely to confer privilege to the king.

Who Sees Gods Face to Face on Minoan Rings?

How may the syntax on the Minoan rings be described?

1. The divinity arrives from the sky in rapid motion or stands on the ground. In either case, he or she meets a single woman or man.
2. The visionary sees god face to face.
3. The epiphany takes place outside a building that can be identified as the house of god (Chapter 5).
4. The visionary shows no sign of being in ecstasy (*pace* Matz and other scholars), and there is no trace of a ritual of invocation or sacrifice.[13]

Given these parameters, we must conclude that the method of invocation of the deity was not of interest to the artist. Rather, what the scenes try to convey is the fact of the *occurrence of an epiphany* at the gates of the house of god.

A few concrete examples will illustrate this. A ring of Knossian origin shows a woman standing before a large, impressive male who has an extended arm and can be identified as a god by his gesture (Fig. 6.3a).[14] His sanctuary is behind him. We may conclude that the god has emerged from his "house."[15] The woman who faces the deity has a modest body posture with folded arms; her head is bent down, which suggests that she is subdued and awed; a large star is between the two figures. Since stars are suggestive of star epiphanies in the Near East (as we see in Figs. 6.2 and 6.5b), we are very close to the conceptual apparatus of Near Eastern epiphany scenes.

Fig. 6.3. Queen (?) sees god.
(a) Knossos ring, now in Berlin.
(b) Knossos ring, now in Oxford.

Another Minoan ring, found near Knossos and now in Oxford, shows a woman with her fist raised to her forehead (Fig. 6.3b).[16] The clenched fist can be defined as a special form of greeting addressed by mortals to gods and has Hittite and Egyptian parallels.[17] The divine figure is shown descending from the sky in rapid motion. The meeting place is the outside the house of god, with his sacred tree visible behind the wall (see Chapter 5). The epiphany also may take place on a mountain, as on a ring from a tomb in Messenia (Fig. 6.4). There, a male visionary witnesses the epiphany of a god descending from the sky.

Ever since it was found, a ring impression from Knossos, named by Evans "Mother of the Mountains," has been used as a key piece for the interpretation of the Minoan goddess. It shows a man facing the deity (Fig. 6.5a), and although the deity has been much discussed, the identity of the male who faces her has

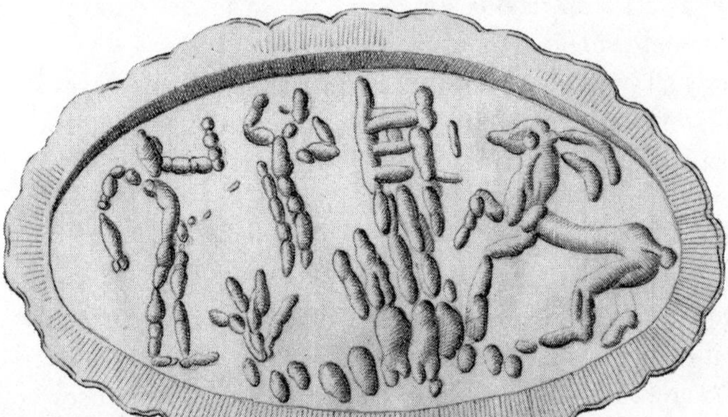

Fig. 6.4. Ruler sees god. Ring from Messenia.

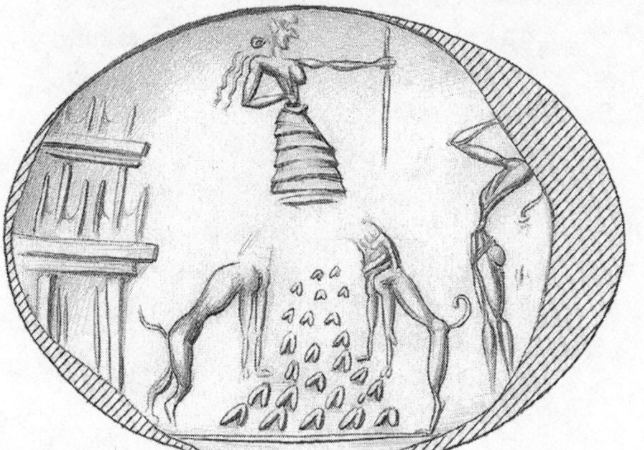

a

b

Fig. 6.5. (a) Ring impression from Knossos. (b) Syrian seal.

been of less interest.[18] Some scholars have noticed that the ring has parallels in Near Eastern representations, especially the investiture scene from the palace of Mari in Syria (Fig. 4.9).[19] I add another comparison: a Syrian cylinder of the mid-second millennium, which has a strikingly similar syntax with the Knossian ring (Fig. 6.5b). Identified by his long mantle with a seam, the figure on this Syrian seal cannot be any other than the ruler.[20]

If we adopt a Near Eastern lens, the males and females who face the gods on the Minoan rings must be kings and queens.[21] It may be argued by the skeptics that this cannot be the case because these figures are not distinguished by any special insignia; they are not wearing a plumed crown or a long mantle. The answer to such an objection is that the dress of the royal personage varies and that, in this instance, the royal visionaries mirror the appearance of the divinities themselves. We have seen this to be the case in Anatolia and Syria, and we have sought the very meaning of kingship in the identical appearance of king and god.

The similarity in the visual syntax between Near Eastern and Minoan images showing king and god cannot be an accident. The privilege of seeing a divinity and advertising this fact is allotted only to special individuals. This last claim may be substantiated with passages from the Hebrew Bible that show that only kings and prophets see God. One individual, especially, is singled out, who is both a leader of his peoples and a prophet: Moses.

Consider the following dialogue between Moses and Jahweh when the former asks to see him: "Now if I have found favor in your sight, show me your ways, so that I may know you and find favor in your sight." God consents, but Moses wants further proof. "Show me your glory, I pray. . . . But, [the Lord] said, you cannot see my face; for no one shall see me and live." Jahweh continued, "See, there is a place where you shall stand on the rock; and while my glory passes by I will put you in a cleft of the rock, and I will cover you with my hand until I have passed by, then I will take away my hand, and you shall see my back; but my face shall not be seen" (Exodus 33:12–23). In this passage, the foremost message is how extraordinary it is for any man to see god and that Moses alone came close.

Of the Israelite kings, Solomon was among the most charismatic, and he, too, saw god, if only in a dream vision: "Then the Lord appeared to Solomon in the night and said to him: I have heard your prayer and have chosen this place for myself as a house of sacrifice (2 Chronicles 7:12).[22]

The Message of the Rings

Why was the subject of epiphany chosen for the rings? Curiously enough, this question has seldom been posed, but perhaps the comparison with the Near Eastern material will help us answer it. The Near Eastern stelai that have been considered here are large-scale public monuments rather than personal items. Yet the rings and seals are also public in some way because they were used to stamp documents and parcels. Thus, they were viewed by many people.[23]

The users of the rings must have shared in the public iconography of prestige, which was disseminated by the royal palace. Such a claim has been made by Irene Winter for Assyrian iconography. As an example, she shows a seal from the reign of Senacherib (704–681 BCE) that represents the king between the gods Assur, on the left, and Ishtar, on the right (Fig. 6.6). Although the king is the protagonist, it does not mean that the seal was wielded by the king's own hand. It was used by a high official, who, by sharing in the royal iconography of power, acquired the authority to act as the king's emissary.[24] The Minoan gold rings were most likely similarly dispensed by the palace to selected courtiers who acted as the king's representatives. The courtiers disseminated royal ideology, bearing the royal seal, as it were.

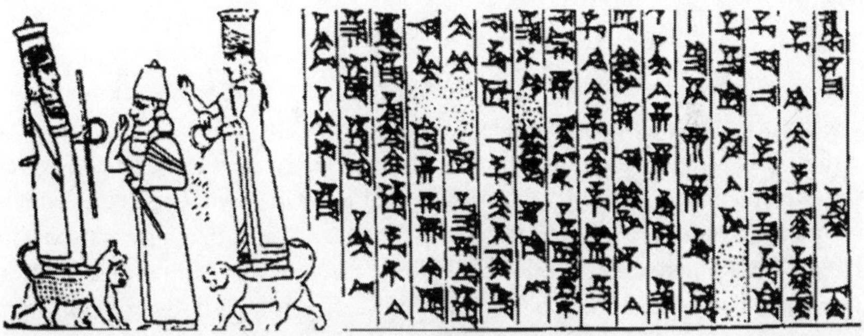

Fig. 6.6. Senacherib between Assur and Ishtar. Assyrian cylinder seal.

The Near Eastern evidence reviewed above demonstrates that the question of who sees the gods is not trivial, but one of great importance. The answer, "worshipper," (usually given in connection with the Minoan scenes of epiphany) is not only inadequate but misses the point of the intended message.

Who sees the gods and why? The answer is this: royal personages who promoted their authority by basing it on intimacy with the gods.

7

Minoan Prophecy and Royal Power

"Among primitive races at the present day the spiritual being constantly descends on the tree or the stone in the form of a bird."

—Sir Arthur Evans

Evans's views about prophecy and divination were colored by his beliefs about *baetyls* and animistic theory. "We have here," he writes about a scene on a ring, "the unique illustration of the primitive baetylic cult of Crete, in which the aniconic image serves as the actual habitation of the divinity and into which, or upon or beside which, he may at any time be brought down by appropriate ritual."[1] Evans here applies Edward B. Tylor's lens on the Minoan representation, namely the idea that spirits enter and exit a human body, tree, or other inanimate object. "To the savage," writes Sir James Frazer, "the world in general is animate, and trees and plants are no exception to the rule. He thinks that they have souls like his own, and he treats them accordingly."[2]

However, Evans wore two sets of lenses at the same time. One was derived from palace cultures of Egypt and the Near East, and the other was the anthropological theory current in his time and principally embodied by Tylor and Frazer. He blended the two lenses, the palatial and primitive, without perceiving the contradiction. The thesis of this chapter is that prophecy and possession occur not only among the "savages," but also in highly sophisticated palatial societies to serve the needs of the royal house.

Let us start from the scenes themselves. There is a group of Minoan gold rings that have divine epiphany as their subject, but this epiphany does not consist of a direct vision nor of an anthropomorphic form of the god, as discussed in Chapter 6. The visions in this second group occur *inside* a sanctuary rather than outside its gate, and the space is marked by a tree or an oval rock.[3] The recipients of the vision are involved in an activity that may be termed ecstatic and that will be further qualified as prophetic.

The visual structure, or syntax, of these scenes has the following basic, important differences with those discussed in Chapter 6:

1. The ecstatic never faces the god.
2. The ecstatic never greets the god with a clinched fist raised to the forehead.[4]
3. The deity rarely has an anthropomorphic guise, and if it does, it is witnessed not directly by the ecstatic, but through the mediation of a figure that I shall identify as a queen.

Much scholarship has been devoted to the interpretation of the action of the figures inside the sanctuary. Most follow Evans's view that the figures worship a tree or a *baetyl* and assume that this is a feature of primitive cult. Clear definitions of *baetyl* are hardly ever offered in contemporary scholarship, and it is taken for granted that the word refers to a stone possessed by a spirit. The word is constructed from Semitic Beth-el, namely "house of God."[5]

We start with the visual vocabulary and the syntax of the rings. The viewer of this group has been mentally transferred *inside* the open-air tree sanctuary that is discussed in Chapter 6; this is probably why its gate is not shown. It is to be suspected that the viewer becomes privy to monuments and associated rituals that were not common knowledge. The holy place can be recognized by the presence of a sacred tree (discussed previously in Chapter 5) or an oval rock, the so-called *baetyl*. To explore the function of the stone we cross the Aegean to Syria-Palestine and Anatolia, where aniconic stone monuments played a substantial role in cult.[6] The Hittites had holy stones called *huwasi*, which were set up in temples or open-air sanctuaries. We know something about them because they are mentioned in inventories, commissioned by the Hittite king Tudhalya IV. They were anointed, like cult images, and sacrifices were performed in front of them.[7]

Rocks as cult monuments are mentioned also in biblical narratives. "Joshua wrote these words in the Book of Law of God; and he took a large stone, and set it up there under the oak in the sanctuary of the Lord" (Joshua 24:26 NRSV). In another story of the Hebrew Bible, Gideon experienced an epiphany of God near a rock on which he had placed an offering: "Then the angel of the Lord reached out the tip of the staff that was in his hand, and touched the meat and the unleavened cakes; and fire sprang up from the rock and consumed the meat and the unleavened cakes" (Judges 6:21 NRSV). From these biblical passages we may conclude that the sacred rock is the spot where epiphanies occur or where oaths are pronounced. Sometimes they are said to be near a tree, which exactly reproduces the scenes on the Minoan rings (see Judges 6:11–19).

The coupling of tree and stone survives even in later times, as shown on a Tyrian coin of the late Roman period: two stone monuments are coupled with a tree and an incense altar in front of them (Fig. 7.1). Many more examples of iconography have been assembled by Tryggve Mettinger; the tradition of stone

Fig. 7.1. Stone and tree in sanctuary. Tyrian coin of the Roman period.

and tree was long indeed in the East Mediterranean.[8] In short, the rock marks the *place* of epiphany and was perhaps conceived as a dwelling place of the god, as Frazer and Evans had envisaged.[9]

Incubation Rituals by the Sacred Rock

Nilsson thought that figures kneeling by a rock worship the *baetyl* without specifying how he imagined the spiritual state of the worshipper. He was apparently confused as to what he really thought, because he sometimes agrees with Evans that the figures are mourners.[10] The *baetyl*-worship theory has major problems. First, the posture does not befit an adorant; it would be strange if worshippers turned their head away from the stone. Second, worship implies offerings, but such offerings are never shown on the rings. See, for examples, Figures 7.2a and b.

Evans and, following him, Axel W. Persson had an alternative explanation. They thought that the rock represented the tomb of a dead god on which a goddess mourned her loved one.[11] The mourning theory originated in the belief that Near Eastern and primitive religions included in their myths the story of a dying young god, an Adonis or a Tamuz, who was mourned by his consort.[12] This scenario, like the possession by spirits, was made popular by Frazer.[13] It reflects a Christian interpretation of Near Eastern myths, but discussion of this subject is outside the scope of this study. Suffice it to say that mourning is rarely, if ever, expressed as a passive state of sorrow in ancient art. Instead, mourners beat their chest and forehead or tear their cheeks and pull their hair.[14] The

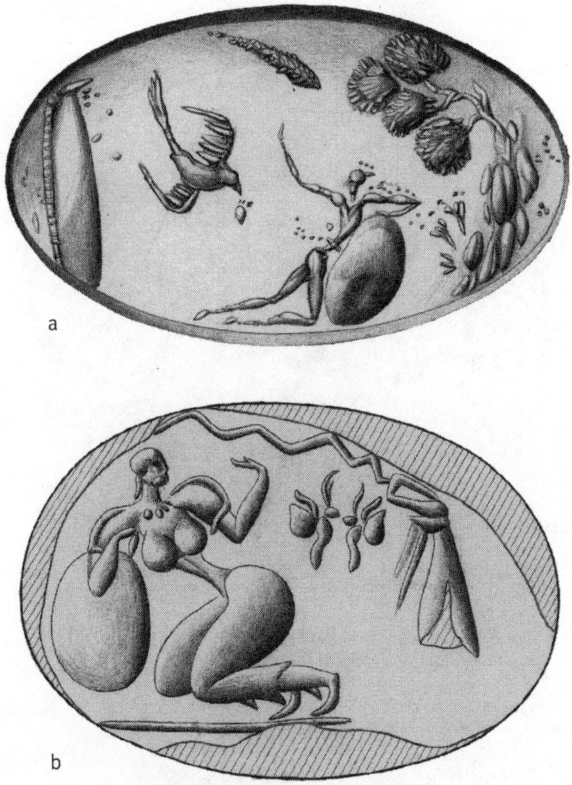

Fig. 7.2. Ecstatics leaning against holy rocks. (a) Ring from Sellopoulo. (b) Ring impression from Hagia Triada.

figures on the rings do none of this. In addition, their backward turned head hardly befits a mourner.

The key to understanding the reclining figures on Minoan rings and seals is furnished by a seal from Knossos that shows a woman resting her head on a stone (Fig. 7.3).[15] The woman is either asleep or, what is more likely, listening to the stone's voice.

In a passage from the *Epic of Gilgamesh,* the sleeper is described as having his chin on his knees. He is half-awake, half-asleep, and experiencs an epiphany:

> Gilgamesh sat with his chin on his knees.
> Sleep, which spills out over people, overcame him.
> In the middle watch he finished his sleep.
> He rose up and said to his friend,
> "My friend didn't you call me? Then why am I awake?

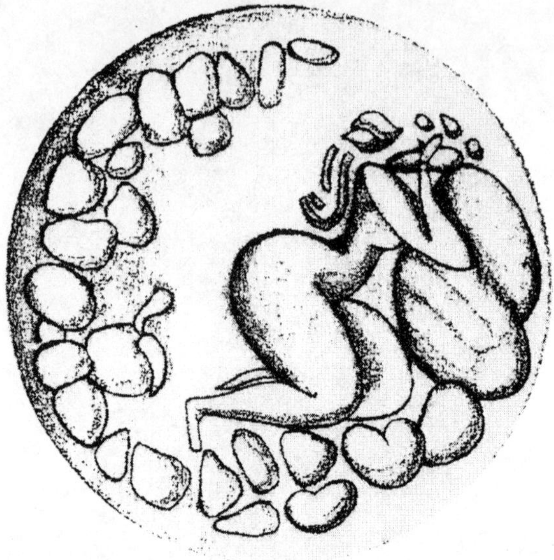

Fig. 7.3. Woman sleeping with head leaning against rock. Seal from Knossos.

> Didn't you touch me? Why am I so upset?
> Didn't a god pass by? Then why is my flesh so feeble?
> Didn't a god pass by?"[16]

The Gilgamesh passage is revealing in many ways. The hero is not reclining, but sitting with his chin on his knees. Also, he is alert because he senses that a god passes by. Gilgamesh experiences the god so vividly that he wakes up, convinced that his friend had touched him. The immediacy of the presence of the divine explains why on the rings the head of the individuals is turned backwards towards a vision: the dreamer "sees" the god and is able to greet him or her by an extended arm (Fig. 7.2). Seeing a deity can be an unnerving experience, as we can infer from the Gilgamesh passage, but note that our Minoan visionaries see not an anthropomorphic version of the god, but a manifestation of the divinity in the form of a bird or an insect or a meteor. We shall return to this.

An equally good text for elucidating dream-visions by a rock is a passage in Genesis, in which Jacob sees God in a dream: "Taking one of the stones of the place, he put it under his head and lay down in the place. And he dreamed that there was a ladder set up on the earth, the top of it reaching to heaven; and the angels of God were ascending and descending on it. And the Lord stood beside him" (Genesis 28:10–13, NRSV).

When Jacob wakes, he anoints the rock with oil and calls it the house of god, *Beth-el* (*baetyl*). This is the passage that supplied nineteenth century scholars with a terminology through which they could understand ancient art: the stone is the god's dwelling place where he can be met, a cult monument *where an epiphany is experienced.*

We may conclude, then, that the rock on Minoan rings was a cult monument, a central feature of the Minoan open-air sanctuary. It was also a place of incubation because at this spot a god might be seen in a dream.[17] The figures resting on the stone may be designated as prophets or ecstatics in a state of incubation.

Shaking or Touching the Tree

Some rings show an alternative mode of ecstatic vision, one induced by the shaking of a sacred tree (Fig. 7.4). The ecstatic is in violent movement, kicking back one leg, as on a seal from Knossos (Fig. 7.4a). We have seen before that touching the sacred tree of god was an experience sought by Minoan worshippers in the wilderness (Fig. 5.8). There are also Near Eastern rituals that involve contact with a tree, although this contact may take diverse forms. Closest to the Minoan rings and seals in concept is a seal from Judah that dates to the Iron Age but does show an ecstatic dance around a palm tree, which, as discussed in Chapter 4, is associated with the sun goddess (Fig. 7.4a and b). Two men kick back their legs in the same manner as the Minoan worshippers.[18]

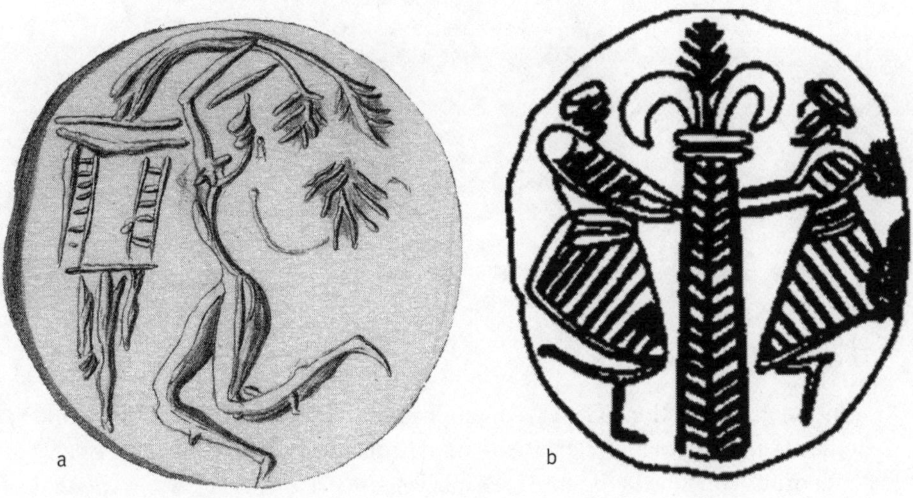

a b

Fig. 7.4. Ecstasy resulting from contact with sacred tree.
(a) Minoan seal. (b) Syro-Palestinian seal.

A biblical passage provides us with a parallel that may serve as an explanation for why the vicinity of the tree was sought by prophets. In the Book of Samuel, David is told by God how to successfully deal with the enemy troops of the Philistines. He should come on the enemy in front of Baka trees, he is told. His instructions are to advance quickly when he hears the sound of marching "at the top of the trees" (2 Samuel 5: 23–24).[19] This implies that the grove of Baka trees was an oracular sanctuary and that if David understood the noise of the trees, he would receive advanced warning about the movement of the enemy. The biblical passage may be a key to interpreting the Minoan rite of tree shaking. The leaves make a sound that the prophet hears and understands. At the same time, contact with the live emblem of the god induces ecstasy (Fig. 7.4). It is noteworthy that on some rings both forms of prophecy are shown, incubation and tree contact (Fig. 7.5).

Fig. 7.5. Woman, perhaps queen, and two ecstatics on ring from Mycenae.

The Mari Prophetic Texts

A substantial collection of letters containing reports about prophecy were found in the royal archives in the palace of king Zimrilim of Mari (1774–1760 BCE).[20] This corpus constitutes the most reliable evidence about prophecy in the second millennium, but unfortunately the archives date to about two and a half centuries earlier than the Minoan rings. At this period, the kingdom of Mari by the Euphrates was strong, although it was destroyed by the Babylonian king Hammurabi shortly after. The prophecy documents are letters sent to the king by either trusted eponymous officials or by his queen.[21] Important to this discussion is that the contents of the letters are relevant to the king's welfare and consist mostly of predictions, warnings, and admonitions.

Note also that the Mari letters are actual records and not fictitious narratives (such as the biblical prophecies). In this they resemble the type of information furnished by Greek oracular inscriptions. They give information about the gender of the prophet, his or her social position, as well as the place where the prophecy took place—aspects that have been lucidly discussed by Martti Nissinen.[22] They constitute a guide to the type of questions we want to ask of the Minoan material, namely, who were the prophets and what was their social status?

In the Mari texts, prophecy takes place *inside* the temple, which is also what we have inferred from the Minoan rings. We also note that incubation is a well-established method of divination. A prophet reports: "In my dream, I, as well as another man with me, was planning a travel . . . Before reaching Mari I entered the Terqa. Having entered [the city], I went into the temple of Dagan and prostrated myself before Dagan. During my prostration, Dagan [i.e., the cult statue] opened his mouth and spoke to me thus."[23] In this report the prophet's spirit wandered in a dream and entered the temple.

From another text we learn that prophecy may have been elicited by some sort of incubation ritual, but unfortunately we do not hear what that ritual was. "D[aga]n, your lord, appeared to me in a dream, even though nobody had performed an incubation ritual on me."[24]

Tree-shaking rites are not attested in the Mari texts, but the following two reports clearly imply a type of ecstasy or trance: "In the temple of Annunitum . . . a servant girl of Dagan-Malik went into trance and spoke."[25] "In the temple of Annunitum, three days ago, Selebum went into trance."[26] In the Akkadian language, the word used for the frenzied prophet, *muhhum* (fem. *muhhutum*), connotes "going crazy."[27] This fits well with the strange activity of kicking on the Minoan rings. We may best explain it as a kind of madness induced through contact with the sacred tree (Figs. 7.4 and 7.5). Physical contact resulting in frenzy also fits well with some biblical passages in which the prophet becomes possessed when the hand of god touches him: "the hand of God came upon him [Elisha]" (2 Kings 3:16).

Two conclusions may be drawn from the Mari texts. First, ecstasy was expected and may have been ritually achieved through psychological preparation, contact with sacred objects, and use of music; it was a performance not a spontaneous occurrence. There are parallels for this controlled prophecy in ancient Greek religion. The Pythia at Delphi prophesied only under certain circumstances, after having chewed the leaves of the sacred tree. Herodotus mentions a man who spent the night in the temple of Amphiaraus in Thebes, presumably with the expectation of receiving a dream vision (Herodotus 8.134).

Second, the Mari texts show that frantic behavior and dreaming were two *alternative* forms of possession. Consequently, the Minoan rings depict practices which are attested elsewhere in the east Mediterranean.

The Message of Stone and Tree in Ugaritic Texts and in Hesiod

The previously discussed passage in Samuel implies that David understood the sound of the Baka trees. The same procedure is referred to in an elusive phrase in the Ugaritic literature of the thirteenth century BCE.

> I have a word that I would say to you,
> a message that I would repeat to you:
> *a word of tree and whisper of stone*,
> the sighing of the heavens to the earth,
> of the deep to the stars,
> I understand the thunder,
> which the heavens do not know, a word unknown to men, and which the multitudes of the earth do not understand.
> Come,
> And I shall reveal it
> In the midst of my divine mountain, Saphon,
> in the sanctuary. [my emphasis][28]

The above comes from the epic of the *Baal Cycle*. The speaker relates a message of the god. The message is "a word of tree and whisper of stone." This is a formulaic pronouncement, a coined expression with reference to a riddle or prophecy. The same rhetorical formula recurs in other Ugaritic texts, and the lacunae may be easily filled precisely because the sentence is formulaic: "I would say to you a message that I would repeat to you [a word of a tree and whisper of stone]." "[For I have a word that I would say to you], a message that I would re[peat to you,]: a word of tree and whisper of stone."[29]

If the expression is formulaic, how did it originate? The coexistence of tree and stone are so evocative of stone and tree on Minoan rings and biblical texts that coincidence is unlikely. Prophetic performance on both sides of the Aegean provides the best explanation for the origin of the proverb. This may be the reason prophets in the Hebrew Bible are often described as sitting under a tree, as is the prophetess Deborah (Judges 4:4) and the "man of God" who sits under an oak tree (1 Kings 13:14).

What is even more remarkable is that the expression is used also by the Greeks some five centuries later. The Greek poet Hesiod (eighth century BCE) claims that the Muses breathed in him a voice divine: "But why all this about [oak] tree and stone?" (*Theog.* 36). In Homer's *Odyssey* we have another version of the proverb: "What is your lineage?" Penelope asks the beggar who is her husband in disguise. "For you certainly did not spring from a tree of the old story or a rock" (*Odyssey* 19.163).[30] Here the oak and tree are linked to a proverbial phrase. Similar expressions are found in the *Iliad* (22.126–28).

I suggest that the expressions in Ugaritic and Greek originate in rituals that go back to the Bronze Age both in the Aegean and the Levant, and possibly also in Anatolia.[31] The oak and the stone refer to divination practices, such as those we witness in Minoan iconography. The oak tree of Zeus played a similar divinatory role in the sanctuary of the god at Dodone.[32] Thus, tree and stone are elements of a Near Eastern *koine*. The expression presupposes knowledge of sanctuaries where rock and tree formed a pair and where prophecies took place. Are the *omphalos* stone and laurel tree of Greek Apollo at Delphi part of the same religious vocabulary seen on the Minoan rings? Indeed, this may well be the case: as coins of later periods testify, *omphaloi* in the shape of oval rocks are depicted throughout the history of the Mediterranean.[33]

The King's and Queen's Involvement in Prophecy

"Write to me whatever oracle is delivered in the temple of god and which you hear," the king of Mari Zimrilim writes to a trusted official.[34] The king was evidently highly interested in receiving positive news from the prophets. On certain occasions he attended the prophetic performance himself. Dressed in a special garment, he entered the temple of Ishtar and sat down."[35] The chanters strike up the *uru-amma-darubi* [chant] of the end of the month. If by the end of the month the prophet maintains his equilibrium and is not able to prophesy when it is time for *mae-u-ruemen* [the chant], the temple officials let the musicians go. If he prophesies, they strike up *ma-eu-re-m[en].*"[36] We further read that the sacred emblems of Ishtar were brought in, no doubt to help the prophet get inspired by signaling the deity's arrival. In any case, the king's presence raised some kind of expectation for performance, although he did not interfere with the inspiration of the ecstatic; indeed, despite the chant, prophecy could not be guaranteed.

Perhaps equally important for the understanding of the Minoan rings is the involvement of the queens in divination matters. We have seen in the Mari texts that the queen sends letters to her husband reporting favorable prophecies and acting as a mediator between king and diviner. Also noteworthy is the fact that the Israelite queen Jezebel hosted some four hundred prophets at her table (1 Kings 18:19). It is not clear why she was the hostess, but it may be suspected that she did so in her capacity as the high priestess of Asherah. The suspicion is further supported by another passage in the Hebrew Bible in which we are told that King Ahab assembled Elijah and all the prophets of Baal at Mount Carmel. They had a contest there, which Elijah won, but this incited queen Jezebel's wrath: "Then

Jezebel sent a messenger to Elijah, saying 'So may the gods do to me, and more also, if I do not make your life like the life of one of them by this time tomorrow.' Then he was afraid" (1 Kings 19:2.). Why Jezebel is so inimical to Elijah is not explained. It is possible that because she was a high priestess of Asherah, the consort of Baal, Elijah undermined her political authority and credibility.

These passages show clearly how royal personages had an investment in prophecy. Having adopted this perspective, we turn to the Minoan rings, where we often see a large female figure with her hands on her hips occupying the center of the scenes; to her left and right ecstatics are dreaming or shaking the tree (Fig. 7.6).[37] On the ring from Archanes, shown in Figure 7.6a, the central figure wears the plumed hat, which has been shown in Chapters 2 and 3 to be exclusively worn by divinities or royalty. The Ashmolean ring, Figure 13.13, may also show the queen. She is to the left of the ecstatic and wears a plume on her head, which is indicated by small dots.

a

b

Fig. 7.6. Woman, perhaps queen, as chief ecstatic and mediator. (a) Ring from Archanes. (b) Ring from Vapheio.

May this central "dancing" figure be the queen? Many scholars, including Evans, have assumed that she is the goddess herself making an epiphany.[38] The difficulty with this interpretation is that a dance posture would be unprecedented for divinities: gods normally have stiff formal stances in Near Eastern and Egyptian art. The central figure on the rings, on the other hand, is a performer, as her bent arms and knees show. The arms on her hips remind one of dervishes whirling around. It is consequently easier to understand her as an intermediary between the prophets and gods than as a deity.[39] If she is the queen, her large size and plumed hat would be explained. It must be admitted, however, that I know of no such precedent for the role of an ecstatic queen in the Near East. The only biblical incident that comes to mind is when the king falls into prophetic ecstasy. This was the case with Saul after he was chosen to be king "and the spirit of God possessed him, and he fell into a prophetic frenzy" (1 Samuel 10:9). I tentatively conclude that the queen or queen mother were participants in ecstasy rituals in their capacity as priestesses of the solar goddess.

The Status of the Prophet

What was the status of the other ecstatics shown on the rings of palatial Crete? The biblical notion of a prophet as a towering or even ascetic figure rivaling the king is completely misleading. Martti Nissinen correctly observes that the men of authority and miracle making in the Hebrew Bible constitute a special case: "Many would avoid the use of the word *prophecy* outside the Biblical context."[40] For this reason, the designation "prophet" must be used with circumspection, and in no way should we associate the Minoan ecstatics with the chosen men of God in the biblical tradition. At the other extreme of the scale of privilege are the prophets of the Mari and Nineveh texts who are mere employees of the palace. When they please the king, they are rewarded with gifts, such as garments, rings, and occasionally donkeys. Even Israelite prophets were sometimes the king's servants, as we can see in the story of Ahab and Elijah (1 Kings 18:20).

On the Minoan rings, the prophets seem to enjoy a status higher than we would expect from a temple employee.[41] First, they wear jewelry, which is always a mark of distinction in Minoan art. Also the formidably curvy bodies of the women resting against the rock on the Zakros and Hagia Triada ring imprints give the impression that they are matrons whose femininity is emphasized (Figs. 7.7a and b). As far as the dress goes, it is worth noting that the women leaning against the rock wear not the flounced skirt, but only an undergarment. Perhaps this minimal dress is a sign of humility in front of the gods.

All in all, it seems that the Minoan ecstatics belonged to an elite class but must be differentiated from the central dancing figure with the plume, which I have tentatively identified as the queen.

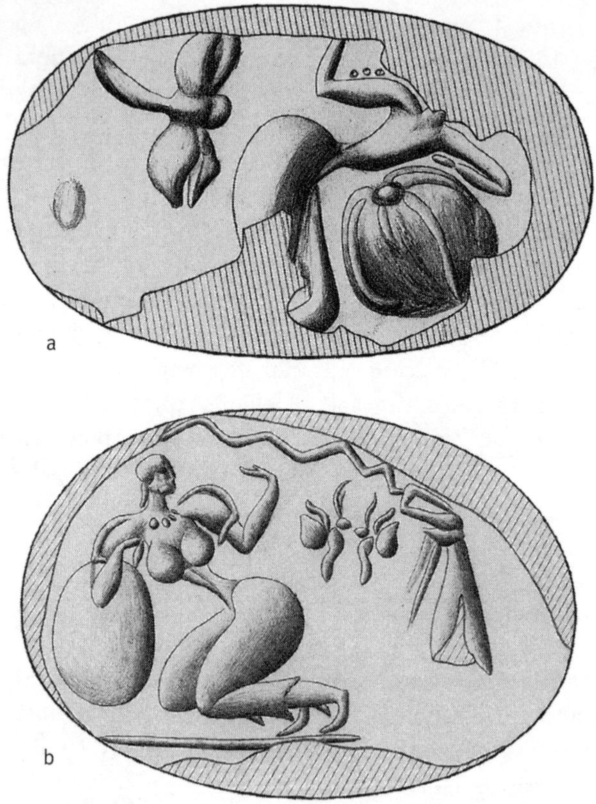

Fig. 7.7. Ecstatic, perhaps queen, having visions of huge dragonflies or butterflies, perhaps epiphany of deity. (a) Ring impression from Zakros. (b) Ring impression from Hagia Triada.

The Visions: Insects, Birds, and Shooting Stars

What do the prophets see? Because the corpus of the rings consists of a handful of scenes, the material is not enough for a complete decipherment. Despite these difficulties, we can discern certain patterns.

The first type of discernible vision to be discussed here are huge butterflies or dragonflies that are so large that they must connote something extraordinary. They occur together with a figure leaning on a rock and are "seen" by the visionary (Fig. 7.7a and b). In one scene (Fig. 7.7b), the two insects are coupled with a sacred garment (perhaps of the goddess) and hover below a zig-zag line that represents the firmament. The insects may well be manifestations of the divine encoded in a symbolic language. What this would mean is that the real form of god is not perceived clearly but that his or her manifestation is the insects.

In another instance (Fig. 7.8), we see a large bull accompanied by a huge dragonfly or butterfly that hovers above his back. There is no prophet here, yet the composition reminds us of the visions discussed previously. One possible interpretation is that the dragonfly is a manifestation of the goddess, her spread wings evoking the form of the double axe (Chapter 9). The insect may thus represent the epiphany of a female deity, whereas the bull may be the sacred animal of a male god. This is all speculative, but this much is certain: the motifs constitute a code that defies literal interpretation.

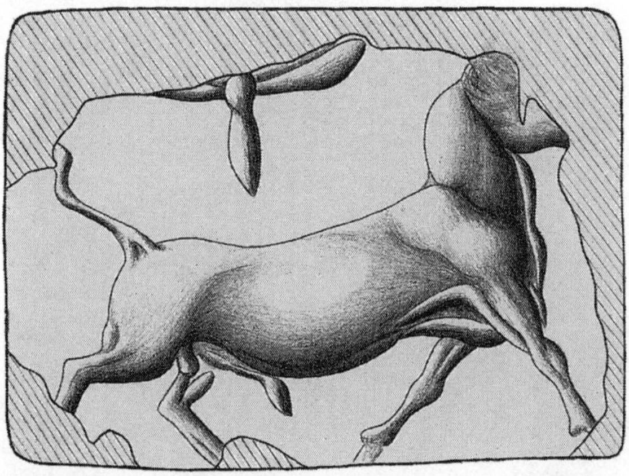

Fig. 7.8. Huge dragonfly above bull. Seal from Zakros.

The second type of discernible vision consists of birds. For example, on two rings shown here the visionaries greet a bird, which is probably another manifestation of a god; this, at least, was Nilsson's view (Fig. 7.9).[42] On the Sellopoulo ring (Fig. 7.9b), the vision includes a sign in the sky, which resembles a sheaf of wheat.[43] This object is most likely a meteor or shooting star, and this is why it appears in the sky, high in the field of the ring. It is attested also in other scenes (see, for example, the Tiryns ring, Fig. 2.25, and the Poros ring, Fig. 7.10).[44]

A few passages from the Greek *Iliad* might aid our understanding of the ancient viewer's perspective about meteor or bird epiphanies. "Athene swooped down from heaven through the air, like a shrieking, long-winged bird of prey" (*Iliad* 19.350). Note that nobody in the Trojan or Greek camp knows that this bird is Athena except the poet himself. In another passage, Athena and Apollo meet by a sacred oak tree. They sit down in the form of vultures on the "tall oak tree sacred to aegis-bearing Zeus" and enjoy the sight of Trojans and Greeks fighting one another (*Iliad* 8.70). In another passage, Athena appears as a meteor:

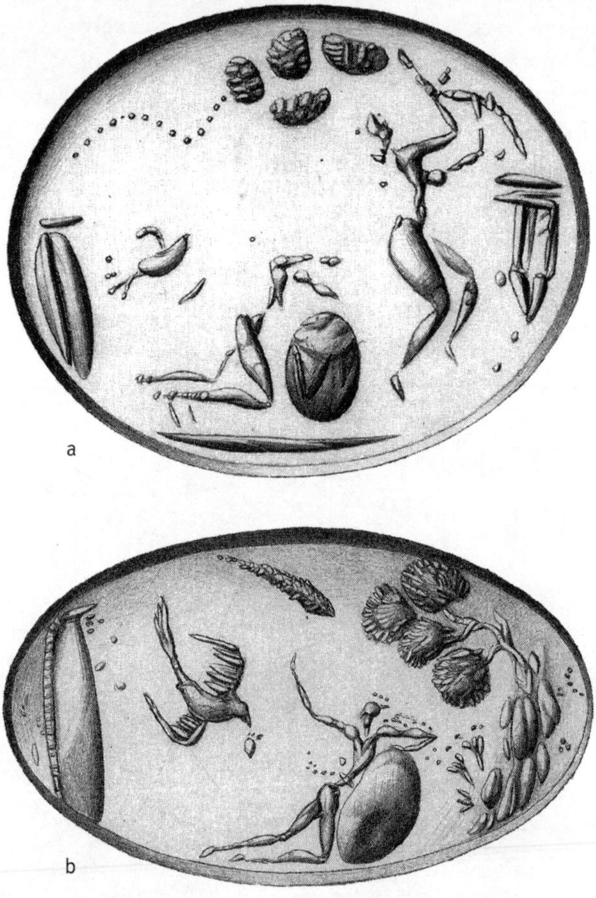

Fig. 7.9. Visions of birds. (a) Ring from cemetery of Kalyvia near Phaistos. (b) Ring from Sellopoulo.

"Athene, who had already set her heart on action, sped down from the peaks of Olympus, like a shooting star that is discharged by Zeus as a warning to sailors . . . and comes blazing through the sky tossing out innumerable sparks" (*Iliad* 4.23; 58–59).

I do not claim that there is any direct continuity between the Minoan ring and the Archaic text of the *Iliad.* Rather, what I assume is that both are documents of a Near Eastern and Mediterranean *koine.* A hovering insect, a sparkling meteor, a swooping bird: all are manifestations of the gods, but none of them in the true form of the divinity.[45]

A third type of vision is different from those previously discussed. It is attested on a gold ring recently found in a cemetery at Poros, near modern Herakleion (Fig. 7.10). The center is dominated, not by a dancing queen, but by an

Fig. 7.10. Seated goddess in mid-air appearing to visionary, perhaps king, who stands on a podium with ecstatic to his right. Gold ring from Poros.

impressive male with a tall hat standing on a podium and extending his arm in the manner of kings and rulers. Is he a god or a king? His status is ambiguous, probably deliberately so. In any case, he faces a goddess seated above the wings of two huge birds. A minute female figure is also hovering above them.[46] To the right, a man is shaking a tree: he is the ecstatic. Note, however, that the prophet does not see the goddess because this is a privilege reserved only for the king or the god. Who the central male with the peaked headdress is cannot be decided on the basis of the iconography because god and king are interchangeable (Chapters 2 and 13).

Prophecy as an Instrument of Royal Bureaucracy and Power

I argued in Chapter 1 that rings are biased material because they were instruments of royal administration and, thus, served the purpose of royal self-presentation and administration at the same time.[47] But how does prophecy fit into this scheme?

In the Near East, prophecy serves the needs of the royal house. The prophetic letters of Mari and Nineveh were kept in temples or in the king's library because, as Nissinen pointed out, they directly or indirectly enhanced the authority of the king.[48] The Minoan rings are different because they record *generic* statements of fact rather than *specific* accounts of individual utterances: a prophetic vision has occurred. This latter fact is the key to the interpretation of the iconography. The message is that prophecy has occurred and that the royal family was privy to it. Without exception, all the Mariot prophecies are addressed to the legal power, says Jean-Marie Durand.[49]

With this final stage of interpretation, we have moved very far from Evans and Nilsson's theory of tree cult and tree adoration: "Tree cult," wrote the Swedish scholar, "is one of the best known features of primitive religion."[50] However, instead of the primitive ecstasy envisaged for Crete by scholars of the early twentieth century, the activity depicted on the rings should be reinterpreted as a feature of a palatial theocratic society.

8

The Cosmic Mountain as a Frontier

The best known pictograms of the ancient world are the Egyptian hieroglyphs. Yet the Egyptians were hardly the only ones to have developed pictographic scripts: Minoans, Luwians, and Hittites had them as well. In all these cultures the signs of the script had a conceptual value as ideograms in addition to their phonetic value. In other words, the sign expressed an idea that helped the viewer instantly to grasp the concept behind the image. This ideogrammatic meaning of signs will occupy us here.

The Minoans developed several hieroglyphic systems during the Old Palace period that were later replaced by Linear A and B.[1] One of Evans's many contributions is his observation that Minoan hieroglyphs were also used as ideograms in art, especially on seals of the Old Palace period. He also noted that many hieroglyphs were common to the Egyptian script.

In the following three chapters, the ideogrammatic meaning of four important Minoan hieroglyphic signs, numbers 36 through 38 in Evans's inventory, are deciphered (Fig. 8.1).[2] It is shown that they can be understood in the context of Minoan cosmology, religion, and kingship.

The Minoan "Sacred Horns": The Reasoning of Evans

Hieroglyph 37 is commonly interpreted as "bull's horns." It also exists as a three-dimensional object found in many places in Crete, the mainland and the Aegean islands. We can, therefore, be certain that it is a symbol of great importance for Minoan cult. But what is it?

One specimen, found in the southern section of the Knossian palace, may give us a first clue (Fig. 8.2). Evans noted that it made a perfect frame for the mountain of Juktas; although its original location is uncertain, the question arose in his mind whether there existed a relationship between the object and the mountain itself.[3]

In the end, Evans rejected this option. He assumed that the shape represented stylized bull's horns, perhaps because he was impressed by the ubiquitous presence of the bull in the palace. It is also possible that he was influenced by the

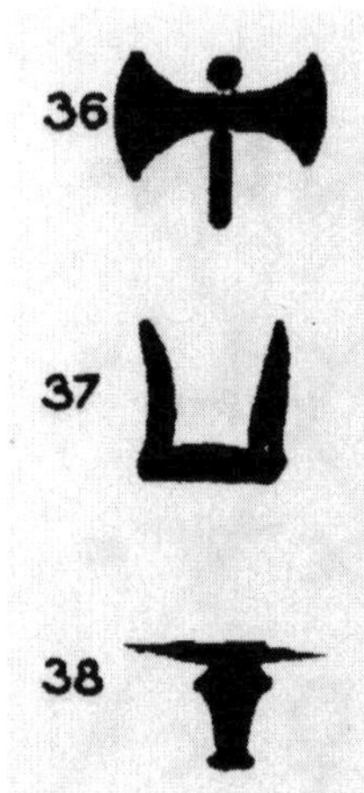

Fig. 8.1. Ideogram of double axe, sacred mountains, and ox head in Minoan hieroglyphs of Old Palace Period. Hieroglyphs 36–38 in Evans's inventory.

Fig. 8.2. Top of mount Juktas viewed from the palace of Knossos. Framing mountain is object that Evans interpreted as bull's horns but may be better explained as "sacred mountain."

biblical description of Hebrew incense altars in Exodus 30:1–3: "You shall make an altar on which to offer incense; you shall make it of acacia wood. . . . It shall be one cubit long, and one cubit wide; it shall be square . . . its horns shall be of one piece with it" (RSV).

Evans knew his Bible well; horns are indeed mentioned there. Yet the context shows that the horns refer to each of the four wooden poles projecting from the corners of the altar, thus defining the cardinal points of the square edifice. *Horns* is used in a metaphorical way in the Exodus passage and has nothing to do with bulls (note also that the altar is an incense altar and not a slaughter table).[4]

Evans had another reason for his interpretation. He looked at a stele from the sixth century BCE (Achaemenid period), which is now in the Louvre, and interpreted it as an altar topped by horns and a bull's head (Fig. 8.3). He assumed that the head was a sacrificial offering, concluding that this was a "complete parallel" to the Minoan usage.[5] He thus deduced that ⊔ on which the animal's head was placed must designate bull's horns.[6]

Fig. 8.3. Royal personage shown twice. On upper level, as king topped by the sun disc; on lower level, acting as high priest, the king stands in front of podium (not necessarily altar) with boukephalion. Stele from Persian period, now in Louvre.

Evans's reasoning is based on the principle of association by contiguity, by which two linked objects mean the same thing. Thus, if a bull's head is shown together with ⊔, then the latter must be its horns. But this is erroneous logic which, if followed strictly, would mean that any two objects shown together (let us say a spoon and a fork) would have the same meaning.

A second problem is that Evans did not illustrate the whole stele but only its lower part, which depicts a male figure in front of the so-called altar. If we look at the entire stele, however, we see that the "altar" is, rather, an object of veneration (and indeed this is what the gesture of the worshipper indicates).[7] If this is the case, the implications are quite different from what Evans imagined. In the next chapter, the bovine head (hieroglyph 38 in Fig. 8.1) will be discussed extensively; it will be shown that it is not a sacrificial animal but a mythical one imagined in heaven.

Let us return to the so-called horns. Nilsson, Evans's critic, followed him in this case: "the use and significance of the sacral horns are established with certainty through the testimony of the representations. They were justly called 'horns of consecration' by Sir A. Evans."[8] Yet Nilsson emended the original theory: "The Minoan horns of consecration are no symbol but a cult implement, the place of consecration for different objects."[9] Having lost its symbolic function, ⊔ now becomes a mere implement of cult. And yet, even a cursory glimpse at the collection of Nilsson's evidence will show that the object in question is almost never a receptacle for offerings, an implement of consecration. For this reason, its function can hardly have been to consecrate, as Nilsson suggested.[10] Rather, it is an embellishment of the palace, enriching its meaning as a cosmic center (Chapter 5).

Interpreting ⊔ as "sacred horns" is not convincing, but Nilsson's acceptance of this interpretation caused the hypothesis of Evans to become fixed in stone. Generations of scholars have relied on these two giants of Minoan religion for the interpretation of the sign as bull's horns, an idea that originated with a biblical passage and a misunderstood image, as has been shown here. Nevertheless, even at the time of Evans, there were alternative views, which Nilsson with his characteristic objectivity, carefully recorded. He cites the theories of the Dutch scholar W. B. Kristensen and the German scholar W. Gaerte, who both regarded the so-called horns as mountains, pointing to the similarity with the equivalent Egyptian ideogram. Nilsson concluded, however, that the hypotheses were wrong.[11] Written in Dutch and German, respectively, these theories found no echo. Occasionally, the similarity between the Egyptian mountain of the horizon and the Minoan "horns" is noticed anew. Barry Powell demonstrated it in 1977, but he did not discuss the cosmological concepts underlying this coincidence of form.[12] In more recent years, Alexander MacGillivray and Vance Watrous have also returned to this view.[13] I endorse it here as well and will add additional visual evidence that makes it unlikely that the symbol is anything but the twin peak mountain depicting the east and west points of the horizon. Given the similar morphology of mountain signs in Crete and the Near East, it would be strange indeed if the Minoan symbol *alone* meant something different.

The Minoan "Horns" Redefined as a Mountain

As noted above, the Minoan symbol (Fig 8.4a) is almost identical to the Egyptian cosmic mountain. The Egyptian symbol consists of two peaks that define the horizon between which the sun disc rises (Fig. 8.4b). On Akkadian seals of the third millennium we find a very similar rendition of the mountain represented as two scaly cones that signify "land" (Fig. 8.4c). In Syria and Anatolia, the twin peaks also symbolize a mountain, sometimes a double one (Fig. 8.4d).[14]

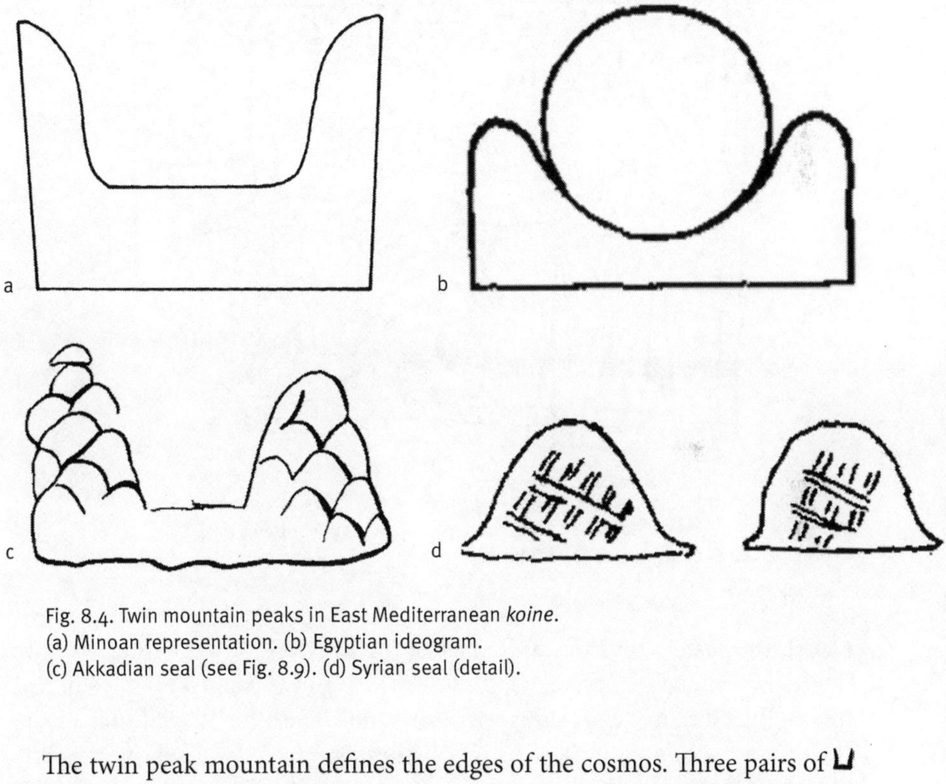

Fig. 8.4. Twin mountain peaks in East Mediterranean *koine*.
(a) Minoan representation. (b) Egyptian ideogram.
(c) Akkadian seal (see Fig. 8.9). (d) Syrian seal (detail).

The twin peak mountain defines the edges of the cosmos. Three pairs of ⊔ would cover three sides of this imaginary cosmic triangle, and four pairs would define an entire square. For this reason, ⊔ occurs in double, triple, or even quadruple numbers (see, for example, Figs. 8.5 and 11.2). A symbol so common to Mesopotamia, Syria, Anatolia, and Egypt and designating "mountain" *must* have had a similar meaning in Crete. Subsequently, our task will be to explore its use in Minoan conceptual thought.

First, Nilsson's theory of consecration ought to be put to the test. It has been previously mentioned that we do not see offerings (bread, meat, incense, etc.) between the peaks of the object that has been redefined as a mountain; therefore, its function cannot have been to sanctify offerings. Instead, the two peaks frame a tree (Fig. 8.5), a double axe (Fig. 9.2a), or a god (Fig. 8.7a). All of these are symbols of cosmic significance and not votives that can be consecrated. Nilsson's view is therefore conceptually inaccurate.

One particular scene, a bronze votive tablet from the cave of Psychro (Fig. 8.5), will be considered next.[15] Three pairs of twin mountain peaks define the

Fig. 8.5. Cosmic tree growing between peaks of sacred mountain and framed by sun and moon above and sea (fish) below. Bronze votive tablet from Psychro.

center, the eastern and western edges of the universe. In the center we have a tree that reaches to the very top of the scene and is framed by the sun and moon. In addition, we see a fish and a bird and some other illegible object. On the ground, a human is dancing or worshiping. Lucy Goodison has cleverly suggested that the sun's journey is being represented.[16] In any case, the central tree is an axis of this cosmic map and it grows between the mountain peaks. If we compare it with an Akkadian seal depicting the rise of the sun god, we find the same cosmic elements: tree, fish, and birds (see, for example, Fig. 8.9b). On a seal from Vapheio, a tree rises between the two peaks of the mountain (Fig.

8.6). Because it is watered by leonine demons, there is little doubt that this, too, is a cosmic tree ensuring the well being of the earth. In summary: the tree rising between the Minoan twin-peak mountain is not consecrated as an offering but constitutes the tree of life. This is the solar palm that has been already encountered in Chapter 4.

On a seal from Cretan Kydonia we meet something even more striking: instead of a tree there is a god standing between the mountain peaks and receiving homage from a Minoan demon and a goat (Fig. 8.7a).[17] The visual syntax of the rising god has parallels in Egyptian art: primeval Geb rises up from a mountain (Fig. 8.7b).[18] In the Hittite sanctuary at Yazilikaya, a mountain god stands atop one (Fig. 8.7c).[19] On Akkadian seals, the sun god Shamash habitually rises between the twin peaks of a mountain (see, for example, Fig. 8.9).

Fig. 8.6. Tree between peaks of sacred mountain, framed by demons. Seal from Vapheio.

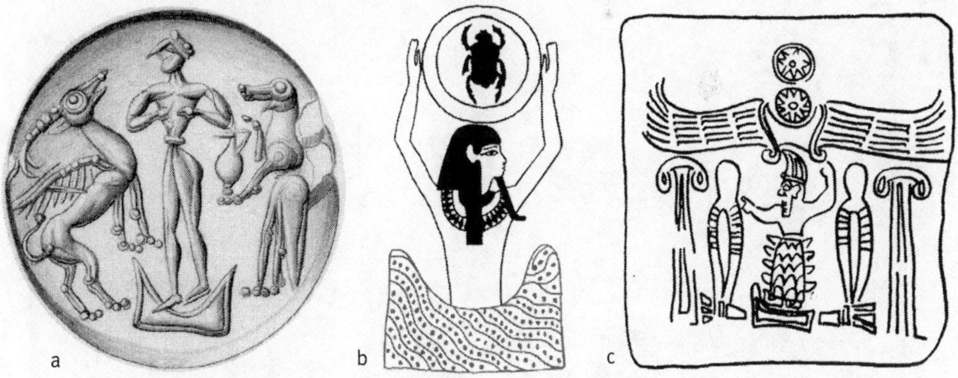

Fig. 8.7. God standing between peaks of sacred mountain. (a) Minoan seal from Kydonia (western Crete). (b) Egyptian image. (c) Relief from Yazilikaya.

All the cases discussed here prove that Evans's and Nilsson's theory that ⊔ is an altar serving to consecrate an object cannot be right. The connection with the sacrificial bull was tenuous and arbitrary. It has been shown, instead, that the morphology of the sign is almost universal and designates the twin peaks of a cosmic mountain. But the story of the mountain is not finished yet; we must investigate the conceptual apparatus behind its inception.[20]

The Mountain as a Gate to the Underworld in Near Eastern Cosmology

Mountains are gates. Strange as this may seem to us, it was a common concept in Near Eastern mythology, and it is a key for unlocking the door of its meaning.

A starting point for our discussion will be a clay votive model of a sanctuary from East Crete excavated by Costis Davaras. It shows a peculiar building that is a blend of fantasy and realism and has the shape of two large mountains, one within the other (Fig. 8.8a; see also Fig. 5.2).[21] In the center, a gate is flanked by more mountains and smaller gates. This highly abstracted construction illustrates how "mountain" and "gate" are conceptually linked in the Minoan world of ideas. The Egyptians constructed similar images: for example, a door is shown on top of the mountains of the horizon sign on a papyrus from the *Book of the Dead*, Nineteenth Dynasty (Fig. 8.8b).[22]

Mountain gates are also present on Akkadian cylinders of the late third millennium that show the rise of the sun god Shamash from the underworld (Figs. 8.9). The gate to the beyond is conceived as a double-peak mountain, sometimes guarded by lions.[23] The Akkadian seals depict an entire mythological topogra-

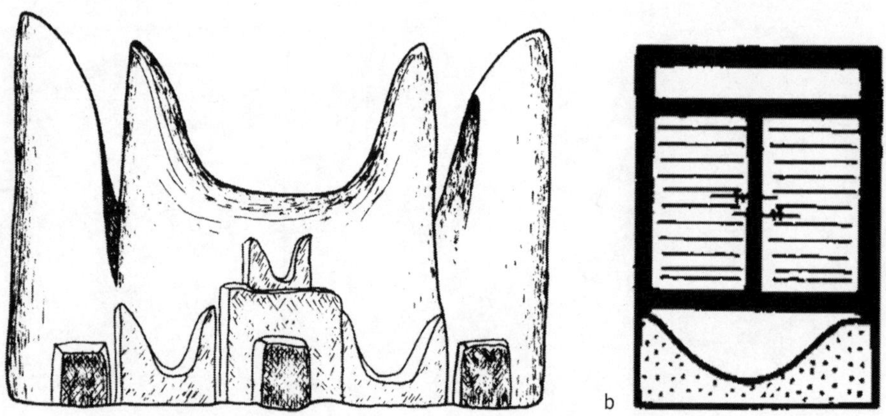

a

b

Fig. 8.8. Mountains as gates. (a) Gates within mountains on Minoan clay model. (b) Mountain and gate on Egyptian funerary papyrus vignette from New Kingdom.

Fig. 8.9. Babylonian god Shamash rising from the mountain gate.
In Akkadian cylinder seals (third millennium BCE).

phy. The sun god rises from the netherworld through the mountain gate and is greeted by Ishtar and other gods. A river flows by. Birds and sometimes animals are there to greet him at sunrise.

The idea that the mountain is a gate to the netherworld is supported by linguistic evidence. The Sumerian word *kur* means both "mountain" and "underworld." This has puzzled scholars because the two meanings seem incompatible if not outright contradictory.[24] The contradiction is removed if the mountain is simultaneously a ladder upwards towards heaven and downwards to the underworld: it is a medium of transition between worlds, which makes it equivalent to a gate.[25]

The Assyrian twelve-tablet version of the *Gilgamesh* epic gives us explicit and lively evidence about the journey of the hero to the edges of the cosmos along the path of the sun. He travels in search of the man who can advise him on matters of immortality: the wise Utnapishtim. The latter is the only mortal who has ever been present at the assembly of the gods and thus knows everything about life and death. He lives far away at the edges of the universe, and Gilgamesh sets out to find him. He must leave civilized cities behind him and proceed in the wilderness, traversing the steppe and killing lions at mountain passes. He comes to the cosmic mount Mashu "which daily guards the ascent and descent of the sun." The mountain is a cosmic gate guarded by a scorpion man whose mien and eyes are terrible to behold and whose function is to stop anybody who wants to enter the gate of the sun.[26] Gilgamesh is questioned by the guard: why does he want to pass the gate? The answer is deemed satisfactory, and he is allowed to go through, although not without a warning of the trials he is to meet ahead. The path of Gilgamesh through the dark tunnel of the mountain is measured in twelve units, which are units of space and time, evidently reflecting the Egyptian model of the twelve-hour sun journey in the underworld. At the end, Gilgamesh arrives at a splendid garden.

This passage is a goldmine of information about Mesopotamian cosmology. First, we learn that Mashu is a cosmic mountain, the root of which is located in the underworld, whereas its peak reaches heaven.[27] We also learn that the sun uses the mountain as a gate. This is important because it corresponds exactly to the images of the sun god rising between the mountain peaks engraved on the Akkadian seals (Fig. 8.9).

The final piece of evidence about the role of mountains as the frontiers of the universe is a Babylonian cosmic map on a clay tablet dated anytime between the ninth and seventh century BCE (Fig. 8.10).[28] Here, the universe is represented as a circle. In the center are cities and rivers. Around the circle is a cosmic river, the *marratu,* (equivalent to the river Ocean in Greek mythology). Beyond this river lie triangular regions referred to in Babylonian as *nagu;* they are usually thought to represent islands. Because of their triangular shape, however, it is more likely that they are mountains. This has been argued by Nicolas Wyatt, and I find this very convincing because mountains are always triangles in ancient art, whereas islands are not.[29] One thing is certain: the triangles constituted the world's frontier.

The model developed here fits reasonably well with the Hebrew Book of Enoch, dating to more than a thousand years later (second century BCE). The mountains that define the borders of the universe in 2 Enoch are twelve: three in the north, three in the west, three in the south, and three in the east.[30] The prophet reaches the underworld through a mountain: "And he showed me to the west a great and high mountain of hard rock, and there were four hollow places in it, deep and very smooth . . . and a fountain of water was in the midst of it. . . . These hollow places are intended that the spirits of the souls of the dead might be gathered into them" (2 Enoch, 22:1–3). Because this work dates much later than our period, it may be used as proof that the conceptual ap-

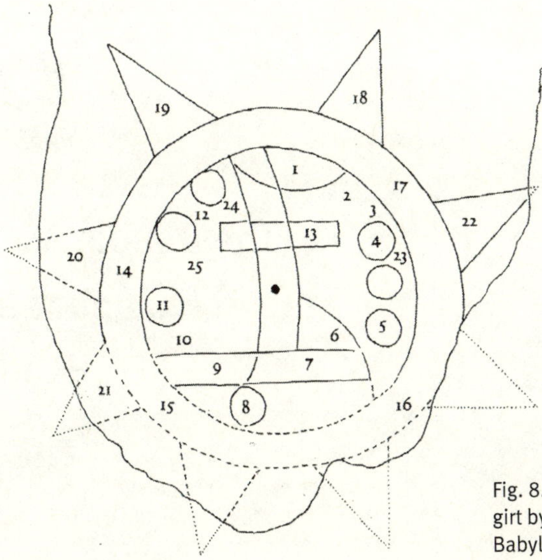

Fig. 8.10. Cosmos as circle girt by river and mountains. Babylonian map.

paratus of the ancient Near East regarded the mountain as "transition between two dimensions" over many centuries.[31]

Near Knossos there is a mountain by the name of Juktas, which dominates the plane south of Knossos. It is not very high, but its conical shape makes it stand out as a special feature of the landscape. Being atop this mountain is an unusual experience. The view of the north coast of Crete and much of the surrounding plane is perfectly compatible with the fantasy that it is a pillar of the universe. The ancient Greeks claimed that it was the tomb of Zeus, thus imagining it as an axis uniting the heavens with the world below. Excavations, which were conducted already by Evans and continued in the 1980s by the Greek archaeologist Alexandra Karetsou, have proven that Juktas was considered one of the most impressive sacred mountains of central Crete. At its top was a monumental sanctuary, which was open to the sky although it contained rooms for storage. Its most salient feature is an altar and a deep fissure in the rock. This chasm, found full of votives, was apparently the entrance to the underworld.[32] The further associations of the mountains with the underworld will be explored in Chapter 11, where the ⊔ motif decorates the coffins of the dead.

In conclusion, the Minoan pictogram ⊔ is neither a bull nor an altar but a mountain. Yet, as we shall see, Evans was not completely off the mark; as usual, part of his intuition was correct. The full significance of the pictogram will be appreciated only when we look at two other syntactically related signs: the ox head (hieroglyph 38 in Fig. 8.1) and the double axe (hieroglyph 36 in Fig. 8.1), to which we turn next.

9

The Double Axe, the Ankh, and the Ox Head

"It is clear that the special aniconic form of the supreme Minoan divinity, as of her male satellite, was the Double Axe."

—Sir Arthur Evans

The double axe is hieroglyph 36 in Evans's grid (Fig. 8.1). "Of all religious symbols and emblems that appear in the Minoan civilization the double axe is the most conspicuous, the real sign of Minoan religion and as omnipresent as the cross in Christianity and the crescent in Islam," wrote Nilsson.[1] Evans was the first to stress this and used the double axe, along with the plumed crown, on the cover of his *Palace of Minos*.[2] His ideas about what it signified shifted in time as his knowledge about the Minoans increased. At first, he suspected that it represented a male Minoan god, but later he changed his opinion. Convinced of the predominance of the Great Goddess, he arrived at the conclusion that the double axe embodied a duality: the goddess and her consort or son.[3]

For the pragmatist Nilsson, the double axe was not a deity at all but a sacrificial instrument, a mere tool of cult.[4] There are two major objections to Nilsson's view. First, the double axe is never depicted as an instrument of animal sacrifice in Minoan or Mycenaean art.[5] Second, it would be unusual in the ancient world if a mere tool were turned into the central symbol of a religious system.

Scholars today follow either of two schools: the pragmatism of Nilsson (symbols originate in practical use), or the imaginative/intuitive path of Evans (the double axe is an abstract emblem of divinities).[6]

Decipherment of the double axe will be made here by a review of its visual syntax in a variety of contexts. The analysis of the syntax will take the form of seven different questions or riddles of the type: "Why is the axe doing this or that?" The riddles will be answered independently of each other; whereas each of the individual answers may be doubted, it will be difficult in the end to reject the one solution that answers all seven questions. Only one hypothesis explains all the riddles.

First Riddle: Why Does the Double Axe Rise from the Cosmic Mountain?

In the previous chapter, we concluded that ⊔ represents the gate of the cosmic mountain of sunrise and sunset, rather than the horns of a bull. If this is indeed the case, the double axe, shown frequently between the two peaks of the mountain, must be semantically related to the mountain peaks. In terms of visual syntax, the double axe is equivalent to the anthropomorphized sun god Shamash rising between the mountains in third-millennium Akkadian seals (Fig. 8.9) and the sun-disc in Egyptian art (Fig. 9.1). The axe, then, occupies the same position as the rising sun in the syntax of the representation: it passes through the mountain gate every morning.

There is a detail that supports this hypothesis in some instances of Minoan art. Birds flank the twin peaks (Fig. 9.2a) or perch atop the double axe, as on a coffin from Giofyrakia (Fig. 9.2b).[7] We may easily understand why birds are

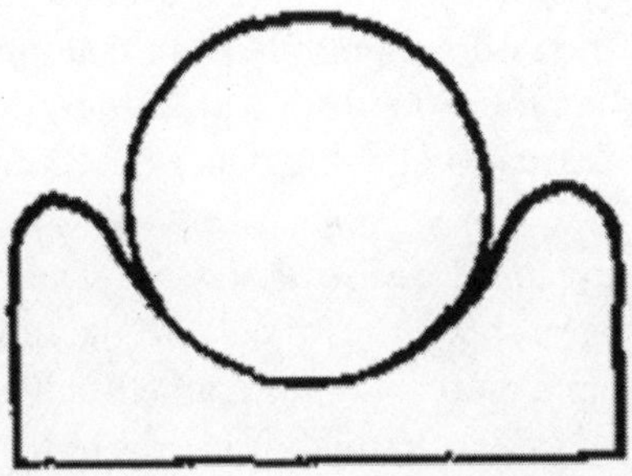

Fig. 9.1. Egyptian ideogram for mountain.

a b

Fig. 9.2. Birds perching on double axes. (a) Minoan clay vessel. (b) Larnax from Giofyrakia (detail).

associated with the sun. They are the first to wake up in the morning and greet the emerging disc; their presence on the same scene as the rising axe is thus quite meaningful.

Why does the double axe rise from the cosmic mountain? The double axe is the sun.

Second Riddle: Why Does the Double Axe Appear Between the Horns of a Bovine Head (Boukephalion)?

The ox head is hieroglyph 38 in Evans's hieroglyphic grid (Fig. 8.1). He noticed that it is related to the double axe because in many cases the double axe is represented between the horns of the ox head. Although the semantic meaning of the horns of the ox and the peaks of the mountain is different, they are *morphologically cognate.* This similarity led Evans to the hypothesis that they are identical and that the mountain peaks are bull's horns. The distinction in their semantic value, however, is essential and must be kept in mind.

Before we proceed to the meaning of the ox head we must clarify that it is not a *bucranium,* as it is often called. Rather it is a *boukephalion,* as Othmar Keel has called it. Namely, it is the head of a live animal with open eyes and ears, not the skull of a sacrificed animal. Once a distinction is made between head and skull, a new perspective opens. The assumption of Nilsson that the axe is the instrument of sacrifice falls apart on the grounds that the ox head is alive. The *boukephalion,* however, is itself a visual riddle that defies the common-sense approach of Nilsson.

In the Near East, the ox and the ox head are manifestations of animals imagined in heaven, and they always have something to do with the sun or moon. In Egyptian mythology, both sun and moon bore the epithet "bull of heaven."[8] Richard Wilkinson says the following: "As a cosmic animal, the powerful bovine appears as the "bull of Re" in the Pyramid texts; and the sun, the moon and the constellation of Ursa Major were all associated with the bull in some way. The young bull calf also occurs as a symbol of the rising sun."[9]

We must also note that sometimes the bull has lunar associations or is a manifestation of Seth, the adversary to Horus.[10] The female cow of heaven is Hathor, and she carries the solar disc between her horns: apparently the entire bovine family was involved in the bearing of the sun. Although we cannot devote further discussion to the whole range of meanings of the bull and cow in Egypt and the Near East, the evidence already cited here shows that we must seek the answer to our riddle in the mythological sphere, not in ritual practice.

Consider one example on an Egyptian Nineteenth Dynasty sarcophagus that shows the journey of the elongated polelike sun bark. It ends in two ox heads and is pulled by deities (Fig. 9.3). Here, the ox heads define the east and west axis of the pole. Thus, in Egyptian imagery the ox heads envelop the sun's course between east and west.

The ox head (or cow's head) appears also on scarab seals, as a carrier of the sun disc.[11] If we compare a Mycenaean gem from Argos with an Egyptian scarab, the similarity of syntax will not go unnoticed, nor the fact that the double axe is interchangeable with the sun disc (Fig. 9.4).[12]

Fig. 9.3. Elongated sun bark with two ox heads and two bulls at each end. Sarcophagus of Seti I.

a b

Fig. 9.4. Ox head as a carrier of emblems. (a) Mycenaean seal from Argos. (b) Egyptian scarab seal (New Kingdom).

A series of Minoan seals show exactly the same thing, although this has gone largely unnoticed: a rayed stellar body is shown between the horns of an ox (Fig. 9.5a and b). This is definitive evidence that the ox head functions as a stellar/solar carrier, similar to the Egyptian bull or cow of heaven. We find the same pattern on the Minoan vessels held by the Keftiu in the tomb of Senmut; the symbol here takes the form of a rosette between the horns (Fig. 9.5c).[13] Thus, there was a *koine* mutually understood by Minoans and Egyptians alike.

The ox head and the bull are associated with the heavens also in the Near East. From Hittite art we have a sealing from Boghazköy on which the disc hovers above the animal's horns (Fig. 9.6).

a

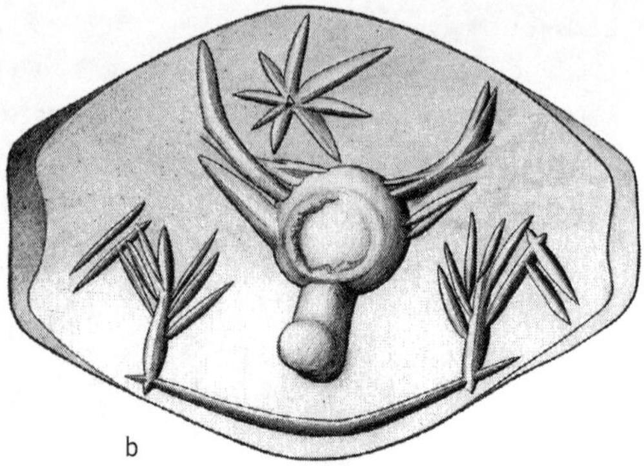

b

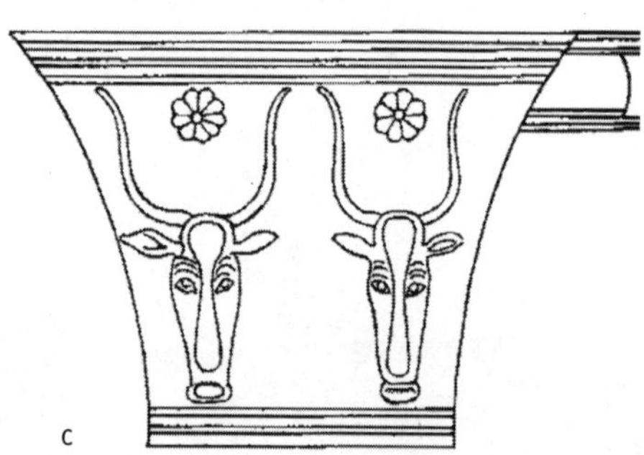

c

Fig. 9.5. Ox head as a stellar/solar carrier. (a) Seal from Mt. Juktas. (b) Seal from Psychro. (c) Vessel carried by Minoan (Keftiu) on Egyptian painting from tomb of Senmut (Eighteenth Dynasty, Hatshepsut/Tuthmosis III).

Fig. 9.6. Ox head as carrier of disc of moon (or sun). Hittite seal impression from Boghazköy (thirteenth century BCE).

Also, in Syria and Ugarit the ox head appears in the sky.[14] On an Old Syrian seal (eighteenth century) the *boukephalion* is situated between two figures identified as rulers. Behind them and to the right is a man holding an emblem with a crescent and a disc; we therefore know that the cult referred to here is a stellar one (Fig. 9.7a). On a seal from Ugarit dating to the fourteenth or thirteenth century BCE, a boukephalion carrying the disc between its horns is behind the seated pharaoh (Fig. 9.7b).[15] These few examples show that in Anatolia, Syria, and Palestine the ox head is a manifestation of a mythical animal and a carrier of the luminaries of heaven.

A ring found in Vapheio in the Peloponnese has a similar syntax with the above Syrian and Ugaritic examples. The ox head is represented in the sky, together with a double axe to the right of a dancing figure (Fig. 9.8).[16] Here we note once more the close association of double axe and ox head. A sealing from Knossos throws further light on Minoan symbolic thought by making the ox head the center of a heraldic composition: two lions flank a large boukephalion (Fig. 9.9).[17] On other seal impressions, lions flank the sun disc.[18]

Fig. 9.7. Ox head in sky.
(a) Old Syrian seal. (b) Syro-Palestinian seal from Ugarit.

Fig. 9.8. Ox head in sky with double axe, above ecstatic (perhaps queen). Ring from Vapheio (detail).

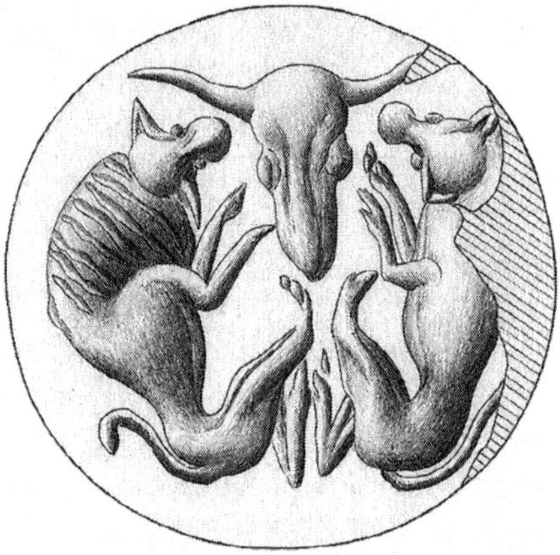

Fig. 9.9. Ox head flanked by lions. Seal from Knossos.

These examples show that in the *koine* of Egypt, the Near East, and Minoan Crete, the bovine head is a carrier of the solar disc (sometimes also the lunar disc, in all cases a heavenly body).[19] If the ox head is a mythical animal imagined in heaven, and if the double axe appears between its horns, then the double axe is the sun.

Why does the double axe appear between the horns of a bovine head (boukephalion)? The axe is a manifestation of the sun.

Third Riddle: Why Does the Double Axe Turn into a Lily?

In Egyptian thought, certain flowers, such as the papyrus and lotus, had regenerative qualities; this is the reason why paintings of the New Kingdom depict the deceased smelling flowers. The lotus flower is considered to have been a primeval plant of regeneration when it emerges from the waters. A spell from the *Book of the Dead* says: “I am this pure lotus which went forth from the sunshine.”[20] Sometimes a child emerges from the lotus bud. This child is none other than the sun of the horizon, sometimes taking the form of a specific person, as Tutankamun (Fig. 9.10).[21]

Evans noticed that lily and papyrus in Crete had similar qualities to Egyptian sacred plants and that sometimes the two merged, resulting in a hybrid flower that he named *waz* after its Egyptian name: “As a decorative motif the flower

Fig. 9.10. Primeval lotus emerging from waters and giving birth to sun deity. Egyptian funerary papyrus.

[lily] is often combined with the upper part of the papyrus symbol or *waz,* intensifying thus the religious value of the symbol."[22]

Evans did not stress the association of the lily with the double axe, although it is evident in many examples. A jar from Pseira, a small island off the East coast of Crete, is decorated with ox heads and double axes, from which lilies are sprouting (Fig. 9.11).[23] How is it possible that an inanimate object gives life to a flower? Evidently there is a process implied here, a "coming forth," as the Egyptian phrase from the *Book of the Dead* puts it. Could it be that the double axe has a regenerative quality? This idea is supported by the scene on the Pseira vase because the double axes occur interspersed with plants (olives). Lilies occur on other representations as well.[24] Sometimes the axe is topped by rosettes rather than a lily (Fig. 9.12).[25]

Fig. 9.11. Ox head as carrier of double axe sprouting into lily. Vase from Pseira (detail).

Fig. 9.12. Pithos from Knossos.

Why does the double axe turn into a lily (or rosette)? The double axe is a regenerative symbol suggesting growth or development. It is the visual manifestation of the Egyptian concept of "coming forth by day" and the equivalent of the lotus giving birth to the primeval sun/child.

Fourth Riddle: Why Does the Double Axe Merge with the Ankh Sign?

A peculiarity of the double axe is that it sometimes blends with the Egyptian ankh, a sign of life (Fig. 9.13). The ankh has many variants, such as the knot of Isis (Fig. 9.14).[26] The Minoan hieroglyphic script includes the ankh as its own sign.[27] Evans noted the similarity of the Minoan and Egyptian hieroglyphs as well as the relationship of the double axe with what he called a "sacred knot," and came to the conclusion that it signified life and divinity.[28] Indeed, the solution is very simple if we adopt a Near Eastern *koine*. In Egypt, Syria, the Levant, and Anatolia, the sign of the ankh means "life."[29]

Fig. 9.13. Double axe combined with ankh sign.

Fig. 9.14. "Knot of Isis," Egyptian ideogram, which has form of ankh.

In the Hittite/Luwian script, the meaning of ankh as life is quite clear.[30] Helmut Theodor Bossert, a Hittitologist and contemporary of Evans, systematically explored the similarity of Hittite signs to their Minoan equivalents and arranged them into a table, shown here as Figure 9.15.[31] In the Egyptianizing seals of the Middle Bronze Age, the ankh also signified life, health and blessing, and we sometimes see the ruler in front of the ankh (Fig. 9.16).[32]

Why does the double axe merge with the ankh sign? It is because they both signify regeneration and life.

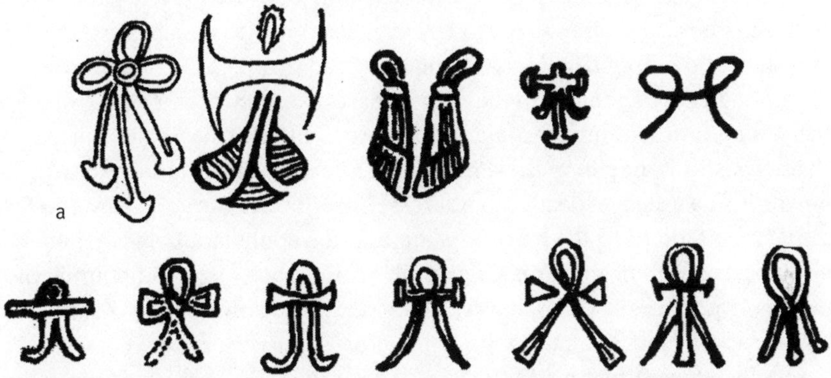

a

b

Fig. 9.15. Double axes and ankh as collected by H. Bossert.
(a) Minoan. (b) Hittite.

Fig. 9.16. Ankh between ruler and god or deified ruler.
Old Syrian seal (eighteenth century BCE).

Fifth Riddle: Why Is the Double Axe Both in the Underworld and the Sky?

The double axe may be found in the depths of the sea. An obvious example of such a depiction is a ritual vessel from Palaikastro and one palace of Knossos that represents a marine landscape replete with conch shells and coral reefs (see Fig. 9.17a). The dominant motif in this seascape is the rayed sun disc in the depths of the ocean.[33] The first reaction of the modern viewer is that this is a paradox: the sun cannot be under water. But, in fact, the very opposite is the truth. In the ancient Near East and Egypt, the sun is the only deity that reaches the depths of the cosmos.[34] "Shamash, your glare reaches down to the abyss so that the monsters of the deep behold your light," we read in a Babylonian hymn.[35]

Although the mythology of the sun is most elaborately documented in Egyptian thought, it is found throughout the Ancient Near East.[36] The principal characteristic of the sun in these mythologies is its cyclical journey around the universe. The waters of death can be crossed only by the sun god Shamash, says the woman Sidouri to the hero Gilgamesh in the eponymous epic: "There has never been a ferry of any kind, Gilgamesh / And nobody from times immemorial has crossed the sea. / Shamash the warrior is the only one who has crossed the sea: apart from Shamash nobody has crossed the sea."[37]

In a Babylonian hymn addressed to the sun god Shamash, he is praised as "never failing to cross the wide expanse of the sea."[38] When the sun god and/or the sun goddess cross the sea, they end up in the netherworld. In the Babylonian hymn, Shamash goes to the underworld to care for the gods there.[39] In Ugaritic religion, the sun goddess Shapshu has the role of taking souls to the underworld and spreading her light there; she is therefore named the "luminary of the underworld." In the epic of *Baal* we read: Baal "was carried away by the luminary of the gods Shapsh . . . into the hands of divine Mot."[40] More evidence comes from Ugaritic liturgical texts in which the sun goddess is asked to go down to the underworld and shine on the dead: "Go down, Shapsh, yea, go down, Great luminary! May Shapsh shine upon him."[41]

Among the Hittites, the sun travels in the sky, the underworld, and in the depths of the sea.[42] A couple of Hittite myths relate how the sun was one time held down by the sea in its depths and could not rise up to the sky.[43] This story expresses a fear of disorder and chaos: what will happen if the sun does not return and follow its course? The journey of the sun from the underworld to the horizon, and his subsequent climb to the sky is expressed in spells from the Egyptian *Book of the Dead.* "Hail to you, you having come as Khepri, even Khepri who is the creator of the gods. You rise and shine on the back of your mother (the sky) having appeared in glory as King of the gods."[44] Another spell hails the sun: "O sun-disc, Lord of the sun beams, who shines forth from the horizon everyday: may you shine in the face of N . . . May the soul of N go up with you in the sky."[45]

We now return to the Minoan vases depicting the depths of the sea and view them through the Egyptian and Near Eastern lens of the *koine.* The sun is shown in the depths of the sea on two vessels from Palaikastro (Fig. 9.17a–b). On one of the two, the double axe is shown next to the sun (Fig. 9.17a). It has an inverted position, as though it is dipping into the sea head down.[46] The juxtaposition of the inverted axe and the rayed sun disc shows that the two entities are cognate but not identical. In other words, the axe is not the solar disc in the sky but its underworld counterpart.

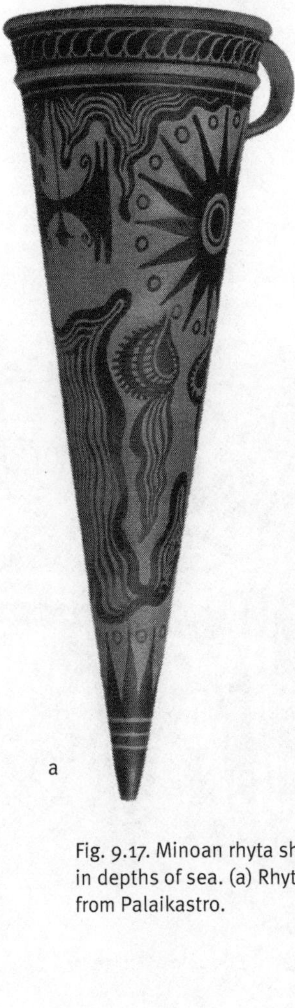

a

b

Fig. 9.17. Minoan rhyta showing sun disc and double axe in depths of sea. (a) Rhyton from Palaikastro. (b) Rhyton from Palaikastro.

The axe also appears in the depths of the sea on the short side of a clay coffin from Kavrochori (Fig. 9.18a).[47] The scene there may be described as a topographical map showing an island bordered by the undulating wavy water lines to the right and the sea with fish to the left. The island incorporates a rectangle, within which we see a double axe. A possible interpretation of this unique scene would be that the axe rises from the caverns of the depths of the underworld. On a clay painted cylindrical vessel from Crete, the painted decoration also corresponds to the cosmological model outlined here (Fig 9.18b). The double axe appears both on the lower half, together with fish, and on the upper half. The vessel may be considered a mini-model of the universe, showing the upper and lower worlds.

Why is the double axe in both the underworld and the sky? It traverses both regions like the sun. In the Ancient Near East it is the sun and only the sun that makes this journey; consequently the double axe must be the sun. Such a hypothesis explains why double axes occur in graves and caves, namely chthonic realms.[48] At Knossos/Isopata there was even a tomb that had the shape of a double axe.[49]

Fig. 9.18. (a) Double axe on larnax from Kavrochori. (b) Double axe on clay vessel.

Sixth Riddle: Why Does the Double Axe Encircle the Cosmos?

The double axe occurs as a decorative motif on several vases; only two very special representations on vases from Pseira will be considered here. The composition on the first example is circular. It is particularly striking because the axe is shown four times around a center (Fig. 9.19a).[50] On a cylindrical vessel from the same site, the entire surface is decorated with axes (Fig. 9.19b).

If the pattern on the Pseira vases were unique, it would not be so crucial to our discussion, but there are other instances. On a ring impression from Knossos, the center of the composition is a rosette surrounded by four double axes (Fig. 9.20). In all cases, the double axes surround the cosmos or travel around it. It is no accident that there are four of these on Figure 9.20. In German, the word *Sonnenlauf* quite precisely captures the notion of the sun's course.

Why does the double axe encircle the cosmos? The answer is that it *is* the sun.

Seventh Riddle: Why Does the Double Axe Occur Together with the Sun and Moon Disc?

On a gold ring from Mycenae, the double axe is represented together with the sun and moon (Fig 9.21). However, the axe is *below* the undulating line (the sky or the horizon in Minoan art). The simultaneous occurrence of the double axe with stellar bodies (see also Fig. 9.17a) leads us to the inevitable conclusion

a b

Fig. 9.19. Double axes in orbit. (a) Lid of vessel from Pseira, east Crete. (b) Cylindrical basket-shaped cultic vase from Pseira.

Fig. 9.20. Four double axes (perhaps representing four points of horizon) orbit central rosette. Ring impression from Knossos.

Fig. 9.21. Gold ring from Mycenae.

that the double axe has some close relationship with the heavenly luminaries, the sun and moon.

Why does the double axe occur together with the sun and moon disc? It is related to the solar disc but is *not identical* with it.

The Hypothesis that Answers the Riddles: The Double Axe Is the Emerging Sun of the Horizon.

"Truth did not come into the world naked, but it came in types and images," says the anonymous Valentinian author of the *Gospel of Philip*. "Every image can constitute a powerful, but, in the last analysis, limited and imperfect expression of the nature and reality," says Eric Hornung.[51] These two authors, one ancient and one contemporary, have expressed the wisdom that images and language are alternative forms of rendering reality and that we need both to articulate truths. The double axe may not be simple to translate in one word into English or any ancient or modern language, but its conceptual range may be grasped in an image.

My hypothesis is that the double axe is the sun, specifically the sun emerging from the horizon. The rayed sun disc in the sky has a different function from the newly born regenerative sun. For this reason the two suns have two forms. Whereas the disc in the sky is luminous and forceful, the sun of the horizon has potential but is not fully realized, expressing the dynamic aspect of the deity. As it rises from the depths of the sea and reaches the mountain gate, it has immense potential for regeneration. It comes forth by sunlight, according to the expression from an Egyptian spell. For this reason it may merge with a lily or a rosette and blossom into a new being. For the same reason it merges with the ankh to signify life. In the form of the double axe, the sun loses some of its power when it goes into the underworld, but it still may revive the dead. This theory explains the prominent role of the double axe on Minoan coffins.

It must be noted that this conceptualization is not unique to Crete. The visual expression of the sun also takes many forms in Egypt: a winged disc, a falcon, a beetle, a child emerging from the lotus plant, even an eye.[52] All these images say something about the nature of the solar divinity, describing its shape, its movement, its force, its ability to regenerate, its growth; yet, none of them captures all these notions simultaneously.

We may ask the further question why the Egyptian sun of the horizon takes the form of a scarab? In Egyptian, the sound (vocalization) *kheper* sounds both like "beetle" and "coming into being."[53] The image thus creates a linguistic/visual pun and reproduces the unique side of the reality of god. I suggest an equation of the double axe with the Egyptian scarab (Fig. 9.22).

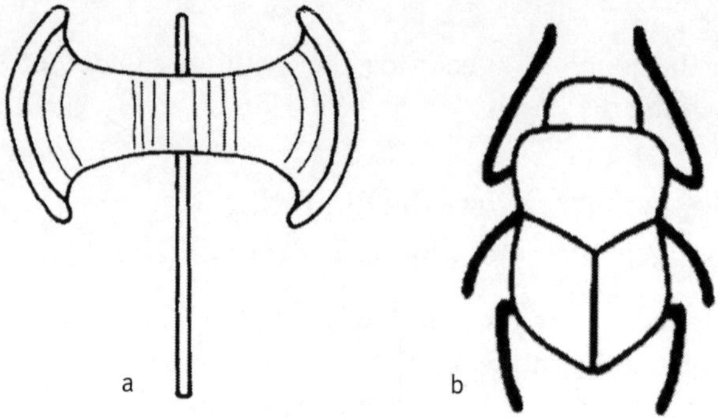

Fig. 9.22. Symbols of sunrise as a "becoming" or "coming forth by day." (a) Minoan double axe. (b) Egyptian scarab.

Two features of the sun have been stressed consistently: its chthonic and celestial sides. Duality is a constant and key feature. I suggest that this duality is made manifest in the two blades of the axe.

The double axe is the sun of the horizon: this is the only hypothesis that explains all seven riddles from the visual contexts where it occurs. It may be tested again and again as new findings come to light.

10

The Rosette, Half-Rosette, and "Incurved Altar"

Evans grouped together a cluster of ideograms that represent heavenly bodies (Fig. 10.1). Thus, it is an undisputable fact that the Minoans utilized solar and stellar symbols as pictograms. Of these ideograms, 108 and 111, the whirled, rayed disc and the lunette, are most obviously identifiable as sun and moon. But the rosette, 110, too is a stellar body, as we shall see; it is an allomorph of the sun.[1]

The Minoan rosette has two forms. It is either a circle with petals or an oval with or without petals. The naturalistic petal version became a popular motif on pottery from the Middle Minoan II A period onward, namely the nineteenth century BCE.[2] It was even more popular in the succeeding phase, the eighteenth century BCE, when the Knossian palace became consolidated during an era of intense international contacts.[3]

The split oval rosette, on the other hand, is a phenomenon of the New Palace period, beginning in the sixteenth century BCE.[4] At that time it became one of the dominant decorative emblems of the Knossian palace, indeed of many Aegean palaces that have been hitherto excavated, including the Egyptian one of Tell el Dab'a, in the Eastern Nile Delta. In the Tell el Dab'a palace, a split-rosette frieze was a major feature of the decorative mural program.[5] Recall the prominence of the split rosette in the west façade of the palace of Knossos and in the Throne Room (see Chapters 2 and 4, Figs. 2.24 and 4.7).[6]

Fig. 10.1. Minoan ideograms and hieroglyphs relating to the cosmos.

Why would a flower be the central emblem of the Knossian palace? We turn to Near Eastern seals for inspiration. There, the rosette is a visual metaphor for heavenly rayed bodies, signifying either a star or the sun.[7] A further development shows that it came to symbolize the sun only. This occurred in the eighteenth century BCE when it fused with the Egyptian winged solar disc, a mutation that coincides with the strong Egyptianization of Syrian seal iconography. The winged rosette may thus be viewed as a Syro-Levantine solar idiom forged under Egyptian influence.

Figure 10.2 shows two Anatolian seals of the eighteenth century BCE on which the rosette represents the sun in the sky.[8] On an Old Syrian seal, the winged rosette is attached to a solar standard flanked by two griffins (see Fig. 4.10a). There is no doubt, then, that in Syrian glyptic the rosette represents the sun.[9]

Fig. 10.2. Solar symbol as rosette in sky. (a) Mitanni seal of the sixteenth century BCE. (b) Seal of Princess Matrunna of Karkemish (eighteenth century BCE).

The Hittites used both the rosette and a winged rosette in their hieroglyphic script. The winged variety signifies "sun," whereas the wingless one signifies "life and health" (Figs. 10.3a–b).

Consequently, if a Syro-Anatolian lens is applied to Minoan pictograms, the rosette is a sun symbol. A crucial key to the decipherment is not only its resemblance to the rayed sun disc of the Levantine and Anatolian *koine,* but its link with the double axe, which was explored in chapter 9. When the two fuse into one body, the double axe becomes a blossoming flower (Figs. 9.11–12).[10]

Such a double axe/rosette is depicted on a vase from Knossos. It stands within a zigzag landscape that possibly suggests mountains (Fig. 10.4).[11] Note that the shaft of the double axe has the undulating shape of a tree trunk. Such trunks belong to palms, because only they have this roughness created by the constant cutting of the dry leaves (Fig. 10.5b).

a

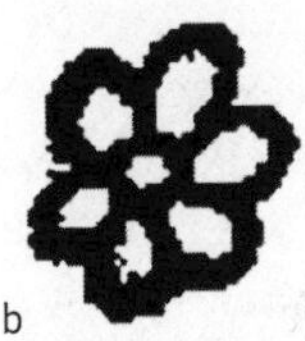

b

Fig. 10.3. Hittite hieroglyphs. (a) Winged rosette signifying sun. (b) Wingless rosette meaning life and health.

Fig. 10.4. Cult standard on Knossos vase.

The peculiar motif of figure 10.4 may be interpreted as follows: it is a palm shaft with a double axe fitted onto it and a rosette topping it. If so, it is a man-made object, a cult standard of a deity combining three different cult symbols of the sun goddess: the palm, the double axe, and the rosette. It resembles the double axe cult standard topped by a bird depicted on the Hagia Triada Sarcophagus (Fig. 10.5a).[12] The pole supporting the axe is a palm trunk from which the leaves have been cut, as may be deduced from the rough texture of the trunk. We can compare this further to the palm cult standard topped by the solar rosette disc on a Syrian seal (Fig. 10.5b). Since the Hagia Triada double axe is itself topped by rosettes on the border above, there can be little doubt that we have here a symbolic visual language common to Crete, Egypt, and the Syro-Levantine area. The formula is solar rosette plus palm. Teissier argues that "the symbolism of the tree with the winged sun disc was developed in the Levant."[13]

The comparisons show that solar cult standards existed on both sides of the Aegean. They must have been quite large, constructed by palm trunks and crowned with emblems of the sun deity.

The combination of the double axe with the rosette is comprehensible if they both allude to aspects of the sun. Yet, it must be stressed that although the axe and rosette have related semantic values, they are not identical. My proposal is that the rosette exemplifies the life-giving qualities of the sun, whereas the double axe represents the regenerative potential of the sun of the horizon.[14] As for the palm tree, recall from Chapter 4 that it is a solar tree in Minoan Crete as it was in the Levant (see also Chapter 12).[15] The final proof that the rosette designates the sun in the Near East comes from Kassite seals (fifteenth century and later) where it is used as a determinative of the sun god Shamash.[16] Finally let us note that at Knossos, the rosette decorates a ceiling.[17]

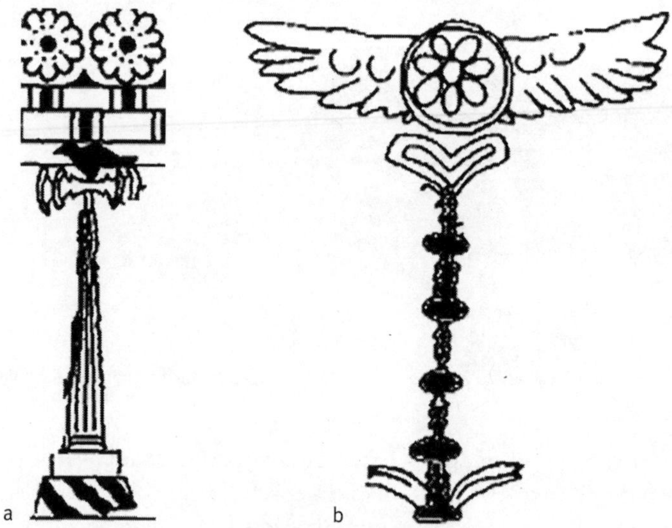

Fig. 10.5. Cult standards. (a) Double axe atop palm tree shaft on Hagia Triada sarcophagus (detail). (b) Solar disc on Syrian seal (Middle Bronze Age BCE).

The Abstract Split Rosette

The story of the rosette is not yet finished, however. Its alternate form, the oval split in the middle, became quite popular in the sixteenth and fifteenth centuries BCE, during the New Palace Period. We have seen already how it occurs in connection with the throne room at Knossos, on the façade of the same palace, and in the Egyptian palace at Tell el Dab'a (Fig. 10.6a).[18] Another instance is the rosette design on the hem of the dress of a female figure from the corridor of the Procession mural at Knossos (Fig. 10.7a).[19]

Comparing the Minoan split rosette (Fig. 10.7a) to a Luwian/Hittite hieroglyph (Fig. 10.7b), we see that the two have the exact same form. Helmut Theodor Bossert was the first to note this similarity in 1932. He was followed by Helga Reusch in 1958, but this striking connection between the conceptual apparatuses of the two cultures seems to have been forgotten.[20] It is unlikely that the similarity is an accident because the signs are too abstract for such a coincidence.

Fig. 10.6. Split rosette. Minoan painting found at Tell el Dab'a, Egypt.

a b

Fig. 10.7. Split rosette. (a) Minoan. (b) Hittite.

The question, then, is how this similarity may be interpreted in a historical context. The Hittite sign is a determinative for "god." This meaning is quite compatible with my suggestion here that the Minoan equivalent designates the solar goddess. I suggest that the commonality of this symbol between Minoans and Hittites may be best explained by intimate contact between the royal courts (see also Chapter 14).[21] Consider also the following two images in which the two halves of the rosette are used to determine a building as sacred. One is the Hittite hieroglyph for "house of God," depicted as an edifice with a split rosette (Fig. 10.8a). The second is a gold plate from the Shaft Graves of Mycenae (c. 1550–1530) that also shows the house of god (Figs. 10.8b). In conclusion, the split rosette is god (or a particular solar deity) and when it is combined with a building it designates the divine palace or its earthly counterpart.

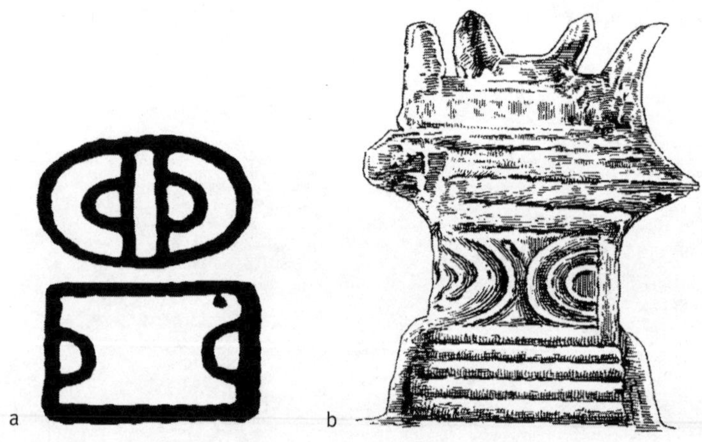

Fig. 10.8. House of god. (a) Hittite hieroglyph. (b) Gold plate ornament from Shaft Graves at Mycenae.

The interstice between two abutting oval split rosettes results in another shape that may be termed an "incurved podium" (Fig. 10.9). As usual, it was Evans who noticed the complexity of Minoan morphology, namely that the combination of two rosettes gives birth to a second form.[22] I suggest that this second form is the sacred pillar of the universe, an axis between the two halves of the East and West of the cosmos. It occurs as a pictogram of the hieroglyphic script, so we can add it to our conspectus of ideograms that are also cult symbols.[23]

First, however, we must note that objects with this shape actually have been excavated in Crete; Evans perceived their sacred nature and called them "altar-bases of the incurved type."[24] He was followed by Nilsson, who noted that in art they are flanked by griffins or lions (Fig. 10.10).[25]

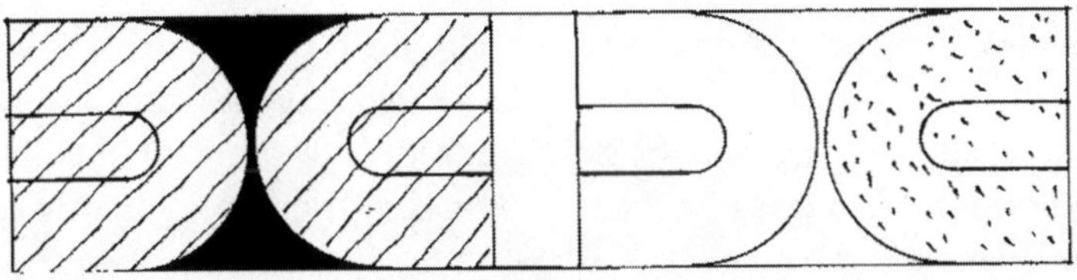

Fig. 10.9. Rosette and incurved design.

Fig. 10.10. So-called incurved altar flanked by griffins. Seal from Mycenae.

We now turn to meaning. The object is not an altar because we almost never see offerings placed on it. As Maria Shaw has shown, it has some connection with gates, and we have seen that gates mark transitions to another world.[26] Still, the puzzle remains: what does this object signify?

Some help may come from the other side of the Aegean. The so-called *weres* is an Egyptian hieroglyph and pictogram with a similar form (Fig. 10.11). Here the meaning is clear: the Egyptian object is without a doubt a headrest with symbolic associations relating to the sun's course.[27]

Fig. 10.11. Egyptian hieroglyph signifying headrest (or support) of sun. It is equivalent to Minoan sign labeled "incurved altar."

Richard Wilkinson explains: "Symbolically, the head-rest was closely associated with solar imagery for it held the head which, like the sun, was lowered in the evening and rose again in the sky."[28] Indeed, in the tomb of Tutankhamun, one of the headrests was personified by an Atlas-type figure, a god who supports the firmament and is flanked by the lions of the horizon (Fig. 10.12a).

I believe that the Egyptian conceptualization of the incurved object as an axis of the cosmos explains well its function in Minoan art. Compare with a seal from Crete on which two lions flank the incurved base, above which is the rayed sun disc (Fig. 10.12b). The coincidence of the motifs is not accidental. The Minoan and Egyptian symbols shared in a *koine* in which the solar cult played a major role. The incurved podium was conceived as a support of the firmament, a pillar of heaven or at least a cosmic axis. Its use as a sacred podium in Minoan imagery may be best explained thus.

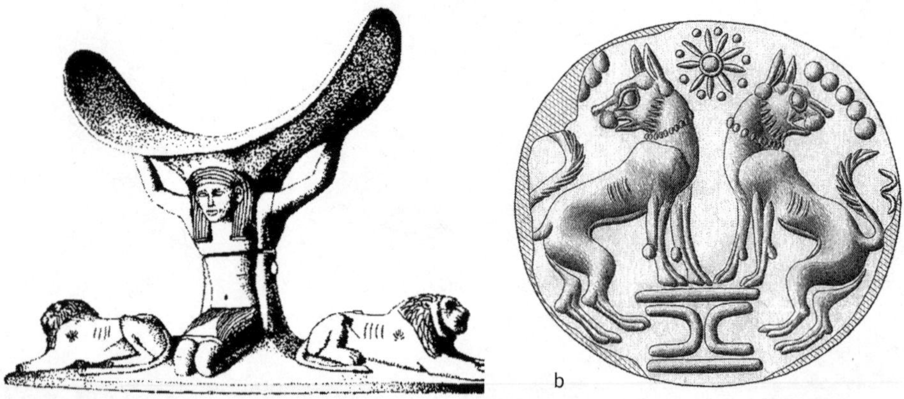

a b

Fig. 10.12. Headrest. (a) From Tutankhamun's tomb. (b) As cosmic pillar on seal from Crete.

Why are so many symbols referring to the cosmos and the sun: the rosette, the split rosette, the double axe, the incurved podium? Each of these visual forms is complementary to the others. We may postulate an entire system of interconnected concepts that cohere first by the nature of their morphology and second by their semantic links. They were used singly or in combination to create a vocabulary of sacredness, most of which revolved around the sun. When a grid is applied to decipher the ideograms, much may be explained, such as for example why the incurved podium is also the center of two abutting rosettes. The split rosette signifies the sun of the East and West; the incurved podium signifies the cosmic pillar in the center. If my thesis is correct, it is clear why the half rosette and the incurved podium are often prominent features of the house of god. See, for example, Figure 10.13, the reconstruction by George

Rethemiotakis of the mansion on the Poros ring, where the sacred mountain, the incurved podium, and two half rosettes (on either side of the podium) are all present (cf. Fig. 5.6). More examples may be found in Chapter 5.

One cannot help but notice that the underlying concept behind the variety of forms is symmetry. We meet this symmetry in the duality of the two peaks of the mountain sign, the split rosette, the double axe, and the incurved podium. Symmetry is essential to cosmic harmony: right and left, East and West, up and down, sky and underworld.

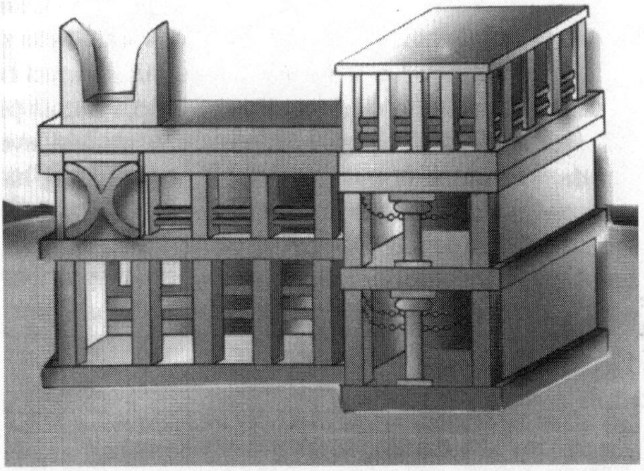

Fig. 10.13. "Sacred mansion" with symbols of split rosette and cosmic pillar. Poros Ring as reconstructed by G. Rethemiotakis.

A decipherment of the Minoan pictograms is possible only if signs from the wider horizon of Egypt and the Near East are taken into consideration. Anatolia, Syria, the Levant, Minoan Crete, Mycenaean Greece, and Egypt were interconnected on the semiotic level. Overlaps are considerable, although not all signs are found in all cultures. For example, Crete has the rosette in common with the Levant, but not the winged disc, which the Levant shares with Egypt. The incurved podium is common to Egypt and Crete, but it is not found in the Levant. The split rosette is common to Luwian/Hittite and Minoan cultures. The double axe as the sun of the horizon is unique to Crete.

This completes the ideogrammatic decipherment of the hieroglyphs. They turn out to be of great importance for the understanding of the vocabulary of the architecture of the palaces and the ideology of palatial religion. A large and complex pictorial dictionary is beginning to emerge, a necessary tool for the comprehension of symbols on both sides of the Aegean. The results are tested in the field of funerary symbolism in Chapter 11.

11

Minoan Afterlife Beliefs

No Minoan texts that elucidate Minoan afterlife beliefs have remained; nevertheless, we are not lacking in eloquent material. This material consists of clay painted larnakes (coffins) dating to the fourteenth and mainly thirteenth centuries BCE, namely a little before and after the fall of the palace of Knossos (ca. 1375 BCE).[1] Unfortunately, we have little funerary iconography before this period because very few royal tombs in the vicinity of the grand palace survived to be excavated by Evans.

The first surviving tomb was a magnificent building at Isopata that was unfortunately destroyed during World War I. The second was excavated as late as 1931 and was the result of Evans's last campaign at Knossos.[2] He called it a Temple Tomb because it combined a grave and a sanctuary within the same building. The pottery shows that it was in use even after the fall of the palace of Knossos; this testifies to a continuous cult of the dead king in the post-palatial period.[3] The temple tomb constitutes evidence that ruler deification was practiced in Crete, as it was in Egypt, Syria, Anatolia, and Ugarit (see also Chap. 3).

Ruler cult vanished shortly after the fall of the palace of Knossos. There are no more structures that may be identified as royal tombs after this period, but this is the time when the larnakes become most popular. We are fortunate that many were found because they constitute an invaluable corpus for Minoan afterlife beliefs of the post-palace period. Strangely enough, neither Evans nor Nilsson seriously considered them as sources for Minoan metaphysical ideas. Since their time, Greek excavators have successively augmented the known examples, and their publications have contributed a great deal to the interpretation of this quaint iconography.[4]

The Function of Coffins as Maps and the Journey to the Beyond

The form of the coffins is rectangular, often with a gabled lid, simulating a house with a roof. A bathtub shape is also attested, especially in East Crete. The iconography of the coffins is quite varied. Sometimes entire landscapes are represented; other times the motifs consist of grazing or hunted animals, bulls, cows, and goats. In a few cases, griffins occur. Humans are rare, but they do occasionally appear as well.[5]

Because the images are so varied, it is not easy to detect a coherent mythology that governs Minoan afterlife beliefs. But we may exclude some possibilities. It is very unlikely, for example, that the scenes on the larnakes are biographical in nature. They do not likely show the profession of the dead or represent excerpts from his life. This kind of biography would be very unusual, if not unique, in the second millennium BCE. Also, it is unlikely that the larnakes depict rituals of sacrifice, as some scholars have argued.[6] The case for sacrificial practices rests on the assumption that ⊔ and the double axe both represent sacrificial implements, but if this postulate is contested (as it has been here in Chaps. 8–10), then the sacrifice scenario cannot hold. There remains a third possibility: that the scenes represent landscapes of the netherworld. This is the position that will be adopted here. My hermeneutical frame will be constructed on the basis of Near Eastern and Egyptian templates of cosmology and netherworld beliefs.

Death in Ancient Egypt and the Near East entailed a difficult journey for the soul through the beyond, with a kind of paradise as its final destination. Yet, *paradise* has misleading connotations to the modern reader. In the second millennium BCE, the netherworld was not a single place, but rather a whole universe with diverse lands and a complex geography: mountains, rivers, and lakes. The journey of the dead was difficult and dangerous because these barriers had to be crossed. For this reason the dead might be aided by instructions in visual or textual form, so they could navigate safely through "the undiscovered country from whose bourne no traveler ever returns."[7] It will be argued here that the scenes on the Minoan coffins are topographical maps designed to guide the dead to the netherworld and show them their final destination.

But let us start with Egypt, where the journey is well documented in sarcophagi, papyri, and murals of the royal tombs. For the nobility and the wealthy members of society, funerary papyri were commissioned.[8] On these papyri we see specific landscapes of the beyond: rivers, fields with plants, and groves with palm trees. The barriers are sometimes conceptualized as gates, a notion that we have already explored in connection with the mountain ⊔ (Chap. 8).[9]

The topography of the Egyptian netherworld is not unique. It shares common features with Mesopotamian cosmology. In Chapter 8 we looked at a clay tablet showing the Babylonian cosmic map on which the circular earth is surrounded by a river and mountains (see Fig. 8.10). These mountains delimit the inhabited universe and constitute barriers to the beyond.[10] The triangles at the circumference of the circle have been interpreted as isles or mountains. On the back of this Babylonian clay tablet there is a textual description of the various regions of the beyond that helps us understand the imaginary geography better. In the texts, it is clear that the netherworld consists of several regions. One of them is said to be enveloped in darkness "where the sun is not seen," another has wondrous trees, and another yet is given the name of the "land of horned cattle" (compare with Fig. 11.3 in the following discussion).[11] It is to be assumed that only a few of these regions are perfectly blissful, the equivalents of the Greek Elysium or the biblical Garden of Eden; others may be frightening or dark.

A journey to the beyond is described in the Mesopotamian *Epic of Gilgamesh*. Assuming a *koine* between the Aegean and the Near East, the vivid description of the hero's adventures may be an invaluable guide to the mentality behind the images on the Minoan larnakes.[12]

After the death of his friend Enkidu, the hero Gilgamesh is desperate to find out the secret of life and death. He seeks the wise man Utnapishtim, who lives at the edges of the world and has taken part in the council of the gods. To find Utnapishtim, Gilgamesh has to travel to the netherworld and follow the path of the sun. In other words, the hero makes a journey modeled on the trip of the dead. He enters the beyond through the sun's gate, which is located in the midst of Mount Mashu. The latter is our familiar cosmic mountain, represented as twin peaks in Egyptian and Minoan art and acting simultaneously as a barrier and a gate to the netherworld. Gilgamesh passes through the mountain gate guarded by a scorpion man and travels in darkness through a kind of tunnel. He races the sun itself and eventually arrives at a splendid garden flooded with light:

> [But the darkness was still dense, there was no light]
> It was impossible for him to see ahead or behind.
> When he had achieved eight leagues, he hurried on;
> The darkness was still dense, there was no light.
> . . .
> He came out in front of the sun
> Brightness was everywhere.
> All kinds of . . . spiky bushes were visible, blossoming with gemstones.
> Carnelian bore fruit
> Hanging in clusters, lovely to look at,
> Lapis lazuli bore foliage.
> Bore fruit, and was delightful to view.[13]

Because the garden is flooded with sunlight and contains marvelous trees, it is evidently a kind of paradise. We are reminded of the Garden of Eden in the Hebrew Bible (Gen. 2:8), which is likewise located east, namely, close to the sun. As we shall see, the Minoan paradisiacal landscape is also close to the rising sun.

The *Odyssey* also shares in the tradition of the *koine* of a cosmic journey. Like Gilgamesh, Odysseus arrives at some kind of paradise at the edges of the world when he reaches the island of Circe "where the sun rises" (*Odyssey*, 12.4). Circe is related to the sun by kinship, and she is the one who directs Odysseus to the island of the sun, where his sacred cattle graze. I have suggested elsewhere that the journey of Odysseus takes place around the cosmos and that it is modeled on the Egyptian journey of the soul's passage to the beyond.[14]

Fig. 11.1. Double axe, sun, and griffin in paradisiacal landscape. Larnax from Palaikastro (fourteenth/thirteenth centuries BCE).

With this background in mind, we return to the Minoan coffins. It is possible to detect in the images the journey in the afterlife: gardens or groves, a sacred tree, rivers, and the sun. To start with the garden, some scenes depict palm groves, lilies, and other curly plants (see, for example, Fig 11.6 in the following discussion). We also meet the sun on a larnax from Palaikastro, (Fig. 11.1, right panel) next to a griffin. Previously, we met the griffin as a companion of the solar goddess in the throne room of the palace of Knossos (Ch. 4). Here we see it again in the metaphysical setting next to the sun disc and a papyrus plant; this scene must be the paradisiacal landscape, the Minoan Elysium. As Evans put it: "We see here an abode of light rather than darkness. We have not here the Hades of primitive Greek tradition—the gloomy Under-World of pale shadows and gibbering ghosts. This is the true Elysion, un-Hellenic in its conception . . ."[15]

We need to consider next what kind of barriers divide the land of the living from that of the dead. We have seen on the Babylonian map that the world is surrounded by mountains and girt by a cosmic river. Thus, both river and mountain constitute boundaries to the netherworld. In the *Epic of Gilgamesh*, the hero must travel across the waters of death to get to the isle of Utnapishtim. But remember: only the sun may cross this body of water.[16]

A river surrounds also the Greek *cosmos*. In the *Odyssey*, the Elysian fields are described as lying next to the river Ocean. The wizard Proteus tells Menelaus: "You will not meet your fate and die in Argos where the horses graze. Instead the immortals will send you to the Elysian plain at the world's end, to join the red-haired Rhadamanthys in the land where living is made easier for mankind, where no snow falls, no strong winds blow, and there is never any rain but day after day the West wind's tuneful breezes come in from the Ocean to refresh its folk" (*Odyssey*, 4.561, transl. Rieu). Consider also another passage in the *Odyssey* in which Penelope expresses the wish to die and reach the river Ocean: "Oh let the storm wind snatch me up and vanish with me down the ways of darkness to drop me where the sea runs into the circling stream of Ocean" (*Odyssey*, 20.63–65). The topography of the netherworld is summed up succinctly in the final book of the same epic. When the suitors of Penelope are killed, their souls have to go past the river Ocean, past the white rock, past the gate of the sun, and past the region of dreams (*Odyssey*, 24.1–14). Hesiod locates the "islands of the blessed" in a distant sea.[17] Finally, Herodotus testifies of an actual map, that of Hekateus, on which the world was surrounded by the river Ocean (Herodotus 2.23).[18]

This digression into Greek myth shows us that we may be certain about the existence of a *koine* between the Aegean and the Near East and that in this *koine* of religious and metaphysical ideas the concept of barriers separating the two worlds is ever present. Furthermore, the barriers are specified as either water or mountains.

This is precisely what we find on the Minoan larnakes: rivers and mountains. To start with rivers, we often find that the scenes of the netherworld are framed by wavy lines, a convention for rendering water or rivers in Minoan art. These lines run vertically across the borders of the coffins, quite often decorating the legs. One example is the coffin from Armenoi, West Crete (Fig. 11.2).

Mountains may encircle the universe, as we have seen in the Babylonian cosmic map (Fig. 8.10). If this map is translated into an image, and if we search for the circle of mountains on a coffin, we ought to find ⊔ surrounding the netherworld. We also ought to find the sun of the horizon rising between the two mountain peaks. Indeed, this is the case on a second coffin from Armenoi (Fig. 11.3). On the lid of this coffin, we see an unusual scene: a bull with his head lowered approaches a double axe. Is this the bull of heaven, the mythological animal the head of which we have discussed as an ox head in Chapter 9? In any case, it cannot be doubted that this is a landscape of the netherworld and that this is a mythical scene and not a ritual one. Consider the following Ugaritic text, where the boundaries of the underworld are defined by two mountains:

> Set your faces toward Mount Trgz,
> Towards mount Shirmegi;
> Towards the twin (peaks) of the
> Ruler of the underworld.[19]

Fig. 11.2. Possible scene of hunt in the beyond, framed by rivers that surround supernatural region. Larnax from Armenoi (thirteenth century BCE).

Fig. 11.3. Mountains and double axes create boundary that enclose landscape of the beyond. Larnax from Armenoi (thirteenth century BCE).

The World under the Sea's Surface

A peculiarity of the Minoan netherworld landscapes is that many of them were imagined as lying in the depths of the sea; this may be the special contribution of Minoan Crete to the topography of the afterlife. The sea surface is also a border between this world and the beyond, but its extent is unfathomable, both on the horizontal and the vertical level. The larnakes depict another universe equally rich and complex as the terrestrial one. This netherworld is located in the depths of the sea, replete with plants, fish, and mollusks. Of the latter, the octopus features prominently. It is a creature that lives in caverns and probably symbolizes the unfathomable and dark depths of the sea.

A scene on a coffin from Kavrochori illustrates the world in the depths of the ocean (Fig. 11.4). To the left, we see a palm and a bird alighting on top of it. Next to the palm is a mollusk; next we see a chariot, the vehicle that transports the dead to the netherworld.[20] This unusual landscape is delimited by rivers on the right and left: the latter constitute the frontier of the realm in which terrestrial and underwater-scapes have been combined to form a new universe. The same combination of terrestrial and underwater creatures is repeated on the lid.

Fig. 11.4. Netherworld in depths of sea. Larnax from Kavrochori (thirteenth century BCE).

On another larnax from Pachyammos, East Crete, we see a juxtaposition of land and sea. On the left half, there is a large octopus that symbolizes the depths of the ocean; on the right, a grove of palms symbolizes the paradisiacal garden. (Fig. 11.5).

On a coffin from Vassilika Anogeia, East Crete, the palm tree grows in the center (Fig. 11.6). Analogous to the biblical passage about Eden, this can be described as the "tree of life" growing in the midst of the garden (Gen. 2:9). Its crest is surrounded by birds, and its lower leaves are surrounded by fish. The palm is thus an axis of the world with its roots in the depths of the sea and its top in heaven.[21]

One important conclusion that emerges from the study of these mixed landscapes is that there is symmetry in the universe; another is that there was a second universe in the depths of the sea. The underwater world was full of regenerative potential. Compare with a passage in *Gilgamesh* where the hero is told by the wise Utnapishtim to dive into the depths of the water to find the plant of youth.[22] He does so, and finds the miraculous plant at the bottom of the ocean. Thus, the plant of youth could only be found underwater.

Fig. 11.5. Sea and land symmetrically juxtaposed. Larnax from Pachyammos (thirteenth century BCE).

Fig. 11.6. Palm as tree of life. Larnax from Vassilika Anogeia, East Crete (thirteenth century BCE).

The Ultimate Goal of the Journey: The Land of the Rising Sun

It is to be suspected that, for the Minoans, the ultimate goal of the journey of the dead was the arrival at the land of the sun, which was embodied in the double axe. Such an idea fits perfectly with the *Gilgamesh* passages: the hero races the sun and arrives at the precious garden flooded by light. It fits even better with Egyptian afterlife beliefs, according to which the sunlight is constantly sought after by the souls of the dead.[23]

If the double axe is the rising sun, as is argued in Chapter 9, then we should expect to find it as a motif on the larnakes. This is, indeed, the case. Consider, for example, a coffin from Giofyrakia on which the double axe rises between the mountain peaks and is topped by a bird (Fig. 11.7). The latter greets the sun at sunrise.

Also, on the coffin from Palaikastro, discussed previously (Fig. 11.1), we noted the sun on the right panel. On the left panel, however, we see the rising sun represented as a double axe emerging from a cluster of lilies. Is it an accident that the disc and the double axe appear side by side? This juxtaposition serves as a further proof of the hypothesis proposed in Chapter 9 that the double axe is the rising aspect of the sun. In fact, the iconography of the Palaikastro larnax may be understood easily if we apply the grid of the Near Eastern *koine*. The double axe is the regenerative sun of the horizon, and the griffin, a creature associated with the sun (Chapter 4), lives in the paradisiacal landscape of the beyond. The rayed disc (which appears also on the lid) and the double axe are *both* features of the sun, and exist in the blissful paradise of the Minoan world. As for the lily, its association with the double axe as a regenerative symbol was previously discussed in Chapter 9. The imagery of the lily of the Palaikastro larnax is conceptually similar to the Egyptian lotus plant giving birth to the sun child (Fig. 11.8).[24]

Fig. 11.7. Axe as rising sun. Larnax from Giofyrakia (detail; thirteenth century BCE).

Fig. 11.8. Sun as god rising from lotus plant. Egyptian funerary papyrus of Ani (New Kingdom).

Thus, a number of ideas converge to form a coherent system pertaining to the afterlife: flowering plants and a double axe signify regeneration; symmetry and duality reflect the terrestrial and sea realms, light and darkness, up and down, East and West. All these concepts would be comprehensible in the Ancient Near East and Egypt although the particularities of the idiom varied.

The Egyptians had a fear of darkness and were terrified by the idea that the soul could be trapped between the doors of the underworld and never reach the sunlight. Consider spell 91 from the *Book of the Dead:* "As for him who knows this spell, he shall become an equipped spirit in the realm of the dead, he shall *not* be restrained at any gate of the West whether coming or going." Also, spell 164 expresses fear of imprisonment in darkness: "His soul shall not be imprisoned."[25]

These passages generate some reflections on puzzles about Minoan afterlife that cannot be conclusively resolved, but that may add a dimension to our reconstructed Minoan netherworld. Is it possible that the Minoans, like their Egyptian, Mesopotamian, and West Semitic neighbors, equated darkness with nonexistence? If so, did they conceive of the deepest levels of the ocean as the abyss of nonexistence? Were the images on the Minoan coffins meant to counteract this negative vision by showing blissful landscapes and double axes emerging from the darkness to the light?

Who Was Buried in the Larnakes?

A final question pertains to the social status of the dead buried in the coffins. The chronological range from the end of the palatial period in LM III A to the one succeeding the fall of Knossos alerts our attention to the fact that in this case we may look for nonroyal ideology in the nature of our material. Were ordinary people given the privilege of possessing painted larnakes? Two issues are relevant here. First, we must consider the frequency of the painted coffins. They were widespread across the whole island of Crete, with each cemetery having several specimens. For this reason, we cannot speak of a restricted elite class who had the privilege of the coffins; rather, we must envision a broader middle class that had access to these ideas and myths. Note, however, that the iconography was present already in palatial pottery and became widely accessible after the fall of the palaces.

Another inference is that the coherence of the images reflects knowledge about the netherworld, which would be difficult to possess without an established and codified mythology. Such a mythology was certainly crystallized during the palatial era. The narrative as well as the visual vocabulary became standard enough to be employable across Crete, even after the fall of the palatial theocracy.

12

The Solar Goddess of Kingship

One of Evans's contributions to posterity was the notion of the great mother goddess. He imagined her as a divinity with powers over the earth, sky, and underworld, responsible for fertility, regeneration, and all aspects of life. He tended to identify her with Greek Rhea (a goddess of very little importance in Greek cult) or with Phrygian Cybele.[1] Subordinate to her was a male, a boy god.

A century later, the mother goddess is still very much alive in both popular and specialized scholarship, although she has taken various guises. She has been linked to Babylonian Ishtar or Syro-Palestinian Astarte by scholars who rightly acknowledge Near Eastern influences on Crete.[2] But even so, she remains the great mother of vegetation and fertility.[3]

Nilsson was critical of Evans's idea of a single goddess, but for unexpected reasons. Because Minoan Crete was primitive, closer to nature than culture, he thought it could not have developed monotheism, which is a mark of high cultures. In Nilsson's view, Crete was primitive and polytheistic, replete with nature gods.[4] The notion of matriarchy we owe less to Evans and more to nineteenth century anthropology. Although he went along with the idea that matriarchies existed in the early history of mankind, he himself mentions the term only rarely.[5]

Matriarchy has never been documented for any Ancient Orient or Mediterranean palatial society of the second millennium BCE.[6] Mother goddesses, on the other hand, exist in all forms and guises but are rarely, if ever, characterized by motherhood alone. Foremost among their roles is the protection of their divine sons and their counterparts, the earthly kings. For example, Mesopotamian Ishtar is often regarded as a fertility goddess, but the most constant feature of her religious identity is her patronage of kings. This characteristic is dominant from the third to the first millennia BCE, and is especially obvious during the

Assyrian epoch. To classify her simply as a fertility or vegetation goddess is to ignore her social role. Yet, if the mythical world has any relevance to real society, we must seek the social paradigms behind the imagery.

Mother and Son

Several gold rings from Crete and the mainland have as their subject an enthroned goddess. The seated posture of the goddess denotes a special type of authority, seniority, and rank within the pantheon. Of the latter there can be no doubt: the goddess is accompanied by mythical or formidable creatures, such as griffins or lions. They attend her or flank her throne (Fig. 12.1). Why is the goddess seated and what kind of authority does this posture denote?[7] The following set of scenes have a semi-narrative character because the seated goddess interacts with a standing male figure. How does this male relate to the goddess?

Fig. 12.1. The enthroned solar goddess.
(a) Ring from Tiryns. (b) Ring from Mycenae.

On a ring from Mycenae, the goddess sits on a throne, the back of which has the shape of a mountain; before her is a standing male who holds a spear (Fig. 12.2). The hands of the two cross, and both have pointed fingers. Apparently they are engaged in an animated conversation.[8]

Evans spoke of intimacy between them, whereas Nilsson interpreted the image as a representation of everyday life: "the scene is claimed as a *sacra conversazione* between the Great goddess and her consort, though for my part, I must admit that the scene strikes me as entirely secular in character."[9] The mountain throne, however, is sure proof that Nilsson was mistaken: mortal women do not have mountain thrones, whereas gods do (Chapter 4). Note two additional elements: First, the size and matronly shape of the body of the female figure indicate that she is a mother; this contrasts with the smaller size of the male, who appears to be younger than her. Second, the seated posture of the female shows her superior hierarchical position. Whatever we say about the nature of the interaction, the relative age difference must be taken into account. Equally evident is the fact that the female figure ranks higher than the male.

A similar pattern is represented on a seal stone now in Geneva. Instead of being engaged in animated conversation, in this case the two figures extend their hands towards each other in a gesture of intimacy (Fig. 12.3). Note however that it is *not* an erotic embrace. Above the pair we see an elongated object best identified as a shooting star or comet (Chapter 7) and a small seated child figure, which I am not able to interpret. Both objects can probably be imagined as being in the sky. If so, the heavens are open, revealing supernatural signs. Surely, then, the figures are divine.

On a ring from Thebes on the Greek mainland, the goddess is seated on a building that has the form of a palace, probably her own (Fig. 12.4). The male god is quite muscular and large compared to those in the previous scenes; both figures are engaged in what may be interpreted as mutual greeting. Above the couple is the horizon line; above the horizon is a rayed sun disc in the sky. This is an indication that the goddess is a solar divinity.

Also recall the Poros ring discussed in Chapter 7 and the Mycenaen ring in Chapter 9. The Poros ring shows a seated goddess facing a standing male. His extended arm is a gesture that typifies rulers and deities (Fig. 7.10).[10] The ring from Mycenae shows a goddess seated under a tree, receiving an armed god who arrives from the sky (Fig. 9.21). The sun and moon in the sky show that the deities are stellar gods; the seated posture shows that the goddess is conceptualized as a queen.

All the rings discussed here juxtapose the seated goddess to a standing god. The former is evidently a major deity of the pantheon because she is enthroned. I suggest that she is not only a divine queen but a figure who is older than the male god.

Fig. 12.2. Goddess and god engaged in conversation, possibly with god receiving instructions. Ring from Mycenae.

Fig. 12.3. Goddess and her son with signs appearing above firmament. Seal now in Geneva.

Fig. 12.4. Goddess seated on her divine palace, facing her son. Sun appears between them, identifying goddess as solar divinity. Ring from Thebes.

The next issue is the relationship of the two deities. The first possibility is that they are partners (as Evans assumed at first); if so, an allegory of vegetation cycle might be implied.[11] Note, however, that Evans had toyed with the hypothesis that they were mother and son. Concerning the ring from Mycenae (Fig. 12.2) he writes: "The impression produced by the design is rather the relationship of a son to a mother than of a husband to a wife or mistress."[12] Evans was right: the ample and curvy proportions of the goddess are deliberately exaggerated to show her matronly aspect. I would further suggest that the images may be interpreted in composite ways: they are both myths and pragmatically based social paradigms. In mythic terms, the mother gives her son instructions and endorses his authority (we shall return to this subject in Chapter 13 when we explore Near Eastern myths). In social paradigmatic terms, the seated deity is the queen mother and the standing male is the king. Seen in this light, the famous ring from Mycenae (Fig. 9.21) may be interpreted as the encounter between the solar goddess and her son, who may well have been a moon god.[13]

Near Eastern Iconographical Parallels for the Seated Goddess

The visual formula of the seated goddess and the standing male god was not unique to Crete. On an Old Syrian seal that dates a little earlier than the rings we have examined from Crete, we see an enthroned goddess seated on an animal; across from her are two gods dressed in kilts and holding weapons, similar to the Minoan god (Fig. 12.5).[14] One of these gods is large and steps on a winged lion. He is the Storm God. The other male deity is smaller and is of uncertain identity. The fact that the goddess is enthroned signifies her queenlike senior (rather than superior) status. Is the smaller god her son?

Another Syrian seal shows the enthroned goddess seated on a bovid and flanked by solar signs (Fig. 12.6).[15] Facing her is a man wearing a kilt and long mantle; behind her is a greeting deity. In this case, the standing figure is most likely the king, rather than a god, because he is *not* stepping on an animal. Note, however, that in Syrian glyptic art it is difficult to distinguish between god and king (Chapter 2).[16] If he is a king, the seal shows us the special relationship of the king with his patron goddess.

On a cylinder found in Cyprus, but in all likelihood of Syrian origin, the enthroned goddess (Ishtar?) holds two palm branches with clusters of dates (Fig. 12.7). She is approached by a worshipper who offers her a live predatory bird; the latter person is most likely the king. To the left, a deity facing the goddess is standing on a bull and can thus be identified as the Warrior God.[17] In this case, both god and king are present, and they are both standing in front of the enthroned goddess.

Fig. 12.5. Seated goddess and Storm God. Old Syrian seal.

Fig. 12.6. Seated goddess, flanked by solar signs, faces ruler. Syrian cylinder seal.

Fig. 12.7. Enthroned goddess faces ruler. Old Syrian seal found in Cyprus.

Finally, on a relief from Malatya from the Neo-Hittite period in the Iron Age, a date later than our Mycenaean rings, the sun goddess is likewise seated. Here, she is also facing the Storm God (Fig. 12.8).

A pattern is beginning to emerge: the seated deity is a major goddess of the pantheon not only in Crete, but in Syria and Anatolia as well. On some occasions, she can be identified as a solar goddess. The standing male whom she faces is the Storm God or his human counterpart, the king.

We now turn to the Hittite reliefs at Yazilikaya (thirteenth century BCE), where the relationship of the goddess and her son is firmly attested. The chief female deity in the Hittite pantheon is *Hepat* (Hurrian name), who is synthesized with the sun goddess of Arinna. The latter is the chief patroness of kingship, the mistress of the land, the greatest of gods, and the protectress of king and queen.[18] She is often (but not in this case) shown seated.[19] On the relief shown in Figure 12.9, she has a central position in the composition and is standing on a feline.[20] Of particular interest is that she is accompanied by her son Sharuma, who is smaller and stands behind her. Sharuma is also the tutelary god of the king and is dressed like him. He stands on a feline, like his mother, and holds a double axe as his emblem. At Yazilikaya, then, we have a clear case of *goddess and son,* the latter being of smaller size.

This brief excursus into Syrian and Anatolian art has shown that the iconographical formula of seated goddess and standing god is not unique to Crete. Moreover, it has shown that the enthroned goddess is a queen. The designation "Great Goddess" is correct; however, it does not necessarily imply a matriarchy. Such a hypothesis is not only unhistorical but it undercuts the role of the king, who, as the fictive son of this goddess, is the hidden protagonist of the mythical paradigm.[21] We have further seen that in most cases in Syria and the Levant the standing god may be identified as the Storm God. We examine him and his Minoan equivalent in the next chapter. We have seen that the seated female in Syrian glyptic art must have some relation to the sun; on several occasions, the Minoan goddess is also accompanied by the sun disc.

If the male god mirrors the role of the king and the seated goddess that of the queen mother, this shows that queens and queen mothers had an elevated social position in Crete, not because Crete was a matriarchy, but because it was a theocracy. Wyatt has made a similar suggestion for Ugaritic and early Israelite queens.[22] This view finds support in a Hittite mythical paradigm in which the sun goddess of Arinna is a mother of both god and king. The Hittite queen Puduhepa prays to her and names the sun goddess as mother of the Storm God of Nerik and of the king alike.[23]

Fig. 12.8. Seated goddess accompanied by winged solar disc faces Storm God. Iron Age relief from Anatolian Malatya.

Fig. 12.9. Hepat followed by her son. Hittite relief from Yazilikaya (thirteenth century BCE).

Mother Goddesses and Queen Mothers in Two Near Eastern Mythical Narratives

Having investigated the iconography in Crete and the Orient we now turn to the mythical side of the paradigm. Two narratives from the Near East illustrate the role of a major goddess of the pantheon as both a mother and a queen. The first example comes from the Babylonian story about the Anzu monster from Nineveh (probably from the seventeenth century BCE). A dreadful monstrous bird steals the tablets of destiny from the gods and causes anarchy and chaos.[24] The gods meet under the leadership of the chief god, Anu. In the council of the divine pantheon, the gods are in despair. Anu proposes that they call the goddess Belet-ili/Mami, to save them:

Have them call for me Belet-ili, sister of the gods,
Wise counsellor of the gods her brothers.
Have them announce her supremacy in the assembly,
Have the gods honor her in their assembly:
I shall then tell her the idea which is in my heart. . . .
Previously [we used to call you] Mami
(but) now [your name shall be] Mistresss of All
gods.
Offer the powerful one, your superb beloved,
Broad of chest, who forms the battle array!
Give Ninurta, your superb beloved,
Broad of chest, who forms the battle array
[then shall his name be] Lord in the great gods'
assembly.
Let him show prowess to [the gods, that his name may
be Powerful].[25]

The role of this goddess is to summon her son, who will champion the cause of the gods and fight the monster on their behalf. Mami was her old name, but now she is given the title Mistress. Her power (which is so great that the collective gods, the Igigi, kiss her feet) derives from the fact that she is a queen mother. Her position in the pantheon is not due to the fact that she is a fertility goddess but that she appoints her son Ninurta to defeat a dangerous monster. The Ninurta epic has an evident relationship to kingship; its composition in the form we have it reflects the royal ideology of the Assyrian king.[26]

This type of narrative is not unique to the Babylonian culture. In the Ugaritic poem of Baal we find a goddess with a similar role. Athirat, the consort of the creator god El, enjoys the respect of all the gods and is accordingly given epithets of power. She is called "the Great Lady who tramples Yam," the sea snake of chaos;[27] she also receives the epithet *rbt* "great." Athirat is also called "the Mother of gods."[28] Like Babylonian Mami, she has an important role in determining matters of succession. For example, when the young Storm God Baal decides he needs a palace (to establish his position in the pantheon) he turns to Athirat, asking her to mediate on his behalf with El. Her approval seems necessary.

In another passage, El himself turns to Athirat. He is desperate because Baal has disappeared and another god/king must be found to replace him. El ask Athirat to appoint a successor:

"Aloud cried El to the Great Lady who tramples Yam:
Listen, O Great Lady-who-tramples-Yam.
Give the first of your sons;
I shall make him king."[29]

Athirat agrees. Her choice is Athtar, a god who eventually rules on earth rather than the heavens. Thus, Athirat's role as a mother of kings is to determine succession. As Wyatt states, the son of Athirat is the apotheosis of the human institution of kingship and Athirat's role in the Ugaritic pantheon reflects the importance of the dowager queen, a key figure in the issue of royal lineage.[30] Moreover, Athirat nourishes future kings by her milk. In the Ugaritic epic of Keret, the king heir, Yasib "will drink the milk of Athirat."[31] Note that Athirat is regarded as a solar goddess; as we shall see, this may be of relevance for interpreting her Minoan counterpart.[32]

Both of these narratives illustrate the exalted role of the mother/queen in the ancient Orient and testify to a common tradition. In Egypt this tradition is represented by the goddesses Isis, the mother figure of Horus and Hathor, whose name literally means "house of Horus." In Minoan religion, then, the goddess is the mother of the dominant male god of the pantheon. At the same time, she is the mythical mother of the king, endorsing his authority. The scenes of the seated goddess and the standing male god can be interpreted through a Near Eastern lens. The seated goddess appoints her standing son in a position of authority and endorses his power. Recall from Chapter 2 that the iconographical similarities between the god and king are *deliberate,* resulting not in confusion but in *intended ambiguity.* It is from this ambiguity that the royal paradigm derives its force.

The Goddess as a Tamer of the Dragon

We now examine some additional Minoan evidence in which a different aspect of the solar goddess is shown. On a ring from Mochlos, a goddess is seated in a dragon boat, and her shrine appears at the edge of the representation (Fig. 12.10).[33] Above the goddess is an oblong rayed symbol of unknown significance that resembles Luwian hieroglyphs designating sun/moon. Moreover, the boat is the vehicle of solar deities in the ancient Near East, especially of Babylonian Shamash and Egyptian Horus. In some cases, the solar bark takes the form of a live dragon, who has been tamed and has become the vehicle of the deity.

As a thought experiment, we may interpret the dragon boat of the Minoan goddess by use of Ugaritic mythology. The chief goddess of the pantheon, Athirat, has the epithet "the Great Lady who tramples Yam," or "the great lady who treads on the sea dragon."[34] Behind the epithet of Athirat lies a story that was unfortunately not preserved. We can assume that the story related how the goddess tamed the sea serpent. What supports this hypothesis is that the solar goddess of the underworld, Shapsh, who is the counterpart of Athirat, navigates over the sea. The sea is the serpent Yam. The Ugaritic goddess has the god Kothar-and-Hasis as a pilot.[35]

Fig. 12.10. Solar goddess transported by sea-dragon boat, arriving at her sanctuary. Ring from Mochlos.

On the sea of the monster and the dragon
Kothar-and-Hasis navigates you
Kothar-and-Hasis propels you.[36]

The Minoan Mochlos ring practically illustrates the Ugaritic text because the sea dragon is the vehicle of the deity's transport. If we look at the Mochlos ring with a Near Eastern interpretative lens, the imagery becomes richer in connotations; this is the point of the thought experiment.

The Mother Goddess as a Solar Goddess

Many paths have led us in the direction of the solar goddess. In Chapter 3, on the sarcophagus of Hagia Triada, we saw that the goddesses on both short sides are related to the cult of the double axe. On rings from Tiryns, Mycenae, and Thebes (Figs. 2.25, 9.21, and 12.4), the seated goddess has been associated with the sun disc, the split rosette, the double axe, or a combination of the three. Note that on the gold ring from Tiryns the sky above the goddess and her demon servants is replete with shooting stars, the sun, and the moon (Fig. 12.11). This iconography defines her celestial aspect. Below her is a row of split rosettes, which are solar signs (Chapter 10). Finally, her throne is decorated with half of a split rosette. Thus, all the inquiries of this study converge on the idea that the principal female deity of the Minoan pantheon is a sun goddess.

Fig. 12.11. Solar goddess and queen of heavens receives libations by leonine demon-servants in her celestial palace. Ring from Tiryns (fourteenth century BCE).

Whose Emblem Is the Double Axe?

If, as discussed in Chapter 9, the correct interpretation of the double axe is the sun of the horizon, then it must be the emblem of a solar deity. That this deity was female was known to Evans as well as Nilsson; "the Minoan double axe is never found as an attribute of a male god," said Nilsson.[37]

The hypothesis is confirmed by the images on a mould found at Siteia in Eastern Crete, an object that was evidently designed for the production of reliefs representing the chief goddess and her symbols (Figs. 12.12). On the one side of this mould, the deity is represented next to the sun disc, holding a rosette in her left hand (viewer's right, Fig. 12.12a). On the other side of the mould, the goddess is displayed holding a double axe in each hand and a rayed disc is also present (Fig 12.12b). Here we see a nexus of images with related meaning: goddess, sun disc, double axe, and rosette flower. That they occur in the same mould and in association with each other, can be considered strong if not conclusive evidence that these images are semantically related and designate the solar goddess and her manifestations. This conclusion may not have come as a complete surprise to Evans. He interpreted the same disc as a "rayed solar symbol of Goddess of Double Axes."[38]

In the post-palatial era, the solar goddess remains important, as is evidenced by a series of clay statues with raised arms. She wears a crown on which the solar disc features together with the sacred mountain, birds, and snakes.[39]

a

b

Fig. 12.12. Solar goddess and her emblems on mould from Siteia. (a) Goddess with rosette in one hand. (b) Goddess with double axe.

The Deities of the Sun and the Underworld on the Hagia Triada Sarcophagus

In Chapter 3 the clay coffin from Hagia Triada revealed the king's and queen's priestly roles. The king made offerings to a divinized ancestor, but we did not discuss the deity in whose honor the sacrifices were made. The key is the presence of double axes on both long sides of the sarcophagus. The repetition of the cult emblem shows that the same deity was worshipped. We can now test the hypothesis that the double axe represents the solar goddess of kingship by investigating the identity of the deities represented on the sarcophagus.

These divinities have an anthropomorphic form but are shown only on the short sides, not on the long ones. On one panel (Fig. 12.13a) a goddess and her charioteer both wear plumed hats and have long robes. They are dressed like the queen, clearly revealing how royalty and gods mirror each other. We know that the figures in the chariot are goddesses, however, because the chariot is drawn by winged griffins.

On the other short side, two more goddesses are represented: they ride a chariot that is drawn by mules or goats (Fig. 12.13b).[40] The two panels of the short sides are very similar, indeed symmetrical. The second, however, has a peculiarity: this scene is located on a *lower level* than its counterpart. This positioning must be deliberate, showing that the deities in this panel are coming from the underworld. Indeed, the closest scene (around the corner) is the tomb of the dead king. Above the deities is an incompletely preserved panel of which the feet of male figures in procession are preserved; perhaps they are images of the ancestors who are joining the festival.[41]

The complete symmetry in the iconography of the panels of the two short sides makes it difficult to avoid the conclusion that the same goddess and her companion, or rather two manifestations of the same divine pair, are represented traveling in two distinct spheres, the sky and the underworld. We might note a further detail: in the celestial scene (Fig. 12.13a) the panel is bordered by rosettes above and below. In the underworld scene (Fig. 12.13b) wavy lines are depicted above the chariot. Thus, the goddesses are below waters. I take these decorations to be topographical indicators, further hints about the location of the divinities in the cosmos; the rosette signifies the realm of the sun, whereas the wavy lines are the waters that constitute the borders of the netherworld. There is only one

a b

Fig. 12.13. Short sides of Hagia Triada sarcophagus.

possible candidate for a divine traveler of this type: the sun, because it is the only divine figure that crosses boundaries and enters both realms. Like the Ugaritic sun goddess Shapshu, who has the role of a *psychopompos*, a leader of souls, the Minoan solar goddess seems to have this dual role as well.[42] Evans, then, was remarkably close to the truth when he posited a dual nature for his Great Goddess. A pair of divinities wearing a plumed hat and traveling in a griffin drawn chariot is shown on a gold ring found in the Peloponnese (Fig. 12.14). This means that the iconography of the sarcophagus was not unique. Note the presence of the palm and the griffin, both of which have been interpreted as solar symbols and inhabitants of the paradiasical landscape (see Chapters 4, 9, 10, and 11).

Fig. 12.14. Divinities with plumed head-dresses in griffin-drawn chariot. Ring from Peloponnese.

The Minoan name of the goddess cannot be securely ascertained but there may be a clue based on the evidence of Linear A tablets and votive stone libation tables, where we see the name *A-sa-sa-ra* several times. We can reconstruct the phonetics by using the sound values of Linear B and transposing them on Linear A. *A-sa-sa-ra* must be the name of a deity to which the objects were dedicated. Who is she? The name does not evoke any figure of Greek mythology.[43] In 1958, Nikolaos Platon timidly suggested that *A-sa-sa-ra* may be a linguistic adaptation of Ugaritic *Atrt* (Athirat).[44] Platon may have been right, although I shall not press this point. Suffice it to say that such an equation would be very convenient for the thesis proposed here.

Using different methods, Lucy Goodison concludes that a sun goddess existed in the Bronze Age; she regards her as a chief deity who was replaced by a male sun god during the Iron Age.[45] Goodison's postulate is based on a developmental view of history, namely that important female deities were in time marginalized and replaced by male ones. I am not convinced of this part of her thesis, because the sun goddess exists already in the second millennium as a major deity of the pantheon in Anatolia and the Levant, where she is a queen and patroness of the king. Despite the divergence of approaches, it must be stressed that Goodison was the first to recognize the existence of a solar goddess in Minoan religion.

This solar goddess, I suggest, had a dual role as a goddess of the underworld and the sky; it may be that she had two different names, each referring to one of her aspects. This duality is expressed on the two short sides of the Hagia Triada sarcophagus and by symmetry of forms inherent in all the sun symbols: double axe, split rosette, and incurved podium.

In the mythological *koine* of the Near East and Egypt the sun goddess is often related to the underworld goddess as a mother or sister (see Table 12.1).

Table 12.1. Relationship between Sun Goddess and Underworld Goddess

Region	Relationship	Names
Mesopotamia	sisters	Ishtar and Ereshkigal
Egypt	sisters	Hathor and Isis
Greece	mother/daughter	Demeter and Persephone
Ugarit	unknown	Athirat and Shapshu

It is likely that the solar goddess had the epithet "great" or "mistress" in the Minoan language. This is pure conjecture, but it is based on the probability that her iconogram as a seated deity corresponds to the epithet "great mistress." The Mycenaeans called her *po-t-ni-ja,* the peoples of Ugarit *rbt,* and the Greeks *potnia.*[46] This "mistress" was not primarily a huntress or a fertility goddess, *pace* Nilsson. She was, rather, the "queen of heavens." Compare also the epithets received by Anat and Astarte in Ugarit, "Lady of Heaven," and see also Jeremiah 7:18 and 44:19.[47] She was also a goddess of the underworld, a dragon tamer, and, most importantly, the mother of the Storm God and the king alike.[48] The throne at Knossos belonged to this solar goddess, but it was the king who sat on it, as if on her lap. It is from her that he derived his power and authority.

13

The Storm God

Although the solar goddess has a primary role in the Minoan pantheon, the male god has a more diverse and more interesting iconography. The standard view is that he is not as significant as the goddess. This is one of Evans's legacies to posterity.[1] He himself detected only one male divinity in Minoan religion. Sometimes he called him a boy god, other times "a youthful divinity, martially arrayed."[2] He died and was reborn; he was a type of Tamuz or Greek Adonis, who was mourned by the mother goddess.[3] This notion is due to his contemporary and colleague, Sir James Frazer, who advanced the idea of the dying god of vegetation. However, today we know that Frazerian narratives are of dubious validity because they are in themselves myths, invented in the nineteenth century to explain ancient beliefs.[4]

Nilsson followed the track of Evans. The Minoan male deity, he thought, was a hunting god and "a relic of a nature demon."[5] But after Erik Hallager's excavation of the ring impression from Chania (Fig. 5.10), Alexander MacGillivray's ivory statue from Palaikastro, and Nota Dimopoulou's three gold rings from Poros, no doubt may exist about the importance of the youthful male god. He must be viewed not as a mere satellite of the Great Goddess, but as an autonomous bright star in the constellation of Minoan deities.[6] Yet despite new discoveries, his mythical persona remains tied to Frazerian notions of fertility religion, death, resurrection, and seasonal allegory.

Because some kind of mythology (ancient or modern) is necessary for thinking about a deity, I suggest we look for models in the Near East, rather than in Greek mythology or anthropological theory about primitive religions. Our first task, however, will be to investigate the typology and morphology of the representations of the chief male god. One immediate observation is that, unlike the solar goddess, he is always standing and never enthroned.

The Morphology of the "Minoan God"

The young god is muscular and youthful, and his bodily vigor is emphasized also by the short kilt he almost always wears. He is very often armed, if only with a spear; sometimes he has a bow and even a shield. When he is not armed, he can be recognized by his commanding gestures (see, for example, Fig. 13.1). Occasionally, he wears a tall, pointed tiara, similar to that of Hittite and Syrian gods (see Fig. 13.3a–d).[7] Note, however, that the tiara is a sign of both royalty and divinity in Syria, Hittite Anatolia, and Minoan Crete. This suggests that the Minoan god was probably conceived as a *king of his pantheon.* It further suggests that we can never know for sure if one particular representation shows the god or the king. Because this ambiguity is deliberate, it need not concern us much (Chap. 2).

The god is sometimes shown as a hunter and a master of animals (see, for example, Figs. 13.1 and 13.2), other times as a warrior defeating enemies. These iconographical categories do not necessarily represent different gods, as Nilsson indicated. He made an erroneous assumption when he stated that morphological categories represent semantic ones. Typology, however, may help us understand something about the *roles* that deities had in the pantheon. How is male power expressed? Against whom do the male gods fight? The possibility that many deities are concealed behind each iconographical type must be left open.[8]

One type is the controller of wild animals. This is expressed in a number of diverse visual ways: sometimes the deity is a hunter (Fig. 13.1), other times he walks by a lion (Fig. 13.1b), and yet other times he grabs an animal as a master of animals (Fig. 13.2). Thus, it is an indisputable fact that male divine power is rendered as domination over wild dangerous beasts.

An alternative way of expressing power is conveyed by the extended arm of the god.[9] On a ring impression from Chania (Fig. 5.10), the god's extended arm shows him as dominant over his own city and establishes him as "lord of the town." On two further images, a ring from Poros (Fig. 7.10) and an impression from Knossos (Fig. 13.1), we meet again the extended arm gesture in displays of authority.

Dominance over animals and authority expressed by the commanding gesture are clearly two types of power associated with the Minoan god but do not necessarily reflect two different gods.

The next step is to investigate Near Eastern divinities with similar morphology. In Figures 13.3, we see deities from Anatolia, Syria, and Crete. When viewed together it is hard to distinguish the Minoan god from his counterparts on the other side of the Aegean. All exhibit a set of common characteristics, including the fact that gods (or kings) are occasionally accompanied by a feline. Note especially the similarity between the Minoan god (Fig 13.3a) and the Hittite god

Fig. 13.1.Ring impression from Knossos.

Fig. 13.2. God as master of animals. Seal from mainland.

Sharuma, son of Hepat, from Yazilikaya (Fig. 13.3b). Likewise, the Syrian Reshep (Fig 13.3d) has iconographical affinities with the Minoan god (Fig. 13.3c).[10]

The investigation of the iconography may lead us to some preliminary conclusions about the role of youthful male deities. Most of the Near Eastern gods shown here are warrior and storm gods, all of which have power over animals as well as men. They are often distinguished by a tall, pointed tiara and are accompanied by felines. The parallelism in the morphology suggests affinities in the way the deity was conceptualized on both sides of the Aegean. If so, we are better off seeking the identity of the Minoan god in the mythology of the Near East than in Greek mythology or in Frazerian anthropological theory of seasonal allegories.

As for the fact that we cannot distinguish between god and king on the Minoan rings, let this be a further proof that their images are conflated.

Mythological Narratives on Minoan Gold Rings

Leaving morphology behind, we proceed to the more speculative ground of narrative content. I believe that several Minoan rings depict stories that reflect lost Minoan myths, but this is a personal view. For the purposes of this discussion, it is important to define what narrative means before proceeding to reflections

Fig. 13.3. (a) God or king on ring impression from Hagia Triada. (b) Hittite God Sharuma on Hittite rock relief from Yazilikaya (thirteenth century BCE). (c) God or king as Minoan statuette. (d) God Reshep. Syrian statuette.

about it. I rather like Dawn Cain's adoption of Genette's definition that "as soon as there is action there is an event."[11] *Action,* then, is a crucial feature of narrative and must be distinguished from *statement.* To make a visual statement, no activity is necessary, a display of relationships is enough. For example, most of the examples in Figures 13.1 and 13.3 are statements about a god but do not constitute a narrative. In order to tell a story, the artist has to include hints about what precedes the action as well as what follows it. The story may be reconstructed in the mind of the viewer, even if not shown explicitly.[12]

How can we proceed from intuition to certainty and actually read the story? This requires a further step, namely the viewer's knowledge of the entire action sequence. It has been a stumbling block in understanding Minoan images because there is a complete absence of Minoan narrative texts. Some would say that the task is outright impossible.[13] However, if we assume that there existed a pool of myths common to the Aegean and the Near East, just as we have shown the existence of a pool of common iconographical motifs, why not attempt to adopt a Near Eastern lens and seek Near Eastern stories behind the actions of gods on the Minoan rings? This method may yield unexpected pay-offs.

The Mythical Biography of the Near Eastern Storm God

Before outlining some of the Near Eastern stories, we look at the mythical persona or, better said, the role of the Storm God in Near Eastern myths. The designation "Storm God" is a convenient descriptive term that fits a number of deities in Mesopotamia, Syria, Anatolia, and Egypt. Among the Hittites, he is Teshub (Hurrian name) or Shantash in the Neo-Hittite kingdom; in Ugarit, he is Baal; in Babylon, he is Ninurta, although Marduk also fits the mold.[14] In Egypt, the Storm God is Seth, who is assimilated with Canaanite Baal in Avaris in the Eastern Nile Delta.[15] On the Syro-Levantine coast, he is Reshep, with the special function to cause and avert plagues.[16] In Greece, the Storm God is Zeus, the king of the pantheon. However, Apollo is also an inheritor of the Storm God, being especially close to the Syrian Reshep; like him, he causes and heals plagues.[17]

According to the pattern presented here, some common points can be established. The Storm God is almost always young; he has enemies, both anthropomorphic ones and monsters; he has to make combat, but he always triumphs in the end and becomes king. However, victory is not won without a price. In the Ugaritic epic, the Storm God Baal is dismembered by Mot and is carried to the underworld by Shapsh, the sun goddess. Yet this is not a final death, and he is restored to his rightful throne with the help of his partner, the goddess Anat. In Hittite Anatolian narratives, the Storm God fights the dragon Illuyanka(s). The formidable serpent manages to remove his eyes and heart and render him powerless.[18] A remedy is found through a complicated marriage system and trickery; eventually the Storm God gets his organs back and can function again. In this story his partner is crucial as well. Babylonian Ninurta has to fight several monsters but he prevails in the end.[19] The Egyptian Storm God, Seth, fights a serpent as well; the image of Seth as a fighter of the dragon is well attested on funerary papyri (see, for example, Fig. 13.10).

These stories demonstrate common patterns that occur in myths of the Ancient Orient. They are not without variations, but there is a consistency that justifies the assumption of a *koine*. This much may be said: the adventures and final triumph of the Storm God constitute a major feature of the mythological narratives associated with him.[20] The view that the young god of vegetation reflects seasonal crises is no longer tenable.[21] Rather, we must look at these myths as *expressions of the ideology of kingship*, an institution that faces potential dangers because orderly transition of generations from the older king to his younger successor may be disrupted or contested by relatives or outsiders.[22] The potential for social disorder is reflected in myth: the young god must fight his adversaries before he can be established securely on the throne. I interpret the mythical paradigm of combat as an expression of the dangers of royal succession.[23]

Another aspect of the Storm God is also closely knit with kingship. One of his roles is to protect the order of the cosmos and his own domain by fighting monsters, wild animals, and all kinds of chaotic forces (*Chaoskampf*).[24] In this respect, he is also a civilizing agent, making the world safe from monsters and wild animals that live in the mountains, the desert, or the sea. His weapon, with which he shoots the animals, is sometimes the bow and other times a spear.[25]

This brief introduction to the Storm God is certainly inadequate; it is impossible to do justice to all the mythical nuances of every story from a large span of time and space in the Near East. Yet these sketchy elements show that there is a consistent paradigm behind the variety of names. The ancients themselves saw these similarities and translated the Storm God of one culture into the religious idiom of the other.[26] Thus, Baal was translated to Zeus Cassios by the Greeks and to Seth by the Egyptians. Yahweh may have been a blend of the Canaanite creator god, El, and the Storm God, Baal (Chapter 14).

As a guarantor of order, the Storm God is the embodiment of the king and is visually assimilated with him.[27] No question then: the Storm God flourishes where there is kingship.[28]

The Ugaritic Baal Epos and Kingship

One specific narrative from Ugarit, the Baal cycle, may be of great value for the investigation of the Minoan Storm God, because Crete had especially close connections with Ugarit. The cycle consists of semi-autonomous episodes, some of which are signed by a person named Ilimilku. Wyatt has argued that this poet was employed by the royal court of king Niqmaddu III-IV and that, quite possibly, he composed the specific form of the text under commission.[29] If so, the Baal texts can be analyzed as documents with an agenda promoting royal self-presentation. In other words, they should not be regarded solely as legends handed down by oral tradition (this is how many scholars speak of myths), but as products of a specific age, commissioned by a specific patron.[30]

We might draw an analogy between mythical written texts and mythical visual narratives, such as the ones on the gold rings of palatial Crete. Might we not say that the scenes chosen for the rings are not random and that their purpose was to underline myths that reinforce the institution of kingship? That they disseminate royal ideology promoted by a dynasty?[31] And that the protagonist is the king, the very prototype of the earthly monarch?

Detecting the Storm God on Minoan Rings

As we have seen, the mythical persona of the Storm God may be behind many of the narratives depicted on gold rings. We now turn our attention to detecting him in the Minoan evidence.

The first example is a figure on a ring from Palaikastro (Fig. 13.4a). On the face of it, the ring shows an ordinary hunting scene with a male hunter in the background and a huge goat attacked by dogs in the foreground. Closer inspection, however, reveals that the scene is too unnatural for a human hunt because the goat is huge. One also suspects that the protagonist is a god because of his commanding gesture, which evokes the smiting posture typical of Syrian and Canaanite deities (Fig. 13.3). It is also important to note that the deity wields a weapon, which unfortunately is not well preserved. See Figure 13.4 for a telling comparison of the hunter deity of the Palaikastro ring (13.4a) with a Syrian deity on an earlier seal from Tell el Dab'a in the eastern Nile Delta (Fig. 13.4b). The deity on the Tell el Dab'a seal steps on a double mountain, which symbolizes his own domain, perhaps even his dominance over the cosmos.[32] Below him is the sea serpent Yam, whom the god defeats with the help of a lion. Both the Canaanite and the Minoan gods have striding postures and smiting gestures. Both attack goats, except that, on the Tell el Dab'a seal, the animal is upside down. Note that in both cases the goats are more than prey: they are wild adversaries that must be dominated. Although the Tell el Dab'a seal dates a few centuries earlier than the Palaikastro ring, the common iconography testifies to a long and common tradition.[33] The establishment of this similarity suggests that the Minoan figure on the Palaikastro ring is indeed a god; if we adopt the lens of the *koine*, he is a Storm God.

A second example is from a ring impression from Hagia Triada.[34] Here the scene is far more dramatic: a male, adorned with a necklace, grabs his adversary by his hair (Fig. 13.5a). He is aided by hounds, which gallop along with their running master. The posture replicates Egyptian images of the smiting pharaoh, a common formula during the Eighteenth and Nineteenth Dynasties (Fig. 13.5b and c). The Egyptian parallel suggests that our figure may be a king, but it is equally possible that he is a god in his capacity as a warrior defeating adversaries. In any case, in Egypt and Syro-Palestine the smiting gesture is possible for either god or king.[35] Keel and Uehlinger have stressed that the iconography of "triumphant and dominant gods" is very popular in the second part of the second millennium; needless to stress once more that these deities are the mythical paradigm for the king.[36] That we should find the image of this aggressive god in Minoan art testifies to a type of kingship in which the king is not only the chief priest but the also the chief warrior. In the New Palace epoch the patron god of the king is the Storm God.

The running, smiting god may be detected in another type of scene, where he appears once more as a victor. On two scenes, one ring impression from Chania (Fig. 13.6a) and one ring from Athens (Fig 13.6b), a male figure drags bound prisoners behind him. In the first scene, the prisoner is a male; in the other they are female.[37] This iconography has parallels in Near Eastern and Egyptian art; one example illustrated here is an ivory piece from Canaanite Megiddo dating later than our rings to the thirteenth or twelfth century (Fig. 13.6c). The king rides his chariot, bringing back captives after a successful war campaign. Naked, bound, and humiliated, the prisoners walk ahead of the king, whose triumph is

a

b

Fig. 13.4. (a) Ring from Palaikastro. (b) Storm God smiting goat (highlighted in black here). Syrian seal from Tell el Dab'a, Egypt (seventeenth century BCE).

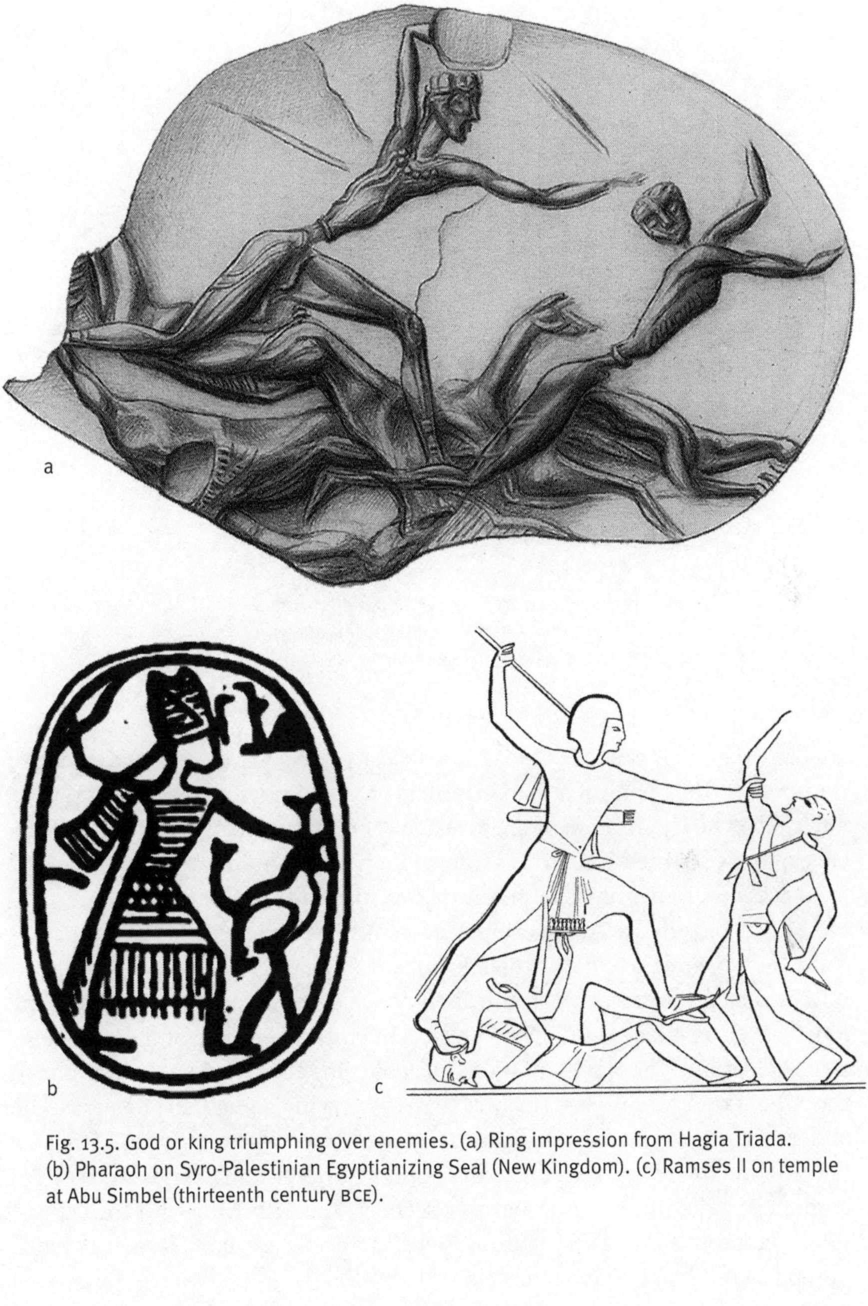

Fig. 13.5. God or king triumphing over enemies. (a) Ring impression from Hagia Triada. (b) Pharaoh on Syro-Palestinian Egyptianizing Seal (New Kingdom). (c) Ramses II on temple at Abu Simbel (thirteenth century BCE).

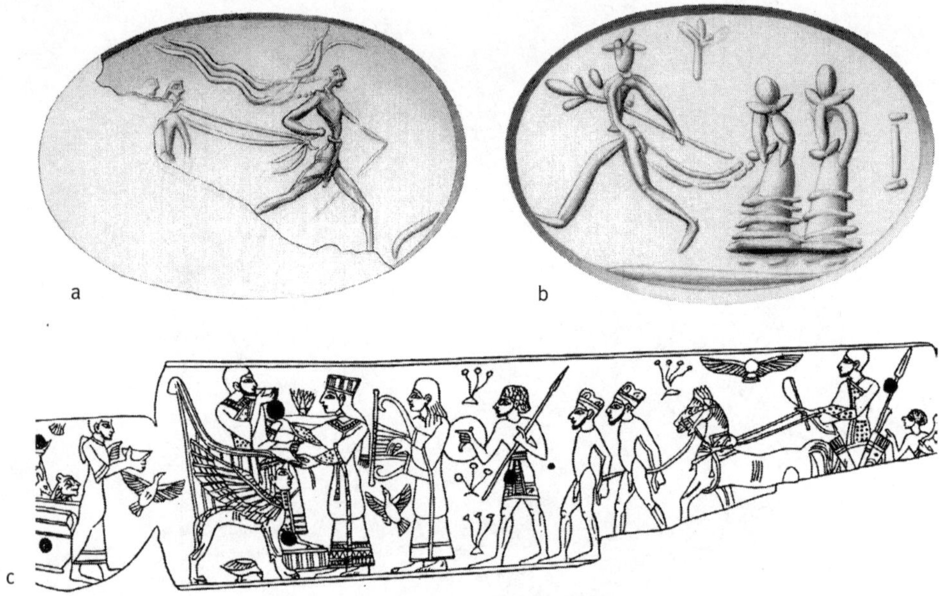

Fig. 13.6. Triumphant god (or king) with bound prisoners.
(a) Ring impression from Chania. (b) Ring from Athens.
(c) Ivory piece from Megiddo (thirteenth century BCE).

confirmed by the presence of his tutelary deity, the solar disc, hovering above the horses.[38] The theme of bound prisoners on the Minoan rings in Figures 13.6a and 13.6b is surely a variant of the royal iconography of victory. The chronological gap between the Minoan and Canaanite pieces should not disturb because there was continuity of visual tradition on either side of the Aegean.

The scene from the Athens ring (Fig. 13.6b) has one puzzling feature, however. The prisoner is female, which is unusual. The only explanation that I can offer is that the narrative is mythical, in which case we may postulate that the female is an adversary of the Storm God. The unusual nature of the scene also struck Nilsson: "The representation on a gold ring found in the excavations in the Athenian Agora is very curious. A man carrying a sceptre (?) seems to be abducting two women, whom he leads by a cord, perhaps as captives" (it seems that Nilsson misread the scene because only one of the females is a captive). He continues: "The interpretation of this scene as the Minotaur with the captive girls is certainly hasty. Persson thinks it to be a predecessor of Hermes Psychopompos who, staff in hand, conducts the dead to the netherworld."[39]

The attempt to project a Greek myth onto this Minoan ring does not work, as Nilsson realized, despite his own propensity towards this very method. It is preferable to turn to the Near East for mythological parallels and remind ourselves that the Storm God often has to face female adversaries.[40]

Our cycle of the Minoan god will close by considering another example of the running deity. He is depicted on a recently excavated ring from the sanctuary of Kato Syme (where it was evidently dedicated and deposited by its owner).[41] The central figure is a runner, as the excavators correctly identify him (Fig. 13.7). Above him is a shooting star, a feature that we have seen on other rings as well, especially in connection with scenes of prophecy.[42] The shooting star thus suggests a divine occurrence of some sort and not an ordinary athletic event (see Figs. 7.6b; 7.10, and 9.8). The runner moves between two figures, a female at the right and a male (?) at the left. The female, who may be imagined as standing at the starting point of the track, raises an arm; the male at the other end displays an object of uncertain significance, shaped like the Greek letter omega.[43] It looks like it is the prize to be awarded to the runner once he has completed his feat. But what kind of prize is it? As will be shown, it is a type of crown but not an athletic crown, such as the olive or laurel wreath awarded to Greek athletes. Our omega object is a headdress worn only by the solar goddess, sometimes in double form (Fig. 13.8). Sometimes it is carried in procession by men, as on a mural found at Thera. On that fresco, the crown is adorned with double axes, namely the emblem of the solar goddess.[44]

The associations of this crown with the goddess allow a tentative conclusion about the identity of the runner. Since he is going to be offered the crown of the solar goddess, he is her protégée. The further inference is that he is either her son, the Storm God, or her fictive son, the earthly king. Perhaps it is helpful to note that the Egyptian pharaoh was depicted as a runner during the Heb-Sed festival because it was important for him to display his strength and bodily vigor.[45]

Our investigation has shown so far that the Minoan Storm God is a hunter, a warrior, and a athlete.

The Serpent Monster and the Storm God

Another aspect of the Minoan Storm God is his capacity to slay monsters. In the Near East, one of his most dangerous adversaries is a serpent residing in the depths of the sea. Because it embodies chaos, it must be defeated.[46]

Precisely such a creature can be detected on a Minoan ring impression from Knossos, although surprisingly little attention has been paid to it, except by Evans first and later by Spyridon Marinatos. Fragmentary though the impression is, Evans recognized a monster attacking a man in a boat (Fig. 13.9).[47] The male figure stands firm, wielding a weapon (which is unfortunately not preserved but which I have attempted to reconstruct); evidently he speared down the monster,

Fig. 13.7. God (or king) running toward prize, the omega-shaped crown of solar goddess. Ring from sanctuary at Kato Syme, Crete.

Fig. 13.8. Solar goddess crowned with omega-shaped object. Seal now in Fogg Art Museum, Harvard.

of which only the leonine head with an open, threatening mouth remains.[48] Since the attack takes place in a boat, the monster is a creature of the ocean.

We could look for parallels in Greek mythology and detect the Homeric Scylla or Charybdis. However, it is preferable to look at the Near East. There is a sea serpent in Ugaritic myth by the name Litanu, which appears also in the Hebrew Bible as Leviathan.[49] Both are adversaries of the Storm God Baal and Israelite Yahweh, respectively.[50] In Egypt, the sea serpent Apophis is combated by Seth, the Storm God. On an Egyptian papyrus, the boat of the sun god is attacked by Apophis and defended by Seth, who is the helmsman of Horus (Fig. 13.10).

Also, the Syrian Storm God is depicted as a snake slayer on Middle and Late Bronze Age seals (Figs. 13.11a and b), whereas in Mesopotamia the sea monster, attested already in the third millennium, continues into the ninth and eighth centuries on Assyrian seals (Fig. 13.11c).

The Weapons of the Storm God

If the mythology sketched above for the Minoan God has any validity, then we must search for his weapons. Divine and royal weapons play a large role in the rituals and the myths of the Ancient Near East. A divine spear and axe are invoked in an Ugaritic prayer for the security of the city.[51] The weapon sometimes guarantees the victory no matter who wields it. For this reason, shields, lances, and other divine weapons were worshipped in the Ancient Near East.

In the Babylonian *Enuma Elish,* a text that goes back to the second millennium BCE, the bow of the Storm God Marduk receives special emphasis because it is the vehicle of the god's victory.[52] Before he goes to battle, Marduk must have a new weapon: "[Marduk] fashioned a bow, designated it as his weapon" (*Enuma Elish,* Tablet IV).[53]

Later, when Marduk has won his battle against his adversaries, and after he has been appointed king of the gods, the bow is praised: "The Lord [Marduk] received the bow, and set his weapon down in front of them [i.e., the assembly of gods]. The gods his fathers looked at the net which he had made, looked at the bow . . . and his fathers praised the deeds that he had done. Anu raised the bow and spoke in the assembly of the gods. He kissed the bow. 'May she go far'" (*Enuma Elish,* Tablet VI).[54]

The importance of weapons for the victory of the Storm God is evident also in the Ugaritic epic of Baal (thirteenth century BCE), which is closer in time to Minoan palatial Crete. The god owes his victory against his sea adversary, Yam, to the magical weapons that the craftsman god Kothar-and-hasis has manufactured for him. Baal uses a mace against Yam. On another occasion he hunts wild bulls and then he uses a bow: "His *bow* he took in his (left) hand and his arrows in his (right) hand."[55]

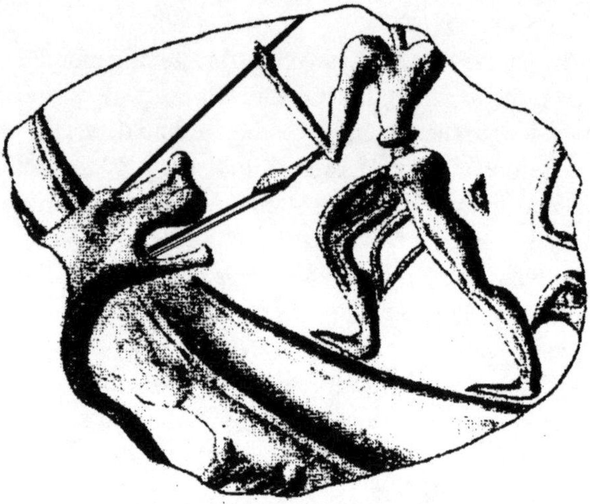

Fig. 13.9. Sea-monster attacks boat of Storm God. Ring impression from Knossos (slightly restored by N. Marinatos).

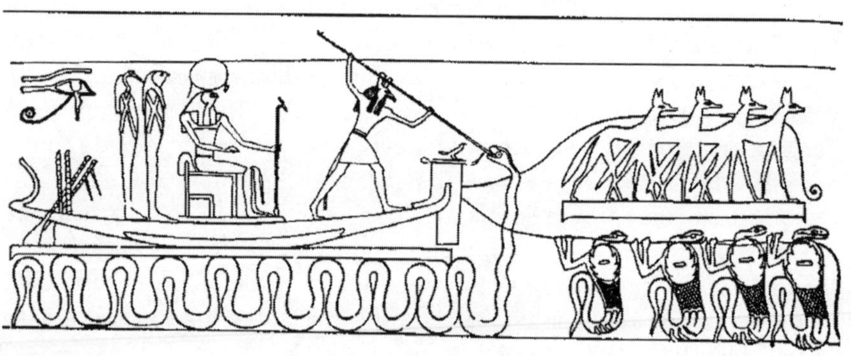

Fig. 13.10. Apophis attacks boat of Horus and is defeated by Seth. Egyptian papyrus (New Kingdom).

a

b

Fig. 13.11. Storm God killing serpent. (a) Syrian seal. (b) Syrian seal (detail).

The motif of the magical weapon is evident also in Greek myths: the armor of Achilles in the *Iliad* is allotted half a book, whereas the bow of Odysseus in the *Odyssey* is the key to the victory of the hero. This shows that Greek mythology was part of a long narrative *koine* on both sides of the Aegean. In this common mythology, sacred and miraculous weapons played a role and were the privilege of gods, heroes, and kings. That Minoan Crete and Mycenaean Greece were part of this *koine* of sacred weapons stands to reason.

On one ring, originally from Crete and now in Berlin (Fig. 13.12), the bow is the central visual motif of the scene. It is held fast by two figures, a male and a female.[56] On the right of the scene we detect an ecstatic, familiar to us from prophetic scenes discussed in Chapter 7. His presence shows that the representation includes both deities and intermediaries. If the male is the Storm God, the female may be the solar goddess, a fact suggested by the double axe hovering above her head. Further signs are the ox head and the shooting star, which have been discussed previously (Chaps. 7–10).[57] In all probability, the central male figure is the Storm God holding his divine weapon. What is the female deity doing? Is she trying to wrestle the bow away from him?[58] Or is she handing it to him? The myth cannot be reconstructed in full, but perhaps we get here a glimpse of genuine Minoan mythology in which the bow plays a central role.

There is further proof of the importance of the bow for defining the identity of the Storm God. It occurs on a ring from Knossos, now in the Ashmolean Museum, Oxford. The god with the bow is a small, floating figure who appears in the sky, displaying his weapon (Fig. 13.13). This is a scene of epiphany. According to what I have proposed in Chapter 7, the scene is one of prophetic vision. The witnesses are the queen (to the left, wearing a plume on her head) and the

Fig. 13.12. Storm God and solar goddess with bow. Ring from Crete, now in Berlin.

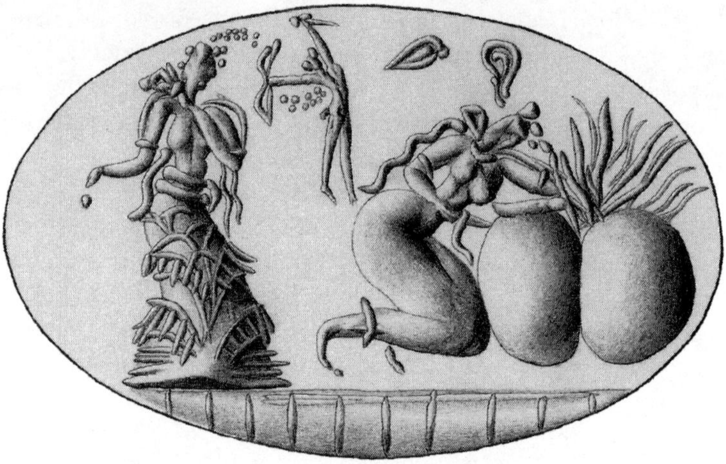

Fig. 13.13. Storm God armed with bow, as seen by visionary. Ring from Knossos, now in Ashmolean Museum, Oxford.

visionary leaning over a boulder.[59] They are most likely the same person shown in two stages of action.

The notion of sacred weapons fits well with the model of theocratic kingship, because the king may claim that they are divine and that through them he rules the world. A text from Mari describes how a priest hands the sacred weapons of the Storm God Adad over to king Zimrilim; this ceremony signals the king's legitimization as the divine representative of the war god.[60] In Ugarit, the ritual association of weapons with the king may be indirectly inferred from the Baal myth, as Wyatt has shown.[61] Note, however, that the weapons of the god are also the weapons of the king: the iconography of the Storm God leads again to royal ideology.[62]

Proskynesis

There is one scene that may serve as the crowning piece of the discussion on the Storm God because it constitutes proof about the existence of the paradigm (if not of the actuality) of divine kingship on Crete. On a ring impression from the palace of Zakros is shown the obeisance (Greek term *proskynesis*) of one male to another. Figure 13.14 shows the ring impression (13.14a) and my reconstruction (13.14b). On the left of the scene, we see a youthful male. He has a posture of authority and holds a staff. To his right is another male who is dressed just like him and bows down to the ground. To the far right are two figures in long robes, witnessing the event.

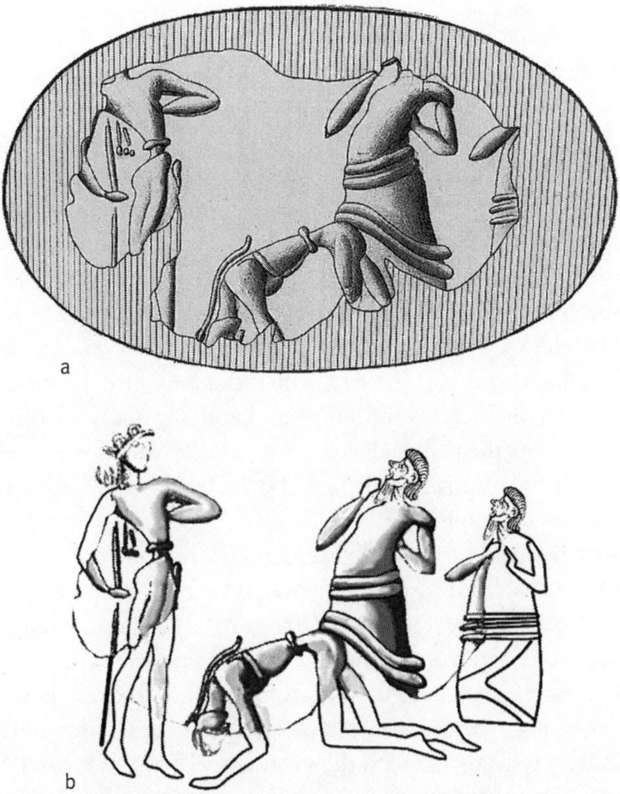

a

b

Fig. 13.14.Scene showing *proskynesis* (obeisance) to god/king.
(a) Ring impression from Zakros. (b) Reconstruction of ring impression.

Texts from Ugarit and Mesopotamia perfectly explain the scene on the Minoan ring from Zakros: it is *proskynesis,* an act of prostration and kissing the ground before the god. In theocratic societies, the recipient may be a god or king, and *proskynesis* is an acknowledgment of the latter's divine or superior status. Consider some passages from the Baal epic of Ugarit where one god says to another one:

> At the feet of Mot bow and fall down,
> pay him homage and honor him.[63]

> At the feet of El she bowed and fell down
> She paid him homage and honored him.[64]

In the seventh century BCE Assyrian Anzu text, the gods kiss wise Ea's feet:

> The Igigi listened to this speech of his
> the Igigi were freed (from anxiety) and kissed his feet.[65]

Proskynesis of a god is found also in a Biblical passage when God tells the prophet Elijah that he will let live only seven thousand in Israel: "all the knees that have not bowed to Baal, and every mouth that has not kissed him" (1 Kings 19:18, RSV).

It is not only in mythical narratives that we find *proskynesis,* however. We also find it as a rhetorical cliché in royal correspondence sent by vassal kings to their superiors, namely kings greater than themselves and thus acknowledged as divine. In the archives of Amarna in the fourteenth century BCE, there are letters written by petty kings of the Syro-Palestinian area to the pharaoh. These vassals usually ask for a favor and they often begin with an expression of obeisance: "To the king, my lord . . . At the feet of the king, my lord, seven times, seven times I fall."[66] "To the king my lord, my pantheon, my Sun-god, the Sun-god of heaven: Thus Widia, the prince of Ashkelon, thy servant, the dirt (under) your feet, the groom of thy horse. At the feet of the king, my lord, seven times verily I fall, both prone and supine."[67]

The Greeks, who did not have divine kingship, rejected the idea of *proskynesis.* Herodotus narrates how two young men from Sparta, Sperthies and Boulis, arrived at the Persian court and were urged by a Persian official to prostrate themselves in front of the Great King: "As they came to Susa and they came to the king's presence, when the guards commanded and would have compelled them to do obeisance (*proskyneein*) to the king, they said they would in no way do it even if they were thrust with the head down. For it was not their custom (*nomos*) to do obeisance to mortal men" (Herodotus, 7.136, transl. A.D. Godley, modified by author).

Whether we interpret the Zakros ring impression as a myth in which we witness the triumph of the Storm God, or as an actual ritual performed in the Minoan court, we must come to the conclusion that Crete had a Near Eastern type of theocracy. This final point may serve also as a definition of sacral kingship. Evans was right after all; sacral kingship did exist in Crete. The monarch (and his mythical prototype, the Storm God) was acknowledged as divine.

Final Reflections about the Morphology and Role of Minoan Deities

It has already been mentioned that the images that have been examined here were all engraved on gold rings. These types were not represented on other media, such as wall paintings or stone vases; the iconography was commissioned for the rings alone.

Many scenes have a narrative character in the sense that some dramatic action with consequences takes place. All rings date to the New Palace period, namely to the sixteenth to fifteenth centuries BCE (according to the traditional chronology).[68] It may be suspected that there is a historical reason why the rings with the Storm God are so evident in the New Palace epoch. They were designed during the period of one royal dynasty (which may have comprised some four to five kings), and this dynasty promoted the Storm God as a patron of kingship. It was contemporary with the Eighteenth Dynasty in Egypt. Many ring impressions were found in the palaces themselves, notably at Knossos and Zakros.

A question that may be raised is why the Storm God has no set attributes. Yet, even in Greek art, attributes were established only in the mature Archaic period, and not before. In the Geometric and Orientalizing times (eighth to seventh centuries BCE) it is impossible to identify deities by names in art: only their roles are evident.

I do not believe that lack of fixed attributes confused ancient viewers; they would have recognized identity by the narrative context, knowing well, as they did, the myths of their culture. It must be further noted that attributes have the disadvantage of being reductive. They force absolute equivalence between name and form (image) of a given divinity; this deprives the image of the very ambiguity that enables conflation of divine and royal imagery. Iconograms, on the other hand (such as the extended arm and stiff posture of the Storm God), are flexible, allowing a dual interpretation of the figure as either king or god. Unfortunately, this ambiguity is rather inconvenient to scholars.

Another consideration is that the ancients did not think of their "gods as god of this or god of that," as Wyatt has well put it.[69] One thing is certain: our categories are *our* inventions. We habitually classify deities as either chthonic or celestial, but this does not necessarily reflect the conceptualization of Minoan, Egyptian, Hittite, Ugaritic, or Greek peoples about their gods.[70] Only images reflect the ways in which the Storm God and the solar goddess were imagined by the Minoans themselves, and these images suggest that the goddess was conceived not only as a nature goddess but also as an enthroned queen, whereas the Storm God was envisaged as a powerful warlike male at the prime of his life. Above all, he was *a king*, as the *proskynesis* scene shows (Fig. 13.14).[71]

That other deities existed in the Minoan pantheon cannot be doubted (perhaps four of them are shown on the Zakros ring impression: Fig. 13.14), but only the solar goddess and the Storm God have a definable iconographical persona. No doubt this is due to their role as primary patrons of kingship.

14

Translating the Gods of the Religious *Koine*

No religion is pure (in the sense that it has totally unique features uncontaminated by other religions) or static (in the sense that it does not change). Religions are dynamic systems that constantly undergo mutations, adapting to new circumstances as they face environmental changes and competition with other religions. Like biological species, they may share a common gene pool that resulted from living and interacting in contiguous spaces century after century.

If we apply this biological model to religious systems, we may speak of a religious gene pool, namely clusters of traits that groups share while still maintaining local identity: this is the *koine.* At any rate, the cliché that religion is conservative must be rethought and perhaps altogether abandoned.

We may define religious mutation a little further. First, there is *synthesis* of religious traits, a term which is preferable to *syncretism.*[1] For example, regional deities may merge with foreign ones. They may acquire new social functions and roles in communal cult and lose others as time goes on.[2] The new traits may be borrowed from similar deities in neighboring cultures. Fritz Graf uses a natural model to explain synthesis, speaking of a flow of "osmotic similarities" between cultures.[3] Einar Thomassen, however, adds that synthesis is sometimes a process that is politically or socially motivated. Rulers, for example, will have an investment in promoting a synthesized cult in a temple because diverse ethnic groups will come together to worship such a god. One example is Serapis, a Greco-Egyptian god of Hellenistic times, who could accommodate both Greeks and Egyptians in the same sanctuary.[4]

Second, there is religious *translation,* which, as Walter Burkert uses it, signifies that deities of one religious system are equated with others belonging to a neighboring religion (see, for example, Table 14.1).[5] Greek Demeter was equated with Isis because both are mothers of important gods.

Translation is not self evident, however. It presupposes common religious perceptions and understandings of the roles of divinities in cult; and because it assumes similar conceptualizations, it is incompatible with complete cultural relativism. In consequence, it is impossible to imagine translation without a religious *koine* in the Aegean and the Near East.[6] And how do we know about the *koine?* Suffice it to mention that without its existence, Herodotus would not have been able to translate Egyptian religion into Greek in the first millennium.[7] For much the same reason, scholars of our times (like Othmar Keel) have managed to create meaningful pictorial dictionaries that encompass Near Eastern, biblical, and Egyptian concepts.[8]

The Role of Royal Policies in the Formation of the Religious *Koine*

The role of royal policy as one of the important factors in the establishment of bridges between cultures has not been sufficiently acknowledged. I shall look at four cases: first, a Hittite/Egyptian treaty; second, an excerpt from a royal letter; third, an Ugaritic image; and fourth, the use of a common symbol between Hittites and Minoans.

We start with an oath between the two great kings of the Hittites and Egyptians:

> As for the words of the regulation [which] the great King of Hatti [made] with Ramses[9] [*Meri Amon*], the great ruler of Egypt, in writing upon this tablet of silver—as for these words, a thousand gods of the male gods and of the female gods of them of the land of Hatti, together with a thousand gods of the male gods and of the female gods of them of the land of Egypt, are with me as witnesses [hearing] these words:
>
> the Re, the lord of the sky;
> the Re of the town of Arinna;
> Seth the Lord of the sky;
> Seth of Hatti;
> Seth of the town of Arinna;
> Seth of the town of Zippalanda;
> Seth of the town of Pe(tt)iyarik;
> Seth of the town of Aleppo;
> Seth of the town of Lihzina;
> [etc.]
> The Queen of the Sky; the gods, the lords of oaths; this goddess, the Lady of the Ground; the Lady of the Oath, Ishara; the Lady (of the) Mountains and the Rivers of the land of Hatti; the gods of the land of Kizuwadna; Amon; the Re; Seth; the male gods; the female gods; the mountains and the rivers of the land of Egypt; the sky; the earth; the great sea; the winds; and the clouds.[10]

The treaty invites a commentary. First, we note that because the gods are witnesses, they must represent both kingdoms, Egyptian and Hittite, in equal measure. This symmetry is coupled with rhetorical hyperbole. No less than a thousand gods from both empires are invoked, and they belong to both genders. The large number is necessary because the more gods there are, the more valid the treaty. The hyperbole of language is mirrored in artistic exaggeration. In the rock reliefs of the great Hittite sanctuary of the gods at Yazilikaya, for example, dozens of identical-looking deities are engraved, divided between male and female.

Another point we should note is that the Egyptian male gods, Seth and Re, prominent in the treaty, are the patron gods of kingship. The choice of Egyptian (rather than Hittite) names is an acknowledgement of the primacy of Egyptian religion; this makes sense because this version of the treaty is Egyptian. We note, however, that the gods of the oath have been adapted to Hittite circumstances because they are localized in cities of Asia. Additional deities are mentioned: they represent mountains and rivers, namely impersonal but powerful personifications of the land itself (see also the invocation of sun and earth in the treaty between Trojans and Achaeans in the *Iliad* 3, 267 ff.).

The Egypto-Hittite treaty is a perfect example of religious translation and synthesis. Re and Seth are perfectly at home in Hittite cities despite their Egyptian names. The result is the creation of a common religion that accommodates both partners of the oath.[11]

The second case comes from a letter written by the Mittani king Tushratta to the Egyptian pharaoh Amenhotep III (fourteenth century BCE.) Here, two mighty emperors establish a common deity: "May Shaushga, the Lady of Heaven, protect my brother and me for 100,000 years, and may our Lady give us great joy. Is Shaushga not my goddess and my brother's goddess?" (transl. W. L. Moran).[12] In this letter we note that the rhetoric employed stresses commonality of purpose: "My brother and me," "our Lady," "my goddess and my brother's goddess."

A third case of religious synthesis is an Ugaritic image of a goddess carved on the ivory lid of a box found in a tomb at Ugarit (Minet el Beida; fourteenth century BCE).[13] Here, the role of royal influence is not so evident, but because the object is a luxury item, it certainly expresses the ideas of an elite class. The deity is represented as a seated mistress of animals, flanked by goats(Fig. 14.1). Although the artistic style is Syrian, the hairstyle, the exposed breasts, and the type of dress are all Minoan features. The seated posture has been defined in Chapter 12 as an iconogram of the senior goddess of the pantheon. This deity could easily be understood in Ugarit as Asherah or Athirat, whereas a Minoan and Mycenaean viewer would have recognized their own solar goddess, whose name may have been A-sa-sa-ra.

Many more examples of synthesized images could be mentioned. One such is the Canaanite naked goddess who appears on Egyptian *stelae*. She wears the

Fig. 14.1. Seated Minoan goddess/mistress of animals. Ivory lid of box from tomb at Minet el Beida near Ugarit.

horned crown with the sun disc. She embodies Hathor, but her Canaanite attributes make her into a new synthesized deity who embodies both Canaanite and Egyptian traits.[14]

A final example of religious synthesis is the Minoan split rosette without petals (Fig. 14.2b). We have already noted how it was used as an iconogram by both Hittites and Minoans (Fig. 10.7). It has been suggested that the split oval expresses the symmetrical nature of the disc of the horizon rising from and setting in the underworld. Yet, there is no way at present to say where the design was first invented, Anatolia or Minoan Crete. I argue that the adoption of the rosette on *both* sides of the Aegean expresses a common concept between the two kingdoms. In 1944, the Hittite specialist H. Theodor Bossert recognized this and suggested that the religions of the Minoans and the Hittites were closely related.[15] I would add here that common symbols were induced by a common royal policy and ideology.

Another symbol used by the Minoans, Hittites, Egyptians, and the peoples of Syria alike is the ankh sign.[16] We have seen in Chapter 9 that it signifies life and the blessings of the sun. The ankh may also be regarded as part of the common language of sun worship, and, because it was utilized on royal seals, it facilitated communication between kings through a common visual language.

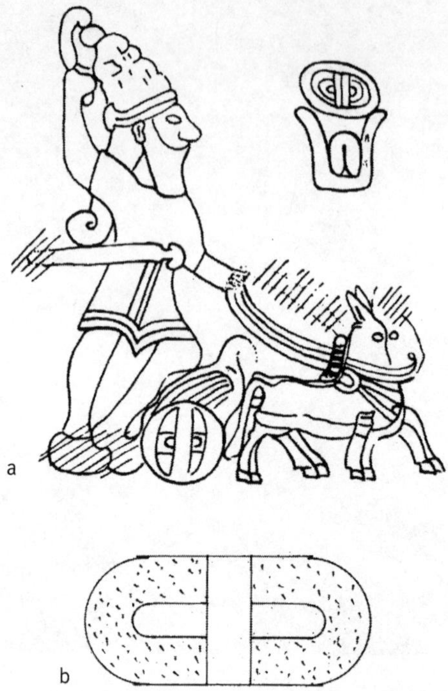

Fig. 14.2. Split rosette design associated with neo-Hittite Storm God Santash. (a) Rock reliefs at Malatya (ca. 1300/1200 BCE). (b) Below throne at Knossos.

The Gods of the *Koine*

The unified world that Bossert envisaged in the 1940s has been recently revived by Marc van de Mieroop, who succinctly and insightfully sketched a history of the entire Near East. Minoan Crete is virtually absent from it, of course, because of its lack of texts, but the Aegean is represented in his work by Mycenaean Greece. Van de Mieroop looks at cultures as being politically interconnected and not mere trade partners.

The rulers of the Near East were aware of belonging to a common system that encompassed the entire region. This is clear from the way they interacted with each other in diplomatic and military terms. They also shared similar ideologies about the social structures within their states and the role of the majority living in them. Although the political organization of the states varied, they were all characterized by an enormous discrepancy in access to wealth and power between the numerically small elites and the mass of the populations. An international elite class emerged, whose participants had more in common with their colleagues in other area states than with the lower classes at home.[17]

It is my belief that communication between royal courts and aristocracies played a major (although not the only) role in the creation of the shared religious *koine*. Especially important was the translation of deities as shown here in Table 14.1.

The table is instructive in many ways. We note that the most translatable deities across the board are the Storm God and the Mother Goddess. Yet the role of the latter is predominantly a *social* role and only secondarily is it connected with fertility. The Mother of Gods is a title that we find even in later Greece (*meter theon*) but she was not directly translatable in any of the deities of the Greek pantheon. In the second half of the second millennium BCE, this goddess is often a solar deity and the patroness of kings and queens.

I would suggest that it is unlikely that the Minoans alone did not possess a Storm God and a Solar Mother Goddess. This statement is made on grounds of *historical plausibility* rather than *iconographical analysis*. And since until now the main method has been the latter, the two methods (historical plausibility and art-historical analysis) converge fully.

It is also evident that positing a common pool of religious motifs for either side of the Aegean works better than projecting Greek mythology onto the Bronze Age. The Minoan solar goddess finds equivalences in the Ugaritic and Hittite pantheons, but not in the Greek pantheon because she cannot be equated with Hera, or with Demeter, or any other major female of the Olympian pantheon. Rhea is a possibility, but the latter was never important in Greek cult, and seldom did she receive her own temple.

Nevertheless, it may be argued that Ares is the war god of Minoan times, with Aphrodite as his partner; Apollo, the young warrior god, is like Ugaritic Baal and Reshep. Apollo's partner, Artemis, is like the virgin Anat, except that she is a sister rather than a lover. Apollo's mother, Leto, the goddess of the palm tree, is a distant echo of the Minoan Solar Goddess.

These are echoes across time, rather than translations. We may be confident that Greek religion has preserved some traits of Minoan and Mycenaean gods, but the system itself has mutated. This is one of the conclusions that emerges fiom the information in Table 14.1.

The table reveals also another fact: solar worship flourishes, especially where there is monarchy. Is this why the sun was never as popular with the Greeks and Jews (Ezek. 8:16–17)? Was the rejection of solar worship a sign of emancipation from kingship?

Table 14.1. Gods of the *Koine*

	Syria Canaan Ugarit	Anatolia	Mesopotamia	Egypt	Crete	Mycenaean Greece, second millennium	Historical Greece, first millennium
Type of Deity							
Storm God	Hadad (Adad) Baal Dagan Reshep	Teshub	Ninurta Marduk	Seth	Young God	Zeus	Zeus Apollo Ares
Creator or Father God	El			Atum	?		Kronos
Queen-Mother and Solar Deities	Athirat Asherah (?)	Sun Goddess of Arinna Hepat	Ningirsu (?) Mami	Hathor Isis	Asa-sa-sa-ra	Po-t-ni-ja	Hera (but not a solar goddess) (translated into the dea Syria Atargatis)[a]
Love Goddess	Anat Asherah Astart Qdsh	Shaushga	Ishtar Inanna	Hathor Isis	?	?	Aphrodite
Male Sun Gods		Sharuma	Shamash Utu	Horus	?	?	Hyperion

[a] According to Lusian, Dea Syria, 31–33. Keel 1998, 23.

15

Conclusions

A Tribute to Sir Arthur Evans

This book began with a map that includes both the Aegean and the Near East and serves as a symbol of the unity of the two worlds. A Near Eastern lens has been adopted for reading the visual code of Minoan culture. The following seven points summarize the most important results of this study.

1. The culture of Crete may only be properly deciphered if it is regarded as part of an international milieu. Knossos had special ties with Cyprus, the Levant, Egypt, and the kingdoms of the Mitanni and the Hittites in Anatolia between 1650 and 1400 BCE. At the end of the fifteenth century, the connections between Knossos and Egypt were especially tight. This is evidenced by the Minoan murals found at the Egyptian palace at Tell el Dab'a in the Eastern Nile Delta, as well by the depictions of Keftiu (Minoans) in the tombs of Egyptian nobility during the times of Hatshepsut and Tuthmosis III. As we have seen, the religious *koine* is, to a great extent, an achievement of kingship (Chapters 1–3, 14).
2. There was, indeed, sacral kingship in Crete. The king was the only legitimate intermediary between the human and divine spheres and served as the high priest of the gods. The distinction between high priest/priestess and king/queen has been shown to be meaningless because in artistic representations the high priest *is* the king and the high priestess *is* the queen.
But what is sacred kingship? The definition given here is one that differs from the notion (developed by James Frazer) that the sacred king is a magician king.[1] My definition entails two aspects: the divinization of the king after death; and the ontological state of being into which the king entered when he was in direct contact with the gods, a state from which he had to exit (desacralization; Chapter 3).

3. Kings and queens associated themselves with the sun throughout the Ancient Orient, and they did so also in Crete and Mycenaean Greece. Solar worship had a political as well as a cosmic dimension; the sun is an appropriate symbol of kingship because it rules over all the domains of the cosmos (Chapters 8–11).
   The major gods of the Minoan pantheon were the Solar Goddess and her son, the Storm God. A mythology for the Storm God and his mother, the Solar Goddess, may be reconstructed by use of a Near Eastern *koine* lens (Chapters 12 and 13). The double axe was the emblem of the Solar Goddess (Chapters 9 and 10).
4. The sacred mountain with its twin peaks, the incurved altar, the rosette, and the double axe are either landmarks in the sun's journey or allomorphs of the sun disc itself. All of these emblems appear in connection with the palace of Knossos, designating it as the center of the cosmos and a house of the sun deity at the same time (Chapters 5, 8–10).
5. The form of each of the Minoan symbols was deliberately construed as a puzzle. The split rosette, the double axe, and the incurved altar are not what they seem at first. The key to their meaning is the symmetry of their form, which reflects the dual world traversed by the sun in its journey in the sky and underworld respectively. Seen in this light, the Minoan symbols are almost as complex as their Egyptian counterparts (Chapters 4–5, 8–11).
6. The iconography of the gold rings reflects the ideology of the rulers because rings were instruments of royal power. The king and the queen (or queen mother) have been detected as the key protagonists in the scenes of many of the rings, especially epiphany and prophecy scenes (Chapters 1, 6–7).
7. This work is dependent on the conceptual apparatus constructed by Evans. Although exploring a completely unknown territory, with much less to go by than we have today, Evans organized and ordered the information in such a way that progress towards decipherment was made possible. Even having misinterpreted some symbols, such as mistaking the mountains for bull's horns, he was not completely off the mark. Indeed, the Minoans intended a deliberate ambiguity between "horns" and "mountain peaks" because both the ox or cow and the mountain embrace the sun in mythical thinking; in some ways they give birth to it. The Minoans deliberately played with the form: horns look like mountain peaks (Fig. 15.1). The Egyptians did the same, as we see on a ceiling from the palace of Malkata (Fig. 15.1d).

Evans noted the "curious reduplication of the axe blades" and interpreted this duality as an image of the divine pair.[2] Contrary to that view, I see the duality of the axe as representing the two aspects of the sun-deity in the sky and the underworld, respectively. Nevertheless, Evans correctly perceived the binary nature of the symbol.

Further, Evans thought that the "Great Goddess" was a mother. He was correct: the major social role of the chief goddess of the pantheon is motherhood (Chapter 12).[3] He also perceived that the religions of Egypt and Minoan Crete were close. It has been shown in Chapters 9 and 10 that the ox head, the double axe, the rosette, and the sun disc are related symbols in Crete. There existed similar visual and conceptual symbols in Egypt. Compare the ox head bearing a double axe on a Minoan cultic vase (Fig. 15.1c) to an ox head bearing a rosette from the palace of Amenhotep III at Malkata (Fig. 15.1d). The comparison will convince even the skeptic that

a b c d

Fig. 15.1. Minoan double axe rising between mountains or horns of ox.
(a) Clay vessel. (b) Seal from Argos. (c) Vase from Pseira. (d) Ceiling from Malkata, Egypt.

the cognitive worlds of the Egyptians and Minoans were related, as Evans always claimed.

Finally, the intuition of Evans about the nature of the theocracy of Minoan Crete was fully justified. It is to him that we owe the first, and historically correct, notion of Minoan sacral kingship.

Notes

Chapter 1: Introduction

Epigraphs: Evans PM I, 15; translated: "The Creto-Mycenaean cultural orbit absolutely belongs to the Anatolian and North Syrian Cultural Community" (Bossert 1944).

1. Most popular books on Minoan Crete immediately associate Knossos with the labyrinth. See, for example, *Wondrous Realms* 1993 and Siebenmorgen 2000.

2. Most scholars think it fairly certain that the Cretans of Minoan times are the Keftiu of the Egyptian and Syrian sources and that Kaphtor is the island of Crete. On some occasions, however, Syria also is called by that name. See, for example, Helck 1979, 26–27; and Sakellarakis and Sakellarakis 1984, 199–202. A collection of primary sources with commentary may be found in the older but still useful books by Bossert (1937, 62–72), Vercoutter (1911), and Helck (1979, 26–35).

3. For Keftiu in Egypt see Evans, PM II, 719; see also note 2 above. Extensive discussion appears in Vercoutter 1911. Biblical references include Amos 9:7, "Did I not bring up Israel from the land of Egypt, the Philistines from Kaphtor, and the Syrians from Kir?" The reference here pertains to the Iron Age.

4. KTU 1.3 vi 15; Wyatt 2002, 89.

5. KTU 1.3 vi 15. Identification of Kaphtor with Crete is not 100 percent certain but it is most plausible. See Wyatt 2002, 89, n. 83. See also KTU 1.100 v 45 and Wyatt 2002, 383.

6. Wyatt 2005a, 19–20. The double name may be a reference to the dual nature of the god as belonging to both this world and the netherworld.

7. *Papyrus Leiden* I, in Bossert 1937, 55; cf. also Helck 1979, 35: Crete was regarded as "*exponent des Westens.*" Helck sees Crete as the western edge of the universe with Punt its counterpart in the East.

8. The dates are very approximate and are based on Warren and Hankey 1989.

9. Scarabs of the period of Amenophis III have been found in an LMIIIA context. Warren and Hankey 1989, 137.

10. The bibliography on chronology is immense and beyond the scope of this work. Basic literature includes Warren and Hankey 1989 and Manning 1999 with criticism by Bietak 2004. See also Wiener 2003.

11. Take, for example, seal and ring iconography. The king riding a chariot motif in LMIA/LHI (Ch. 13) does not appear in Egypt before the Eighteenth Dynasty (Figs 2.19–2.22).

12. Moran 1992, xv–xxvi; and Cline 1995.

13. Van de Mieroop 2004, 130–35. He speaks mainly of the period between 1500 and 1200 BCE.

14. Ibid., 121–25. See also Aruz 1995 and Caubet 1999.

15. Evans PM II, 564.

16. Ibid., 571.

17. For a sample of the criticism of the methods of Evans see Hitchcock and Koudounaris 2002, 48–50. For support see Alexiou 1987.

18. Annals of Tuthmosis III and Leiden papyrus I, 344, 8. See Bossert 1937, 55.

19. Evans PM II, 740–41. The discussion of Bossert 1937, 62–72 with pls. 536–50 about interconnections in the Aegean remains fundamental. See also Helck 1979, 33; Sakellarakis and Sakellarakis 1984.

20. The relationship of the pharaoh to his vassals in the Levant and Asia Minor is evident from the Amarna letters (Moran 1992, xvi–xvii).

21. See the excellent discussion in Munn 2006, 178–221. It is quite possible to see Croesus' involvement with Solon as concealing an attempt to secure Athenian aid, although Herodotus reports that Croesus sought Sparta's alliance. The relationship of Egyptian Amasis and Persian Darius with the ruler Polycrates of Samos (who possessed a strong navy) is well attested in Herodotus (Hdt. 3, 128). Most illuminating is the relationship of the Athenian Peisistratids with the Persian court.

22. West 1997, 4. See also Wiesner 1968, 141–73.

23. Cline 1987, 20.

24. Evans PM IV, 942–44.

25. For similar skepticism concerning the end of the Mycenaean palace culture see Hall 2007, 54–55.

26. Personal communication with Floyd McCoy, whose lab work suggests that the eruption was much more destructive than envisaged a decade ago.

27. The volcanic destruction of the Minoan palaces was proposed by Spyridon Marinatos (Marinatos 1939). The theory has been contested on the grounds that LMIB pottery is absent from Thera. See the summary of C. Renfrew after the Theran conference of 1989 in Hardy et al. ii 1990, 11–12. However, the fact is that both styles LMIA and LMIB coexist in several sites as at Sklavokampos and most clearly at Zakros. The inevitable conclusion is that they are close in date and are not fifty years apart, as assumed by Evans. This argument is being developed at length by Lefteris Platon.

28. Evans PM IV, xxiii.

29. Ibid., 882.

30. Tuthmosis III dates are 1479–25 BCE; Bietak 2007, 13–43.

31. Evans PM IV, xxiii, 884–87

32. Evans's thesis has been labeled "pancretism" or "pan-minoanism," somewhat disapprovingly, but his reasoning is very solid. He and his assistant Duncan MacKenzie both saw that there was homogeneity of iconography and style in the pottery and artistic representations of the LMI and LMII periods, and that LMII pottery attests to homogeneity of style between Crete and the mainland. Thus, the most reasonable conclusion was that this style betokened a unified territory during the *pax minoica* when Crete was a leader. The break between this era and what followed came at only at LMIII, after the fall of Knossos, and not before. To explain this homogeneity, we need not posit a Minoan dynast ruling Mycenae, but neither do we need to posit a Mycenaean dynast ruling Knossos. For discussion of the Creto-centric view, see Fitton 1996, 132–34 and MacGillivray 2000c, 272–75.

33. For a standard account see Hood 1971.

34. Evans PM IV, 1018.

35. Chadwick 1970, 67.

36. Methodically compiled by Keel in his dictionary (Keel 1978).

37. West 1997; Burkert 2004a.

38. Burkert 2004a, 124. See also Karageorghis and Stambolidis 1998; Karetsou 2000.

39. Moran 1992, 44; EA no. 19.

40. Moran 1992, 84–86; EA no. 26.

41. Moran 1992, 39; EA no. 16.

42. Moran 1992, 43; EA nos. 1, 24, etc.

43. Moran 1992, 19; EA no. 3; Redford 1984, 41; Van de Mieroop 2004, 133.

44. Moran 1992, 19; EA no. 10.

45. Wyatt 1997, 775.

46. Doumas 2000, 34, claims that the Therans had an indigenous bureaucratic system that was not dependent on Crete. According to him, the presence of Minoan sealings on Thera signify that goods were imported from Crete. This theory does not explain the fact that rings stamped not only goods but also documents. And if so, then the sealings are firm evidence of Minoan administration on the island of Thera.

47. Hallager (1996) believes that the rings were state owned. Very valuable observations are made by Pini in CMS II. 6 XXI-XXIX; Pini does not commit himself to any theory about the identity of the ring bearers.

48. See Chapter 6, note 24.

49. Plutarch writes that Artaxerxes gave his ring to a friend as a sign of recognition (Plutarch, Artaxerxes, 18).We are told about the image on the ring: dancing Karyatides. This story indicates that the images are not inherently related to the person who wears the ring but that the relationship is arbitrary and culturally constructed. I am grateful to D. Kyrtatas for this reference.

50. No distinction in the iconography of the Minoan and Mycenaean rings is evident in Younger's compilation of themes (Younger 1988), and Pini has said that he has difficulties in finding criteria for distinction between Minoan and Mycenaean rings on iconographical grounds.

51. Matz 1958.

52. Marinatos 1993, 5.

53. Burkert 2004a.

54. Wyatt 2002, 11–24; West 1997, 84.

Chapter 2: The King and Queen in Art

1. See, for example, Beckman's entry on Hittite festivals in Johnston 2004, 336–39.

2. Hood (1971, 146) takes kingship for granted although there is no discussion devoted to it.

3. In a book devoted to rulers in the Bronze Age (Rehak 1995a), nobody except the present author accepted Evans's notion that sacral kingship existed in Crete, although Mycenaean kings were readily acknowledged. Krattenmaker (1995a, 58) comes to the conclusion that the palace represents authority but that kings themselves are nowhere evident. The logic of this argument is not clear to me. See also Farnoux 1995; Preziosi and Hitchcock 1999, 120–22.

4. Evans PM IV, 942.

5. For a method of reading Greek myths, I selectively mention here Burkert 1979 and Vernant 1980. For Ugaritic myths, see Wyatt 2005a.

6. Evans PM I, 2.

7. Hägg and Marinatos 1984; Laffineur and Niemeier 1995; Hamilakis 2002a. See especially Koehl 1995a, 23–35; Koehl 1986, 1997; Hitchcock 2000.

8. See collection of articles in Hägg and Marinatos 1984.

9. Marinatos 1984c, 167–76; Marinatos 2000.

10. Pelon 1995; Cultraro 2000.

11. Betancourt 2002, 211.

12. Davis 1995. See also the comments of Kopcke in the discussion following the paper of Crowley 1995.

13. The shape of the head itself suggests that it was topped by a crown.

14. Poursat 1977, pl. XXXVIII no. 350; and pl. XLVIII.

15. Evans PM II, fig. 506a.

16. Teissier 1996, 80–84; 87–88. Jean-Claude Poursat (1977) suggests that the sphinx is a Mycenaean, not a Minoan idiom. The thesis here is that it arrived at both Crete and the Mycenaean mainland through Syria, and it is connected with royal ideology in both cultures.

17. Teissier 1996, 80–88, no. 142; 192–95.

18. Evans PM II, 774–90.

19. Niemeier 1987.

20. Shaw 2004.

21. It is no accident that Mycenaean royalty borrowed this very emblem, although, to date, only females in Mycenaean art, i.e. queens or goddesses, are represented wearing it. For an overview of paintings where the plumed hat appears, see Immerwahr 1990, 114–21, pls. 58, 61, 62, 92. For ivories, see Poursat 1977, pls. 12; 28; 53.

22. Schroer 1985, 53–115.

23. Winter (1983, 170, n. 415) suggests that the man with the long robe on this particular seal is a ruler because of his curved scepter, which is reminiscent of that of the Hittite king.

24. The scarab seal is discussed in Schroer 1985, 53–115. Winter (1983, 244) identifies the figure from Qatna as a god because of the small horns engraved on the headdress. Similar seated sculptures of men wearing long mantles are found in Ugarit and are identified as either gods or kings (see, for example, Schroer 1985, 72, figs. 23–24).

25. See Evans PM IV, figs. 341–43 for figures carrying such insignias.The dolphin is also a royal emblem; this is why dolphins decorated the palace of Knossos (see Immerwahr 1990, 48, pl. 31; 80, fig. 23; and CMS II. 8, 258; see also Rehak 1994).

26. Betts 1981, 74–83; Davis 1995, 15; Koehl 1995a, 30–31. Koehl acknowledges that the axe is an emblem of royal nature and argues that the head priest and chief may be the same person in chiefdoms or proto-states. Catalogue in Younger 1995, 162–65. Most recently, Cultraro 2001, 265.

27. Rehak 1995b, 111.

28. Evans PM IV, 419–21; Kilian-Dirlmeier 1987; Koehl 1995a, 31, pl. XIIIb; Cultraro 2001, 263–64. For Syrian axes, see Matthiae 1984, 61, fig. 13.

29. Evans PM IV, 412; Marinatos 1993, 129.

30. For debates regarding the attire, see Evans PM II, 341, fig. 194; Nilsson 1950, 160–62; Demargne 1949; S. Marinatos 1967, A27, fig. 4; and Cultraro 2001, 259–60 with recent bibliography. Sapouna-Sakellaraki 1971, 78 no. 181, 107.

31. Evans PM IV, 219; Nilsson (1950, 160) calls him "a headman with a cuirass." S. Marinatos (1976) calls him a "local ruler." See also Sapouna-Sakellaraki, 107, 123–29, pls. 44–45, 52.

32. Demargne 1949, 280–88.

33. Keel 1978, 278–79.

34. On the forelock (*hornfrisur*), see S. Marinatos 1967, B12.

35. Betts 1981, 74–83; CMS II.3, 13 and 196; VIII, 110 a–c; IX, 6D; X, 278. S. Marinatos (1967, B7) however, identifies them as rulers. I must correct my previous view (Marinatos 1993, 127–33) that they are priests.

36. CMS IX, 6D and CMS X, 278.

37. For example, Seti I and Ramses II are represented with their crown princes (Kitchen 1982, 34, fig. 12; Lange-Hirmer 1956, pl. 219).

38. This man is not an African, as originally interpreted by S. Marinatos, but a ruler (N. Marinatos 1987, 137–41 with bibliography).

39. Stevenson Smith 1965, 22–23; Keel and Uehlinger 1995, 68.

40. Chariots do not appear before the Eighteenth Dynasty: Wiese 1990, 81–87; Keel 1995, 202; Teissier 1996.

41. Karo 1933, 29–35; Vermeule 1964, 90–94; Hood 1978, 96–98. Karo and others after him did not understand that the lion is a companion of the king and saw the two scenes as inorganically connected. For Egyptian parallels in Eighteenth and Nineteenth Dynasty art, see Saleh and Sourouzian 1986, no. 178 (Tutankhamun accompanied by lion); Kitchen 1982, 167, fig. 52; Keel 1978, 86–87, fig. 103.

42. Three imprints have been found at Sklavokampos and Hagia Triada in Crete and at Akrotiri, Thera. They are made by the same ring (Marinatos 1976, 16–17, pl. 115; Pini in CMS VS.3, 391).

43. Evans (PM IV, 812–25) collects chariot scenes but does not discuss the Knossos

fragments. For a reconstruction, see Cameron (1967, 330–44) who builds on a previous one by S. Alexiou. See also Crouwel (1981, 145 with bibliography) and Marinatos (1986, 32–33, fig. 21).

44. Cameron 1967.

45. Evans PM II, fig. 450; Boulotis 1987, 145–56; Marinatos 1993, 51–54.

46. Reusch (1958, 334–58) explains the symbolic value of the throne room frieze but does not link it with the female of the procession fresco.

47. Lang 1969, 85–86, col. pls. 31 D, N. The rosette was adopted also by Mycenaean kings and was used emblematically in the palaces and tombs of Mycenae (Lang 1969, pl. 139; Evans PM II, 695–96).

48. Stemming from different periods: Evans PM II, 290, 695; Hägg 1987, 129–34.

49. There were other paintings with a similar design within the palace, such as a stucco relief ceiling where the rosettes are interspersed amidst whirly spirals that probably indicate clouds. Evans PM III, 24–31, pl. XV. Evans noted that there exist similar ceilings in Egypt with astral signs. See Shaw 1970.

50. Evans PM III, 46–65; cf. also Marinatos 1993, 58–61.

51. Karo 1933, 76, pl. XLII, no. 263.

52. Jakob-Rost et al. 1992, cat. no. 109.

53. Collon 1987, 187.

54. Crowley (1995, 190) notes the paradox of the lack of royal iconography: "There is a tension between the iconography that does not exalt kingship in an unambiguous manner and the archaeological evidence that reveals a bureaucratic system." For the most recent discussion see Maran and Stavrianopoulou 2007, 285–92.

55. Marinatos 1995.

Chapter 3: The King and Queen as High Priests

Epigraph: Evans, PM I, 3.

1. Vermeule 1964, V69–70.

2. There are records in Egypt that show that the office of priest was hereditary and that priesthood was a career culminating in the high priesthood. For an example, see the career of a certain Bakekhons at the time of Ramses II (Kitchen 1982, 170–71). However, we are not to assume that such an office overshadowed the high priesthood of the pharaoh himself. Rather, the office entailed supervising construction works, as we may tell from Bakekhons's own boastings. For priests in the Mycenaean Linear B texts, see Gerard-Rousseau 1968, 108–11.

3. Pardee 2002, 2.

4. For the interpretation of the portraits as priests, see Betts 1981, 74–83, and CMS II.3, 13 and 196, VIII, 110 a–c; IX, 6D; X, 278. I must here correct my own previous view that they are priests (Marinatos 1993, 127–33).

5. Kitchen 1982, 168.

6. Ibid., 169.

7. Pardee 2002.

8. Ibid., 47 no. 12.

9. Gerard-Rousseau 1968, 22–23; Ventris and Chadwick 1973, 462–65. It is noteworthy that a separate offering is made to All of the Gods (*pasiteoi*), as in the Ugaritic text.

10. Lang 1969, pl. 119.

11. Rethemiotakis 1999 and 2002. See also Driessen et al. 2002.

12. Palaima 1995.

13. Wyatt 2002; KTU 1.41, 348–55; Pardee 2002, no. 15, 63–65.

14. Wyatt 2002, 352, n. 35.

15. Ibid., 354; Pardee 2002, no. 15, 65.

16. Wyatt 2002, 354–55; Wyatt 2006, 16–17.

17. Pardee 2002, 65.

18. "The king is to wash himself thoroughly," appears as *yrhs mlk brr.* Wyatt (2006, 16–17) has a list of where the phrase, "the king is desacralized or set free," occurs. Pardee (2002, 3) notes that purification always takes place prior to the preparation for the king's participation but leaves it at that and draws no further inferences.

19. Wyatt 2006, 17.

20. ANET, 358–59.

21. KBo iv, 9; ANET, 358–61; i. 25.

22. Güterbock and van den Hout 1991, 59–60.

23. KBo iii. 5.

24. Ibid., ii. 42.

25. Ibid., vi. 20.

26. See, for example, discussion on the *hb-sd* robes and the pharaoh in the festival of Sokaris at Medinet Habu in Bleeker 1967, 51–86, 107 with fig. 3. See also Wilkinson 1992, 80, fig. 1.

27. Van Gennep (1960, 83, 105, 106–7) cites various instances. His description of the Egyptian pharaoh's sacrality, 111–12, however, is too general to be useful. See also Turner 1967, 93–111.

28. Nilsson (1950, 155–64) has a thorough account, but he includes garments that belong to the gods, which obfuscates the issue. For Syria, see Fleming 1992.

29. Evans PM IV, 219.

30. Reeves 1990, 73.

31. Turner 1967.

32. Meissner 1920–1925, II, 55.

33. For the importance of gates in sanctuaries and biblical references, see Keel 1978, 120–27.

34. See Chapter 4 for the enthronement of the king.

35. Paribeni 1908; Marinatos and Hirmer 1974, pls. XXX–XXXIII; discussion in Long 1974.

36. Original publication is in Paribeni 1904; Nilsson 1950, 426–40; and Matz 1958, 398–407; extensive discussion can be found in Long 1974 and Pötscher 1990, 171–79. For theoretical discussion on cult, see Renfrew 1985, 24–25.

37. Designation of priestess is found in Nilsson 1950, 426–43 and Long 1974, 35.

38. Markoe 1985, 278–83; Wiesner 1968, 197–200; West 1997, 99–100.

39. Jakob-Rost et al. 1992, 160–61.

40. Reade 1983, 58, figs. 85–86.

41. Gaballa 1976, 89: "the king, the main actor in the event (i.e. the Opet festival at Luxor) is seen and involved in more than one incident"; Bleeker 1967, fig. 3.

42. Evans PM III, 182–89.

43. It may be objected that if he is the king, why is he wearing the same garment as those following him? This objection is easy to answer: the two men following may be closely associated members of the royal family. In the Near East, the entire royal family took part in the festival. Or perhaps his role in the specific ceremony involved his acting as the head of a group.

44. ANET, 358.

45. I do not quite agree with the clever suggestion of Pötscher (1990, 171–91) that background colors on the sarcophagus designate day and night. Yet, I am sure that he is right in detecting movement in space and time.

46. Pardee 2002, 75.

47. Pardee 2002, 121.

48. The cup in the shape of a fist perhaps reflects a ritual gesture (Güterbock and Kendall 1995).

49. Güterbock and Kendall (1995, 93) think the rosettes indicate a flowery meadow, but I very much doubt this interpretation given the ideogrammatic use of rosettes as sun symbols.

50. Opinions vary as to whether he is a vegetation god, or a dead person (Matz 1958, 400), a mummy (Paribeni 1908), the deified dead (Nilsson 1950, 428–43), the spirit of the deceased (Long 1974, 50), or a yearly god of regenerative powers similar to Hyakinthos of Greek mythology (Pötscher 1990, 183–87). Long (1974, 40) suggests that funerary rites are the subject. One of the least fortunate guesses of Evans (PM I, 438–39), is that he is a dead mariner because of the boat that is being offered.

51. KBo, iv, 9; ANET, 359.

52. Wyatt 2002, 314–23; KTU 1.20–1.22; Pardee 2002, 123–25. Comments may be found in Wyatt 1999, 562; Wyatt 1999–2000, 139; and Wyatt 2006.

53. KTU 1.20–1.22; Wyatt 1999, 562; Wyatt 1999–2000, 139; Wyatt 2002, 314–23; Wyatt 2005b, 202–5; Wyatt 2006.

54. Wyatt 2005b, 191–220, especially 203; Pardee 2002, 195–201.

55. Evans PM II, 278–79; PM IV, 988–1018.

56. Even in Classical Greece, which was not a theocracy, the deified king is often closely allied to the cult of the gods. A good example is the cult of Pelops being closely allied with the sanctuary of Zeus at Olympia.

57. Bin-Nun 1975, 198; for a more recent assessment, see van den Hout 1998, 41ff.

58. Such was the case with kings Mursili and Hattushili in the thirteenth century BCE (Bin-Nun 1975, 184–89 and van den Hout 1998, 44–46).

59. van den Hout 1998, 53.

60. Ibid., 46.

61. Bin-Nun 1975, 196–98.

62. Wyatt 1999, 544–45; Andreasen 1983.

63. Wyatt 2001, 168.

64. For iconography of sacred palms, see Teisser 1996, 69, fig. 94; 87, fig 163; 97, fig. 187; and 121, fig. 268. Wyatt 2005b, 127.

65. Troy 1986, 56–58, 72–77, and 86–87. See also note 64, above.

66. Ibid., 55.

67. An exception to this assumption is found in Goodison 1989.

68. Long 1974, 50.

69. The arguments about the solar significance of the double axe are reviewed in Chapter 9. Evans in PM I, 447, thought similarly: "The cult of the deceased and heroized members of the line of Minoan priest-kings was associated with that of their divine Mistress in the palace sanctuary of Knossos."

70. Sargon of Akkad and Naram Sin seem to have received a cult while they were still alive (van de Mieroop 2004, 64–65). The status of the Egyptian pharoh in this respect would have varied as well.

71. Pardee 2002, 2.

72. Houwink den Cate in Hoffner and Beckman 1986, 95–110.

73. Houwink den Cate in Hoffner and Beckman 1986, 110.

74. van den Hout 1998, 73–78.

75. Bin-Nun 1975, 130–31, 168–72; van den Hout 1998, 46–53.

Chapter 4: Thrones of Gods—Thrones of Kings

Epigraph: Sir Arthur Evans, PM I, 5.

1. Evans PM IV, 901–46.

2. Evans PM IV, 935.

3. Evans PM IV, 920. The throne room included a sunken chamber, which Evans called a lustral basin. These sunken rooms were probably chapels to the underworld goddess (who is the other side of the sun goddess). For the redefinition of *lustral basin* as an adyton see Marinatos 1993, 78–87.

4. Contacts attested in Mari archives: Dossin 1939; Van de Mieroop 2004, 96, 117, 133; Van de Mieroop 2005, 65–66. Syrian seals on Crete: Davaras and Soles 1995.

5. Reusch 1958, 351–52. See also Mirié 1979.

6. Males appear in the company of griffins as well, as indicated previously in Chapter 2.

7. Reusch 1958, 357.

8. Hägg (1986) follows Matz in distinguishing two types of epiphany, an ecstatic and a performed one. For discussion and bibliography on the subject, see Marinatos 1993, 107nn154–59.

9. Niemeier 1986. For a recent reevaluation of the problem, see Maran and Stavrianopoulou 2007, 287–90.

10. Evans PM I, 3.

11. ANET, 359, ii.40.

12. ANET, 359, iii.25–30.

13. ANET, 359, iii.30–35.

14. A different scenario is suggested by Maran and Stavrianopoulou 2007, 290. They suggest that the king was symbolically united with the goddess in a union of sacred marriage or that he embodied her. I see conceptual difficulties with this. Sacred marriage when the king marries a goddess is attested only in Sumerian culture and not any other. For a good description of Hittite inner sanctuaries and the activities that took place there see Alp 1983.

15. Troy 1986, 54–59.

16. Frankfort 1948, 171–73.

17. Evans PM IV, 939, fig. 910.

18. Evans PM IV, 935–36. Libations are attested in Mycenaean throne rooms as well, as the one at the palace of Pylos in the southern Peloponnese. Blegen and Rawson 1966, 76–92, pl. 73.

19. KTU 1.14 iii 52; Wyatt 2002, 198; see also Wyatt 1999–2000, 138: "Every time the king entered the holy of holies . . . it was by virtue of repeated deification that the rituals were rendered effective."

20. Niemeier 1986, 63–66.

21. Evans PM I, fig. 312 a–b; Demargne 1949, 280–88 with parallels. See also Marinatos 1986, 58–61, where I speak of a votive garment, whereas it is almost certainly a cult emblem, an iconic form of the deity.

22. See also ring impressions from Hagia Triada: CMS II. 6, 7–13. The carrying of sacred emblems, namely axes and sacred garments, must have constituted a cycle of rings made in the same period, perhaps by the same engraver.

23. Marinatos 1987, 135–43; Marinatos 1993, 76–111.

24. Evans PM IV, 902; Marinatos 1993, 106 with notes 148–49.

25. Attested in Hittite texts: Beckman in Johnston 2004, 336.

26. Nissinen 2003, 83, no. 53.

27. Nissinen 2003, 88, no. 60.

28. Pardee 2002, 56: RS 24.250. A vacant stone throne was found at Ugarit (RS 90. 1). Discussion in Wyatt 1998.

29. Frankfort 1948.

30. Keel 1978, fig. 353, Drawing by Hildi Keel Leu.

31. Keel 1978, 263.

32. The anteroom painting was decorated with the hooves of a charging bull. For this reason it has received little attention and any detailed interpretation would be risky: Evans PM IV, 904; Marinatos 1993, 74.

33. Evans PM IV, frontispiece. Pl. XXXII of the same volume depicts the mural without the palms. They are visible, however, on a photograph PM IV, 915, fig. 889. Cameron's reconstruction is published in Cameron 1987, 322, fig. 3.

34. Platon 1971, 164–69; Platon 2003, 341.

35. 1 Enoch 25:3. In Ugaritic literature there are similar phrases: Wyatt 2001, 147–48.

36. Parrot 1958, pls. XI, XV; Stevenson Smith 1965, 18; Keel 1992, 149, fig. 119; Al-Khalesi 1978.

37. Teissier 1996, nos. 189–93; 202, 207.

38. Ibid., 98–99, no. 193.

39. Ibid., 98.

40. Ibid., 101.

41. Ibid., 89–90.

42. Pini 1971.

43. Winter 1983, 436 with note 1184.

44. Danthine 1937; Morgan 1988, 24–28; Marinatos 1984b, 115.

45. Winter 1983, 486–90; Keel and Uehlinger 1995, 258–72; Wyatt 2001, 168; Olyan 1988.

46. For the incurved podium, see Chapter 10. For this seal, see Hägg and Lindau 1984, 67–77.

47. I have mistakenly identified this figure as a god previously (Marinatos 1993, 174). He cannot be a recipient of the cult, however, because he is facing the palm as a devotee would. Had he been a god, he would have had his back on it, as though it were his home. A more compelling reason is that the palm is never connected with a male god, even in the Near East or Greek mythology. It is Leto's tree not Apollo's, for example.

48. Goodison 1989; Goodison 2001.

49. Goodison (2001, 77–88) sees the cult of the sun as a development of early Cretan and Cycladic religion when (she assumes) there existed a dominant female deity. This developmental approach is a product of modern evolutionist theory. I prefer to see the solar goddess as an element of the institution of kingship. There is thus a substantial difference in our approaches.

50. Wyatt 1999, 544, 559; Wyatt 2005b. For visual evidence on Canaanite seals, see Ornan 2001.

51. van den Hout 1998, 74.

Chapter 5: The House of God

Epigraph: Sir Arthur Evans, PM I, 4.

1. For Near Eastern temples, see Meissner 1920–1925, 2:52–101; Gurney 1952, 144–55; Biran 1981; Badawy 1966; Frankfort 1954.

2. Town shrines and nature sanctuaries (following the traditional classification) in Marinatos 1993, 112–26.

3. Rutkowski 1986, 229. See also Hood 1977, 158–72, who is bothered by the lack of temples and posits that their function was fulfilled with house shrines. On house shrines, see Gesell 1985, 19–40.

4. Haran in Biran 1981, 31–37.

5. Platon 1971, 161–69. For full bibliography, see Platon 2003.

6. For the symbolism of the wilderness, see Keel 1978 and Wyatt 2005a, 38–54.

7. Platon 1971; Shaw (1978) reconstructs the building as a façade within an enclosure; Rutkowski 1986, 81–85. Most recent and thorough analysis in Platon 2003.

8. The Ugaritic god Athtar (a double of Baal) goes into the uttermost parts of the sacred mount Saphon and sits on the throne of Valiant Baal. KTU 1. 6. i 56–58: Wyatt

2002, 132; Wyatt 2001, 154. Also compare with Isaiah 14:13: "I shall sit in the mount of the assembly in the recesses of Sapphon." Translation and discussion, Wyatt 2005a, 105. For further discussion of the mountain, see Chapter 8.

9. Shaw (1978) reconstructs the building as a façade within an enclosure; Rutkowski sees it as a peak sanctuary: Rutkowski 1986, 81–85. Platon (2003) suggests it is a royal tomb.

10. Bloedow 1990.

11. Davaras 2003, 254, fig. 25c; Marinatos 1993, 122, fig. 86.

12. I owe the insights about gates to discussions with Clairy Palyvou. See Palyvou 2005.

13. The bibliography on the Minoan Tripartite Shrine is considerable and goes back to Evans and Nilsson. See thorough discussions in Shaw 1978 and Krattenmaker 1995b.

14. Evans PM III, 463–64; fig. 323. The columns possibly allude to cosmic pillars because the latter feature in a variety of East Mediterranean cosmologies.

15. Humans *always* face the sacred building because they have approached it from the outside, whereas deities have their back on it.

16. The interstice of half rosettes forms a novel shape, the so-called incurved altar (Chapter 10); see the excellent discussion by Shaw (1986).

17. Steel 1994, 201–12; Buchholz 1999, fig. 97. The vase dates to the Mycenaean period, more than a century later than the neopalatial representations discussed previously.

18. For the similarity between real and imaginary-abstracted buildings, see Palyvou 2005.

19. Rethemiotakis 2003.

20. Shaw (1986) discusses the utilization of the design in buildings and above gates.

21. For the importance of the palace as a medium of prestige, see van de Mieroop 2004, 96–98 and van de Mieroop 2005, 65.

22. KTU 1. 148 R. 20; Wyatt 2002, 428.

23. Pardee 2002, 69, text 18.

24. The back and forth of the procession is well attested in Egypt and is depicted also on the walls of the temple of Luxor. For this possibility of travel and return of effigies of deities in Ugaritic palace or temple, see Pardee 2002, 67–69, text 17. For more parallels, Pardee 2002, 69–70.

25. RS 24. 250; Pardee 2002, 55, text 14.

26. Bittel in Biran 1981, 63–73.

27. Evans PM I, 495–523.

28. Ibid., 463–85.

29. Haran in Biran 1981, 31–37; Bittel in Biran 1981, 63–73; Lebessi and Muhly 1990.

30. See also Chapter 7 for the types of rituals that took place in the sanctuary. For aniconic cult images, see Evans 1901, 123: "The epiphanies and visions of the divine presence beneath sacred trees are most familiar means of Old Testament revelation." Anthropomorphic cult images in Crete were rare, see Marinatos and Hägg 1983, but I now think that some statues may have existed.

31. Haran in Biran 1981, 35.

32. The Jahwehist polemics are dated to the end of the tenth century or later. They were particularly inimical to Asherah and were opposed to all cult places except for centralized Jerusalem. Keel 1998, 54–57; Wyatt 2001, 168–69; Wilson in Johnston 2004, 378–83.

33. Marinatos 1989, 127–43.

34. In the form of three men or angels.

35. Evans PM I, 159. For recent discussion and bibliography, see Cain 2001.

36. Alexiou 1964; Alexiou 1969b.

37. Collon 1982, pl. xxiv, no. 167; Collon 1987, 166, no. 766.

38. Wyatt 2001, 152–53.

39. Hallager 1985.

40. For a different reading, see Palyvou 2005, 194–97.

41. Marinatos 1995. See also Cultraro 2001, 244–70.

42. In Ugaritic, *hkt* means both the house of king and the temple of god.

43. Platon (Nikolaos) 1951 and 1954; 428–83. Gesell 1985; Peatfield 1983; Peatfield 1987; Peatfield 1990; Peatfield 1992; Rehak and Younger 2001; Watrous (1995) rightly speaks of extra-urban sanctuaries.

44. Renfrew 1985.

Chapter 6: Who Sees the Gods Face to Face?

1. Nilsson 1950, 278–88 and 330–40. These are two distinct chapters, the latter dealing exclusively with birds.

2. Matz 1958.

3. Niemeier 1987; Niemeier 1989; Sourvinou-Inwood 1971; Sourvinou-Inwood 1973; Sourvinou-Inwood 1989. Goodison 1989, 107; Cain 2001, 37; Wedde 1992; Wedde 1999.

4. About Hammurabi's self-presentation as a dispenser of justice, see van de Mieroop 2004, 104–9 and van de Mieroop 2005.

5. I endorse here the remarks of van de Mieroop (2004, 107) that the laws of Hammurabi propagate the fact that the king is just.

6. Oates 1986, 75.

7. Van de Mieroop 2004, 59–69 at 65, fig. 4.1.

8. ANET, no. 837; Dalley 1998, 153.

9. Parallel scenes in Unger 1922, figs. 33, 39–40, 42–43.

10. ANET, 562–63, v. II (1975), 109.

11. Teissier 1996, no. 23.

12. See also Winter 1983, 247, figs. 234–36, 238, etc.

13. Matz 1958. The ecstacy theory is represented by almost all standard works, see for example Alexiou 1969a, 76 and Dickinson 1994, 264–65.

14. CMS XI, 28. This ring was formerly in Schliemann's possession and is now in Berlin. The style shows that it belongs to a Knossian group.

15. Nilsson reads the scene in exactly the opposite way "A small gold ring . . . showing a man adoring a goddess," he writes (Nilsson 1950, 266). Obviously, he was intent

on seeing the great goddess everywhere and seems to have been less sensitive to the meaning of the commanding gesture of the male. Matz, however, argued that the male figure is a god (Matz 1958, 15–16). More recently Niemeier defined the commanding gesture as one of epiphany (Niemeier 1985, 171; Niemeier 1987). Pini, who published the ring in CMS XI. 28, is noncommittal.

16. Evans PM I, 159.

17. For Egyptian parallels, see Wilkinson 1992, 54–55. Note especially the clenched fist of monkeys or baboons greeting the sun. Also, the clenched fist is the shape of a Hittite silver rhyton: Güterbock and Kendall 1995, 55. Evans (PM III, 461) interpreted this gesture as one of adoration, and this is a view adopted by most scholars. I think adoration and greeting are different categories. For an examination of gesture as a carrier of social meaning, see Morris (2001, 247) and Wedde (1999), who discuss the methodology of reading gesture. Their analyses are precise but inconclusive. That the clenched fist is one of greeting is suggested also by the iconogram on a Syrian seal (see Fig. 6.5b).

18. Evans implied that the goddess was similar to the Phrygian Cybele: Evans PM III, 463.

19. Pelon 1995, 309–21 and Cultraro 2001, 312–16.

20. Winter 1983, 250, fig. 240.

21. Sourvinou-Inwood (1989, 250–51) and Krattenmaker (1995a, 57–58) see the male figure as a god greeting the goddess.

22. For an analysis of Jahweh in a historical setting, see Albright 1968; Keel and Uehlinger 1995; and Smith 2004, 402–3.

23. Hallager 1990, 121–42.

24. Winter 2000, 51–87.

Chapter 7: Minoan Prophecy and Royal Power

Epigraph: Evans, PM I, 105.

1. Evans PM I, 160.

2. Frazer 1949, 111 (first edition 1922).

3. For the differentiation of space inside or outside the sanctuary, see Sourvinou-Inwood 1989; Marinatos 2004.

4. See Chapter 6, note 17.

5. The application of the term *baetyl* to Minoan studies goes back to Evans (1901, 112–13). The oval rock has been investigated by Sourvinou-Inwood (1971, 68, and 1973, 155). See also Warren 1986 and 1990. Decisive objections against Warren's interpretation have been advanced by Jung 1989, 91–109.

6. Mettinger 1995; Olyan in Johnston 2004, 429–30.

7. Haas 1982, 115–17 with fig. 29, and Mettinger 1995, 129–30 with references.

8. Mettinger 1995, 84–90.

9. Evans 1901, 112–13.

10. Nilsson 1950, 277.

11. Evans 1901, 169; Evans PM I, 159–62; Nilsson 1950, 401–403; Persson 1942, 39 and passim.

12. Frazer 1949, 324–81 (first edition 1922).

13. Frazer 1949 (first edition 1922).

14. Examples can be found in Ancient Greek, Egyptian, and Near Eastern art: Vermeule 1979.

15. The excavator, Peter Warren (1990, 199, fig. 14), interprets the stone as a *baetyl* that is worshipped (Marinatos 2004). I owe the suggestion that the diviner is dreaming to Dimitris Kyrtatas.

16. *Epic of Gilgamesh,* Tablet IV, I; Dalley 1989, 67.

17. Similar cult monuments consisting of stones or stelae are characteristic of Near Eastern hypaethral sanctuaries: Mettinger 1995, 129. Note that all the female worshippers resting against a rock wear a simple skirt that contrasts with the flounced garment. According to Persson (1942, 32, 36) some of the figures are kneeling against a *pithos.* See also Hood 1971, 138, and Sourvinou-Inwood 1973. The *pithos* identification is rejected by Niemeier (1989, 174–175).

18. Keel and Uehlinger 1995, fig. 233.

19. I thank Thomas Staubli for the reference.

20. This chronology is adopted by van de Mieroop 2004. See also Teissier 1996, 5: 1775–62.

21. Nissinen 2004, 17–37.

22. Nissinen 2003 and 2004.

23. Nissinen 2003, 63, no. 38.

24. Ibid., 61, no. 37.

25. Ibid., 48, no. 24.

26. Ibid., 47, no. 23.

27. For Mari see Durand 1997, 119; Nissinen 2003, 6–7.

28. KTU 1.3. iii 21 ff.; Wyatt 2002, 78.

29. KTU 1.7. v 30–32; Wyatt 2002, 150.

30. This expression has been taken to mean that you are not made of wood or stone, namely you must have a human lineage. But given the evidence here supplied, another interpretation seems possible: Penelope says to Odysseus that he is not made of the substance of legend or prophecy or rumor.

31. Nissinen 2003, 1–11.

32. Compare to *Odyssey* 14.328; Johnston in Johnston 2004, 384.

33. Mettinger 1995, 53, fig. 2.12, 85 fig. 5.3.

34. Nissinen 2003, 27, no. 6.

35. For the sacrality of the king and change of dress, see Chapter 2.

36. Nissinen 2003, 81, no. 51.

37. Nilsson 1950, 276–77.

38. In addition to Evans, this view was accepted by Niemeier (1989). I took the view that the women are high-priestesses (Marinatos 1993, 283), but I now think that the high priestess is the queen. See also Cain 2001, 42.

39. Nilsson 1950, 275, and others saw the figures as dancing adorants, a noncommittal view. "In the middle is a woman with flounced skirt and open bodice with her hands held towards her waist. This attitude belongs to the dance." See also Sakellarakis 1967 and 1971.

40. Nissinen 2003, 4.

41. Wilsson in Johnston 2004, 378.

42. Nilsson 1950, 330–40; see also Burkert 2004b, 5–9.

43. Popham 1974, 217, 223, fig. 14D; Herakleion museum no. 1034.

44. This is also the conclusion by G. Rethemiotakis (personal communication).

45. See also Burkert 2004b, 9–14; and Ezekiel 1:1.

46. Dimopoulou and Rethemiotakis (2000) suggest that the same goddess is depicted in two phases of epiphany in cartoonlike fashion. For a summary of the discussion on minute figures, see Rehak 2002 and Cain 2001, 36–37.

47. Collon 1987, 123.

48. Nissinen 2003, 5; Nissinen 2004.

49. "Toutes ces propheties Mariotes sont des encouragements sans reserve addressés au pouvoir legal," Durand 1997, 132.

50. Nilsson 1950, 262.

Chapter 8: The Cosmic Mountain as a Frontier

1. Evans PM I, 276–89; and PM IV, 665–763.

2. Evans PM I, fig. 214.

3. Evans PM I, 151–63; and PM II, 159, fig. 81.

4. The same shape is found on the top of altars in Syro-Palestine and Cyprus. Yet this does not constitute proof that they are animal horns, but simply means that there was a *koine* of altar symbolism. See, for example, Figure 8.3.

5. Evans 1921, fig. 214, no. 37.

6. Evans 1921, 136–37.

7. Illustrated by Perrot and Chipiez 1887, 392, fig. 206. Inscription dating from the time of Darius I, 521–485 BCE.

8. Nilsson 1950, 183.

9. Nilsson 1950, 189. See in general 165–93.

10. Nilsson 1950, 119: "Altars . . . must be recognized by their form." This is a serious methodological error confusing form and function. Altars may differ in form, especially if we are to apply an interregional comparative perspective, but their function will remain the same: they are offering places for the god. The confusion in Nilsson's categories is evident if we look at figs. 35, 61, 73, 77, 78, 80, 83, 85–87, 142, 162.

11. Gaerte 1922; Nilsson 1950, 187–88.

12. Powell 1977.

13. MacGillivray 2000a, 123–30; Watrous 1989, 23.

14. Dijkstra (1991) sees the two mountains as representing specific topography which may well be right but the ideogram must have indicated also a general cosmic topography. Laroche 1960, 125, no. 228.

15. Evans PM I, 632, fig. 470; Nilsson 1950, 171, fig. 72.

16. Goodison 1989, 74, fig. 133.

17. CMS V, 201; Evans PM IV, 467, fig. 392; Nilsson 1950, 148, fig. 56; Marinatos 1993, 169.

18. Also, the cosmic serpent rises between the mountain peaks in the tomb of Sennedjem: Wilkinson 1992, 132, fig. 1.

19. He is incorporated in the royal *aedicula.* Bittel et al. 1941, 214, fig. 249; Haas 1982, 49–54.

20. For the mountain as a cosmic center, see Clifford 1972; and Wyatt 2001, 147–57.

21. Davaras, Hagios Nikolaos Museum, fig. 31.

22. Keel 1978, 23–24.

23. Lions also guard the horizon gate in Egyptian art: Wilkinson 1992, 68–69. Shamash steps with one foot on a mountaintop as though he conquers it: Collon 1982, pl. xxiv, nos. 168; Collon 1987, 166, no. 766; discussion on p. 167. On other seals with similar iconography the sun god appears through a regular gate that frames a twin-peak mountain. For further examples, see Keel 1978, 22–26, fig. 8; Collon 1987, 34, no. 103; 126, no. 537, etc.

24. See Black and Green 1992, 114, under *kur.* The authors are puzzled at how the same word can have such diverse meanings; they suggest they possibly have different origins.

25. "Certainly in some myths the mountains (*kur*) are treated as an other-worldly locale": Black and Green 1992, 114. On cosmic mountains in Canaan: Clifford 1972; and Burkert 1996, 83.

26. Hecker et al. 1994, Tablet XII, col. ii.

27. *Gilgamesh,* Tablet IX, col. ii, 1–5. For the cosmic geography of Gilgamesh, see Horowitz 1998. The cosmic mountain is also the house of Belet-ili, the Mistress of the mountain: Meissner 1920–1925, 2:120

28. Meissner 1920–1925, II, 378–79; Horowitz 1998, 20–42; and Wyatt 2001, 81–82.

29. Wyatt 2001, 82.

30. Between each set of three is an extra fourth one, which is the throne of god. The Book of Enoch makes use of ancient Mediterranean cosmography according to Nickelsburg (2001, 279–80).

31. Wyatt 2001, 154.

32. Evans PM I, 154–56; Karetsou 1981, 137–53, esp. 142–43, figs. 5–7, 145, fig. 10; Rutkowski 1988; Peatfield 1987; Peatfield 1990; Watrous 1995; Jones 1999.

Chapter 9: The Double Axe, the Ankh, and the Ox Head

Epigraph: Evans PM I, 447.

1. Nilsson 1950, 194.

2. The double axe has been associated with the palace of Knossos, and rightly so. What is more dubious is the assumption that it was called *labrys* in Minoan times, a theory that cannot be established securely. On the contrary, if the phonetic values of Linear A correspond to those of Linear B (a reasonable assumption), then the double axe has the phonetic value "a" and not "la." For *labrys,* see Plutarch, *Quaestiones Graecae,* 302A. See also discussion of labyrinth/labrys in Nilsson 1950, 223–25 with note 34. The association of the double axe with the labyrinth is commonly made; see for example Alexiou 1964, 91; Alexiou 1969b; and Pötscher 1990, 60. Note the reservations of Davaras (1976,

73), who calls the Anatolian connection "obsolete." More recently the question has been reviewed by Sippel 1986a and Sippel 1986b. Good critical discussion of the history of the concept can be found in MacGillivray 2000, 213–14. There is a Mycenaean word in Linear B, *da-pu-ri-jo,* which is viewed as linguistically equivalent to *la-by-ri-nthos* and Anatolian *labrys.*

3. Evans PM I, 447. Some scholars have followed this view, accepting that a deity or a unification of two deities are represented by the axe, although there is disagreement as to whether the deity was a female chthonic goddess or a male weather god. See in particular Pötscher (1990, 151–60) who postulates that the axe stands for a male god but the birds perching on it are female and the whole complex signifies sacred marriage between gods and goddess.

4. Nilsson 1950, 227; criticism of Evans: 223–25. See also Dietrich 1988.

5. Marinatos 1986, 22–25; 51–72; Varschoonwinkel 2004.

6. Rutkowski (1981, 91–97) rightly stresses that the double axe is an emblem of kingship. See also Davaras 1976, 71–74.

7. For a different interpretation of the double axe as a sacrificial symbol on the larnakes: Watrous 1991, 302–5 with pls. 82 a; 87 c; 88 f;

8. Lurker 1980, 36.

9. Wilkinson 1992, 57; see also the *Introduction to the Book of the Dead* by Hornung 1990b, 33. For solar cow, see Wilkinson 1994, 72–73 and fig. 45.

10. For the associations of the bull with the moon god, see Bernett and Keel 1998, 62–93.

11. Fribourg Biblical Institute collection: Keel and Schroer 1998, Tafel III b.

12. Evans PM I, fig. 312. The Mycenaean seal is flanked by sacred garments, which, in my view, represent a cult emblem of the goddess (see Demargne 1949). On the Egyptian scarab seal the motifs are hawks, the sacred birds, and the manifestation of the sun.

13. Evans PM II, fig. 338.

14. Keel (1998, 34–40) has shown that the disc is sometimes a lunar one.

15. Winter 1983, fig. 213.

16. See recent discussion in Kyriakidis 2005, 151–52, fig. 21.

17. Evans, PM IV, 597 B, g.

18. CMS II. 8, 326.

19. In Hittite myth and iconography the firmament is carried by two bulls, Herri and Hurri, in the sanctuary of Yazilikaya: Bittel et al. 1941, nos. 28–29. See also Black and Green 1992, 49.

20. Faulkner 1985, 79, Spell 81A.

21. Reeves 1990, 66.

22. Evans PM II, 473, 483.

23. Evans PM II, 475.

24. Niemeier 1989, pl. 8, XVII A1.

25. Evans PM IV, fig. 286; Niemeier 1985, 117; Betancourt and Davaras 1995, 35–36.

26. Wilkinson 1992, 201.

27. Evans PM I, 200, 280–81.

28. Evans 1901, 178; PM I, 434–35; Nilsson 1950, 207–12.

29. Wilkinson 1992, 177. The origin of its visual form is still uncertain.

30. Laroche 1960, 195, no. 369.

31. Bossert 1932. See also Evans 1901, 178, fig. 54; Laroche 1960, 195.

32. Teissier 1996, 158–61.

33. Scholars normally identify this as a sea star, but this is impossible because it is suspended in space, does not crawl at the bottom, and is too large.

34. See Chapter 11.

35. Lambert 1996, 129, lines 37–38. This Babylonian hymn, found in Ashurbanibal's library, probably goes back to the second millennium.

36. Frankfort 1948, 105–23; Keel 1978, 15–46; Hornung 1990a; Wyatt 2001, 184–87.

37. *Gilgamesh,* Tablet X, ii; Dalley 1989, 102.

38. Lambert 1996, 129, line 36.

39. Lambert 1996, 127, lines 31–32.

40. KTU 1.6; Wyatt 2002, 134.

41. KTU 1.161 R15; Wyatt 2002, 437.

42. Götze 1957, 138.

43. TUAT, 811–15 nos. 3, 4. Transl. Ahmed Ünal. For an analysis of that and similar myths, see Pecchioli Daddi 2001, 407.

44. Hymn to the sun god, Faulkner 1985, 27. See also Hornung 1990b, Spell 15b, p. 57.

45. Spell 15 in Faulkner 1985, 41.

46. Bosanquet and Dawkins 1923, pl. XX; Bossert 1932, pl. 166. Bosanquet (50) recognized the star as the sun.

47. Rethemiotakis 1979, 228–59.

48. Buccholz 1959.

49. Evans 1914, 1–59.

50. Nilsson 1950, fig. 97; Betancourt and Davaras 1999, 136.

51. Hornung 1982, 125.

52. Wilkinson 1992, 57, 127; Hornung 1982, 125–35.

53. Keel 1995, 21–22.

Chapter 10: The Rosette, Half-Rosette, and "Incurved Altar"

1. Evans recognized the sun as the rayed disc: Evans 1909, I, 221, no.107a; cf. also Davis 1967, 179, fig. 133; 205. The rosette is a pictogram, also on the Phaistos disc: Davis 1967, 88–94.

2. Evans PM I, 241, col. pl. II; 585, fig. 428; Pendlebury 1939, 112–13, fig. 17, no. 9; fig. 18, no. 30; Betancourt 1990, figs. 44–45. Niemeier 1985, 84: "Die Rosette zählt zu den ältesten Motive der minoischen Kunst." Note its occurrence on the Phaistos disc as sign no. 38: Evans PM I, 652.

3. Crete (Kaphtor) is mentioned in the correspondence of king Zimrilim at Mari. Durand 1997, 159; Guichard 1999, 167–77.

4. It is absent from the hieroglyphic grid, Evans PM I, 282, fig. 214. See also Davis 1967, 182.

5. Bietak 1996, col. pl. iiib. Bietak, Marinatos, and Palyvou 2000, 77–90; Bietak, Marinatos, and Palyvou 2007.

6. See Chapter 2, notes 46–49.

7. Teissier 1996, 101, 111. She considers it a symbol of Ishtar and connects it with femininity.

8. Collon 1987, 49, no 180. That the rosette is the sun in Syrian glyptic is established also by Otto 2000, 230ff.

9. Otto 2000, 230.

10. Several vases of the New Palace period in Crete and the island of Thera furnish such examples; see Niemeier 1989, 119, fig. 57. Niemeier (1989, 117) calls the rosette a knob or handle: "Knauf."

11. Evans PM II, fig. 254.

12. The green leaves were clearly observed by the first excavators and commentators. See Harrison 1962, 162.

13. Teissier 1996, 71.

14. The interpretation of the rosette as life is suggested by its meaning as "life" in Luwian/Hittite hieroglyphs.

15. Teissier 1996, 71; Keel 1998, 20–36. Keel, however, does not stress the solar aspects of the palm.

16. Collon 1987, 58.

17. Evans PM III, 30–31, col. Pl. XV. Evans rightly stresses the comparative material from Egypt.

18. Bietak, Marinatos, and Palyvou 2000, 78–79. For another view with which I disagee, see Weißl 2000.

19. Evans PM II, fig. 450.

20. Bossert 1932; Reusch 1958, 351–352.

21. We may draw some further cautious inferences. In the same Luwian/Hittite hieroglyphic script, the sun is rendered as a staff with a triple split rosette. This suggests that the basic symbolism of the rosette is solar and that this meaning was extended to denote "god": Laroche 1960, no.191.

22. Evans PM II, fig. 381.

23. Evans PM I, fig. 214, no 55.

24. Evans PM IV, 613.

25. Nilsson 1950, 253.

26. Shaw 1986, 108–23.

27. Wilkinson 1992, 159.

28. Ibid.

Chapter 11: Minoan Afterlife Beliefs

1. Discussion of these materials can be found in Rutkowski 1966; Mavriyiannaki 1972; Alexiou 1972; Watrous 1991; Rethemiotakis 1995; Immerwahr 1995; Marinatos 1997.

2. Evans PM IV, 964–78.

3. The sanctuary has been largely reconstructed: Evans PM IV, 964–68.

4. I would like to mention especially the work of Alexiou 1972, Rethemiotakis 1995

and Davaras 1986, all of whom rightly refer to a Minoan version of the Greek Elysium in their publications of specific larnakes. See also Mavriyiannaki 1972; Tzedakis 1971; Kanta 1973, 315–21. Vermeule's study focuses on hunting. The killing of the animals, she argues, makes them holy and gives them a spiritual intimacy with nature: Vermeule 1979, 66–67. I find this logic difficult to grasp. More sober is Immerwahr 1995. See also Marinatos 1993, Ch. 11. The most synthetic work is by Watrous 1991, who stresses that the iconography of Minoan larnakes has an affinity with Egyptian funerary iconography.

5. Some of the motifs on the larnakes were foreshadowed by Palace Style pottery: see Niemeier 1985.

6. Watrous 1991, 303.

7. Shakespeare, *Hamlet,* Act 3, Scene 1, lines 79–80.

8. Most stem from the Nineteenth Dynasty: Budge 1906. The best recent analysis supplemented with pictures is that of Hornung (1990a).

9. For the Egyptian gates of the beyond, see Hornung 1982, 1990a, and 1990b.

10. Meissner 1925, II, 378–79; Horowitz 1998, 20–42; Wyatt 2001, 81–82.

11. See Horowitz 1998. For the dark region, page 33. In Akkadian, *milu* and *zinu,* but this word is difficult to interpret. Instead of wondrous trees, it may signify a region of high rainfall or flooding (38). For the land of horned cattle, see page 39.

12. The *Epic of Gilgamesh* has a long tradition that spans the entire Bronze Age and comes down to the time of King Ashurbanibal in the seventh century BCE.

13. Tablet IX.v; Dalley 1998, 98–99.

14. Marinatos 2002.

15. Evans PM III, 155–56. He was discussing there the forged ring (of Nestor). Yet, his description is very applicable.

16. *Gilgamesh,* Tablet X, ii; Dalley 1998, 102. Utnapishtim's island may be likened to that of the Phaecians in the *Odyssey:* it is a region for semi-divine peoples and cannot be reached by ordinary humans except under very special circumstances. Its inhabitants, like the Phaecians of the *Odyssey,* may consort with the gods. The island of Utnapishtim, then, is a frontier to the habitat of the gods; see Strasburger 1998.

17. Hesiod, *Erga,* 171.

18. Herodotus writes in the middle of the fifth century BCE but embodies views that go back a century earlier.

19. KTU 1.4 viii; Wyatt 2002, 112.

20. Rethemiotakis 1979, 228–59.

21. Marinatos and Hirmer 1976, pl. 130; Marinatos 1993, 231–32.

22. *Gilgamesh,* Tablet XI, lines 209–307.

23. Hornung 1990a and 1990b, 55–57, Spells 15, 17, 18.

24. Derived from the Ani papyrus. See Faulkner 1985, 79 and Wilkinson 1992, 121 with references.

25. Faulkner 1985, 160, Spell 164.

Chapter 12: The Solar Goddess of Kingship

1. Evans PM III, 463–68.

2. Sugaya 2000, 273–82; Owens 1996a and 1996b, 209–18. In Owen's account, Astarte is hardly differentiated from Anat and Ishtar.

3. Most influential is Gimbutas (1995) who generalizes the concept to include Neolithic Europe. More moderate are Alexiou 1969a, 70–71: "Equally the creative power of nature assumed the traits of the Great Mother"; Hood 1971, 131: "The Chief deity worshipped by the Bronze Age Cretans was evidently a goddess; either a single goddess under different aspects, or a group of goddesses with different names but basically similar in character. The Cretan goddesses were versions of the Goddess of Fertility worshipped throughout the Near East in earlier times"; Owens 1996b, 212: "The Great Goddess has been seen as common to every culture in her many guises"; Kourou 2001, 34: "Most tree cults are extreme in their realism often directly implying a personification of the Great Goddess as a tree." The other extreme is represented by skepticism towards mythological interpretation. Thomas and Wedde (2001) discuss iconography as well as Linear B (Mycenaean sources) and conclude that "although visible in the written sources, no clear characterization of *potnia* emerges from Linear B sources. The written evidence cannot be equated with archaeological sources." For criticism of the approaches to the great goddess, see Lapatin 2002, 66–90.

4. Nilsson 1950, 393.

5. Evans PM III, 406. For a recent reassessment, see Keel and Schroer 2006.

6. The idea of matriarchy is due to J. J. Bachofen (original edition appeared in 1861) who, however, spoke of *Mutterrecht* not matriarchy. Due to Bachofen, an entire school of social evolutionist history was founded, which had an impact on Evans, Jane Ellen Harrison, and many other scholars. Discussion and evaluation of the history of (the now outdated) idea of matriarchy for the Near East can be found in Lapatin 2002, 66–90; and Winter 1983, 416–20. Matrilineality, on the other hand, is another phenomenon. It is very probable for Ugarit, at least for the royal family: Wyatt 1999, 544.

7. Rehak 1995b.

8. I have previously sided with those who see the male grasping the wrist of the goddess as an erotic gesture (Marinatos 1993, 1990 with notes 73–75); I no longer think this likely. Recently Koehl 2001, 237–43.

9. Evans PM III, 464. Nilsson 1950, 405. See also Evans PM III, 464 and Dimopoulou and Rethemiotakis 2000.

10. Niemeier 1987 and 1989.

11. Nilsson's thesis is that the Great Goddess portrays the decay and revival of nature: Nilsson 1950, 401–3 with discussion.

12. Evans, PM III, 464.

13. Such an interpretation is suggested by two pieces of evidence. First, a gold ring from Poros, Crete, which I have seen thanks to the kindness of the excavator Nota Dimopoulou and Giorgos Rethemiotakis, shows a seated goddess and a standing god.

Above the goddess is the sun; above the god is the moon. Second, in Egypt the moon is conceived as the son of the sun god.

14. Collon 1994, 81–88, fig. 5. Collon suggests that the motifs can be connected with Alalakh level VII, namely the seventeenth century BCE. Our scenes would be two centuries later according to the traditional chronology, but the new chronology (based on scientific evidence of the volcanic Thera eruption) and adopted by W.-D. Niemeier, would make the Minoan new palace period almost contemporary with Alalakh. I opt for traditional chronology.

15. See also the parallel iconography on a late Egyptian relief of the time of Nectanebo II: Cornelius 2004, 43, fig. 33.

16. Winter (1983, 452) assumes he is a king. The similarity of dress and attributes of god and king have been discussed in Chapter 2. They are a big subject in the discussion of the Hittite deities at Yazilikaya: Bittel et al. 1941, 67 (where god 34 looks exactly like the king).

17. Winter 1983, 449.

18. Bittel et al. 1941, 86; Götze (1957, 136–37) includes citations from hymns.

19. Bittel 1976, fig. 198. A relief at Alaca Hoyük, however, shows the goddess as seated, approached by three males: Bittel 1976, 192, fig. 216.

20. See Güterbock 1943, 307; Götze 1957, 139–46. The relief in question probably dates to the reign of king Tudhaliya IV: Bittel et al. 1941, 86; and Bittel 1976, 167.

21. Cornelius also reaches this conclusion for the Ugaritic Athirat. Cornelius (2004, 100) cites all available iconographical evidence.

22. Wyatt 2001, 168–69.

23. ANET, 393.

24. The narrative exists in an early second millennium and a first millennium version, the so-called Standard Babylonian, which is the one cited here: Dalley 1998, 203.

25. *Anzu* I in Dalley 1998, 210–11.

26. Annus 2001; Wyatt 2006, 5.

27. KTU 1.6 i 45, 48: Wyatt 2002, 131–32.

28. Two of the many examples: KTU 1.4 iv 33 in Wyatt 2002, 99; KTU 1.8 ii 2 in Wyatt 2002, 152.

29. KTU 1.6 i 44–47 in Wyatt 2002, 131.

30. Wyatt 1999, 540–44; Wyatt 2002, 132 with n. 75.

31. KTU 1.15 ii. 27 in Wyatt 2002, 209.

32. Wyatt 1999, 544.

33. This ring has been lost, but a replica was produced and has survived. CMS II. 3, 252; Nilsson 1950, 269–70; Sourvinou-Inwood 1973; Niemeier 1989, 182; Marinatos 1993, 162–63, fig. 150.

34. *rbt atrt* ym. Albright 1968, 105; Wyatt 2005a, 18–37; 38–54.

35. Wyatt 2005a, 18–37 at 19–20.

36. KTU 1.6 iv 45–52 in Wyatt 2005a, 20.

37. Nilsson 1950, 223.

38. Evans PM IV, 94.

39. Notably the goddesses from Gournia and Gazi: Alexiou 1958, pls. E3, Z; Marinatos 1993, 226, fig. 229.

40. Long 1974, 54–55.

41. Long (1974, 73) suggests they are men, but men would not be depicted along with goddesses. Therefore, they must be the dead.

42. Consider also the following texts, which show that Shapshu goes to the end of the world: "Mother Shapshu, take a message to Ilu at the headwaters of the two rivers, and the confluence of the deeps," or, "Mother Shapshu, take a message to Kotaru-wa-Hashishu in Caphtor (Crete)." For RS 24.244 see Pardee 2002, 174, 177–79.

43. Spyridon Marinatos thought that she may have been *A-ka-ka-lis,* basing his conclusion on the fact that one syllable is duplicated in both the Linear A word and the Greek mythological name.

44. In addition to Platon 1958, see more recently Hiller 2000, 107–35; and Owens 1996b, 209–18.

45. Goodison 1989, 173–76. See also Moss 2005.

46. Burkert 1985, 43–46.

47. Cornelius 1994, 80–81.

48. Munn 2006.

Chapter 13: The Storm God

1. Cf. Alexiou 1969a: "The powerful gods of Olympus—Zeus, Poseidon, Apollo—seem foreign to the small pantheon of Minoan religion dominated by female deities." See the summary statement of Burkert 2000, 23: "The warrior figure is strikingly absent from the Minoan civilization of Crete."

2. Evans PM III, 464.

3. Evans PM III, 464–65; compare with Frazer 1949, 327–29. Note that the source of Frazer's Adonis is the Roman author Macrobius. For criticism of fertility theories, see Mettinger 2001; Wyatt 1999; and Wyatt 2005b. For a recent interpretation of the Minoan god as a year god, see Otto 2001, 27–48.

4. Discussion in Burkert 1979.

5. Nilsson 1950, 400–12, esp. 411.

6. Hallager 1985, as well as Niemeier 1987; Niemeier 1989; Marinatos 1993, 166–74 with bibl.; and Dimopoulou and Rethemiotakis 2000. MacGillivray 2000a.

7. Keel and Uehlinger 1995, 66–68, fig. 35; 66–67, figs 56–67. See also Cornelius 1994 for the iconography of Canaanite male deities.

8. Hornung 1982 has a seminal discussion of the "one and the many" in connection with Egyptian religion and iconography. Scholars of Greek religion, on the other hand, debate endlessly if the Mistress of Animals on a given Geometric or Archaic piece is Athena or Artemis or Hera. The issue of identity may be solved once and for all if we acknowledge that roles may overlap with names and admit that art gives us information about the latter and not the former.

9. Niemeier 1987; Niemeier 1989.

10. The god and lion: Cornelius 1994, 195–208, pls. 49–51. See also Fulco 1976.

11. Genette 1980; Cain 2001, 29. A more complex view is offered by Lebessi et al. 2004, 22–23.

12. Cain 2001, 29.

13. Cain 2001.

14. For the various Hittite storm gods, see Götze 1957, 130–34. For the Standard Babylonian version c. 720 BCE see Annus 2001.

15. Bietak 1996, 41; Dijkstra 1991.

16. Cornelius (1994, 258) argues that Reshep never has an enemy and he is a defensive god—an averter of plagues—unlike Baal. Reshep is primarily a healing god and a god of pestilence. See also Burkert et al. 2003, 3–4; Collon 1972.

17. Burkert 1975, 51–79, reprinted as Burkert et al. 2003, 22–25.

18. Götze 1957, 139; TUAT 808–11; for an analysis of the myth on a comparative basis, see Haas 1982, 118–25; Burkert 1979, 8–9; and Uehlinger 1995; ANET, 125–28.

19. Annus 2001.

20. Discussions of *Chaoskampf* (war against forces of chaos) in the Near East in Keel 1978, 47–56; Haas 1982, 118–125; Uehlinger 1995; Annus 2001; and Wyatt 2005.

21. This view is still widely held today. See Otto 2001, 27–48.

22. An exemplary discussion of this issue concerns Ninurta, which Annus 2001 connects with kingship.

23. Wyatt 1997 and Wyatt 2005b.

24. Uehlinger 1995; Wyatt 2005b.

25. He usually has seven or twelve adversaries. Heracles and Ninurta share this in common: Annus 2001, 109–21; Burkert 1979, 78–88.

26. For refined analysis, see Keel and Uehlinger 1995, 55–109. Summary and perceptive comments can be found in Burkert 2000.

27. Keel and Uehlinger 1995, 134–38; Wyatt 2006.

28. The political dimension is explored by Uehlinger 1995, 13–16.

29. Wyatt 2006.

30. Wyatt 1997, 778–79 with further refs.

31. That the time span of the rings coincides with the New Palace period has been cogently argued by Pini 2000, 239–44.

32. Dijkstra (1991) identifies the two mountains as specific topographical locations, but it seems to me that they rather signify dominance over the entire world.

33. Porada 1984, 485–88; Bietak 1994, 57; Dijkstra 1991, 127–40.

34. Originally published by Levi, 1925–26b, no. 114. Also see Pini 1989, 203, fig. 1; CMS II. 6, 16. Pini suggests that the god's weapon was a sword. It may be argued that the Minoan smiting figure is a king, but since king and god are interchangeable in Minoan art (Chapter 2), this makes no big difference.

35. Keel 1978, 293–97; Keel and Uehlinger 1995, 84–92.

36. Keel and Uehlinger 1995, 129.

37. Bossert 1937, fig. 400 f.; Nilsson 1950, 40; CMS 5:173 with bibl.

38. Loud 1939, pl. 4; Wiesner 1968, 190, fig. 39.

39. Nilsson 1950, 40.

40. For example, Marduk faces Tiamat in the *Enuma Elish,* and Nergal has to "tame" Ereshkigal: Dalley 1998, Tablets iv–v, 165–77; 255–60.

41. Lebessi et al. 2004, 21–29. I disagree with the interpretation of the excavators that the owner was an athlete.

42. This identification is proposed by Kyriakidis 2005, 137–54; see also Lebessi et al. 2004, 30. For comets in the Greco-Roman world, see Ramsey 2006.

43. The omega object has been variously interpreted as a snake frame or a pair of horns: Evans PM IV, 175; Nilsson 1950, 363–64, figs. 62–65; Hägg and Lindau 1984, 66–77. The objective description of Lebessi et al. 2004, 18–19, is excellent. Concerning the garment there is *no evidence* that it typifies sacrificial priests *pace* Lebessi et al. 2004, 18, 23.

44. The painting comes from the mansion Xeste 4. It is unpublished; I owe this information to Christos Boulotis and Andreas Vlachopoulos.

45. Decker 1987, 38–42.

46. Keel 1992, 195–32; Uehlinger 1995. For Mesopotamian third millennium dragon gods, see Amiet 1980, 177–81, pl. 106.

47. Evans PM IV, 952, fig. 921.

48. Marinatos 1926, 51; Nilsson 1950, 37.

49. KTU 1.5. i 1; Wyatt 2002, 115.

50. Wyatt 2002, 115.

51. KTU 1.65; Wyatt 2002, 363–65.

52. Dalley 1998, 228–32.

53. Ibid., 251.

54. Ibid., 263.

55. KTU 1.10. ii 6–7; Wyatt 2002, 156.

56. CMS XI, 29, with previous bibliography.

57. Pini 1981, 135–57; Kyriakidis 2005, 140–41; see also Chapter 7.

58. There is an Ugaritic text where a bow is contested by a goddess and the young hero Aqhat. Wyatt 2002, 246–312; Wyatt 2002, 272–78. It is tempting to link the Minoan depiction with the Ugaritic text, but the match is not precise.

59. The females may be one and the same person (the queen) who has changed garment for the incubation procedure. The iconograms in the field above the visionary—an ear and an eye—may be signs that she sees and hears the god.

60. Wyatt 2005b, 151–89.

61. Wyatt 1999–2000, 135–36.

62. A cult of weapons existed also among the Hittites; it is textually attested that offerings were made to a shield deity at Dala: Bossert 1944, 57. The painted tablet from Mycenae probably shows shield cult.

63. KTU 1.4. viii 27–28; Wyatt 2002, 113.

64. KTU 1.4. iv 25; Wyatt 2002, 99.

65. *Anzu* I, iii; Dalley 1998, 210.

66. EA, no. 250, ANET, 264. Transl. W.F. Albright.

67. EA, no. 320, ANET, 483–90. Transl. W.F. Albright.

68. Pini 2000, 239–44.

69. Wyatt 1998, 39.

70. Wyatt (1998) notes that some of the Ugaritic categories are fecundity ("the seventy sons of Athirat"), habitat ("heavenly ones"), and hierarchy ("great gods").

71. For my first reflections on how the chief female goddess and male god of the pantheon were perceived by the Minoans, see Marinatos 1993, Chapter 7.

Chapter 14: Translating the Gods of the Religious *Koine*

1. Thomassen 2004.

2. For example, Hermes is a god of flocks and shepherds, but he is also a god of the underworld or a god of puberty rites. There is no necessary logical relationship between his functions; they are a result of many years of religious synthesis. The roles of each god are reflected in his/her epithets; for example, Zeus xenios, Zeus chthonios, etc.

3. Graf 2004, 5.

4. Thomassen 2004. The examples may be easily multiplied; see Herodotus, 2. 41.2; 43.1; 46.1; 48.1; 51.1, etc.

5. Burkert 2000, reprinted in Burkert et al. 2003, 17–36. For the general problem faced by anthropology regarding translation of one culture into the other, see Evans Pritchard 1951.

6. This counters the argument of Evans Pritchard (1951) who said that the main issue facing anthropologists was one of translation—finding a way to translate one's own thoughts into the world of another culture.

7. Herodotus ii. 41–63. It is interesting that he translates Egyptian gods into their Greek equivalents with great confidence. Amon is Zeus, Osiris is Dionysos, and Isis is Demeter. It is interesting, however, that when it comes to customs (i.e. animal sacrifice) he stresses differences, rather than similarities as though customs cannot be precisely translated.

8. Overview in Keel and Uehlinger 1995; Cornelius 1994, 1–11. See also Burkert 1992.

9. Ramses II is meant here.

10. Transl. J. A. Wilson; ANET 200–201. This is the Egyptian version of the treaty engraved on the walls of the temple of Amon at Karnak and the Ramesseum. There exists also the Hittite equivalent.

11. Interestingly enough, the Hittite sun goddess of Arinna, one of the most prominent deities of the Hittite pantheon, is not mentioned, presumably because, being a female sun deity, she was not translatable into the Egyptian religious idiom. Instead, we meet the male god Re and his Hittite counterpart, the male sun god of Arinna.

12. Van de Mieroop 2004, 129, 61–62.

13. Cornelius 2004, 110–11 with bibl.

14. Stadelmann 1967; Keel and Uehlinger 1995, 29–48; Cornelius 1994; Cornelius 2004, 20–21.

15. Bossert 1944, 10: "[die] Religionen beider Länder[waren] auf engste miteinander verwandt."

16. Black and Green 1992, 74.

17. Van de Mieroop 2004, 137.

Chapter 15: Conclusions: A Tribute to Sir Arthur Evans

1. Frazer 1927, 229–35; 1949, 84–91.
2. Evans 1901, 108.
3. Evans PM III, 464.

Bibliography

Abbreviations

Abbreviations for journals follow the abbreviations system of the *American Journal of Archaeology.*

ANET	*Ancient Near Eastern Texts Relating to the Old Testament,* edited by J. B. Pritchard, 3rd ed. Princeton: Princeton University Press, 1955.
CMS	*Corpus der minoischen and mykenischen Siegel,* edited by F. Matz, H. Biesantz, and I. Pini. Mainz, Berlin: Akademie der Literatur and Wissenschaften, 1964- .
Evans PM I–IV	Volumes 1–4 of The Palace of Minos: a Comparative Account of the Successive Stages of the Early Cretan Civilization as Illustrated by the Discoveries at Knossos by A. Evans. London: Macmillan, 1921–35.
KBo	Keilschrifttexte aus Boghazkoi. Berlin: Gebr. Mann.
KTU	*Die Keilalphabetischen Texte aus Ugarit. Einschliesslich der Keilalphabetischen Texte Ausserhalb Ugarit. Teil 1 Transkription,* edited by M. Dietrich, O. Loretz, and J. Sanmartin, with H. W. Kisker. Alter Orient und Altes Testament 24. Kevelaer and Neukirchen-Vluyn: Verlag Butzon & Bercker, 1976.
RS	Ras Shambra.
RSV	*Holy Bible.* New Revised Standard Version.
TUAT	*Texte aus der Umwelt des Alten Testaments,* edited by K. Hecker, W. G. Lambert, G. G. W. Müller, W. von Soden and A. Ünal. Volume III. Mythen und Epen II. Gütersloh: G. Mohn, 1983–1994.

Albright, William F. 1968. *Yahweh and the Gods of Canaan: A Historical Analysis of Two Contrasting Faiths.* London: Athlone Press.

Alexiou, Stylianos. 1958. "I minoiki thea meth' ypsomenon xeiron." *Kretika Chronika* 12:179–299.

Alexiou, Stylianos. 1964. "Minoikoi Istoi Simeon." *Kretika Chronika* 17:339–51.

Alexiou, Stylianos. 1969a. *Minoan Civilization.* Trans. C. Ridley. Herakleion: Crete.

Alexiou, Stylianos. 1969b. "Istoi Minoikon Ieron kai Aigyptiakoi Pylones (Supports des sanctuaires minoéns et des pylons égyptienes)." *AAA* 2:84–88.

Alexiou, Stylianos. 1971. "Nea Parastasis Ploiou epi Minoikis Larnakos." In *Pepragmena tou Tritou Diethnous Kretologikou Synedriou, Rethymno, 18–23 September 1971*, 3–12. Rethymno: Dimos Rethymnis.

Alexiou, Stylianos. 1972. "Larnakes kai Aggeia ek Tafou para to Gazi Irakleiou." *Archaiologike Ephemeris,* 86–98.

Alexiou, Stylianos. 1987. "Minoan Palaces as Centres of Trade and Manufacture." In Hägg and Marinatos 1987, 251–53.

Al-Khalesi, Yasin. 1978. *Court of the Palms: A Functional Interpretation of the Mari Palace.* Malibu: Undena.

Alp, Sedat. 1983 *Beiträge zur Erforschung des hethitischen Tempels. Kultanlagen im Lichte der Keilschrifttexte. Neue Deutungen.* Ankara: Turk Tarih Kurumu Basimevi.

Alram-Stern, E. and Georg Nightingale, eds. 2007 *Keimelion.* Band, Vienna: Österreichische Akademie der Wissenschaften. Denkschriften.

Amiet, Pierre. 1980. *La Glyptique Mésopotamienne Archaique.* Paris: CNRS.

Amiet, Pierre. 1992. *Corpus des Cylindres de Ras Shamra-Ugarit II. Sceaux-cylindres en Hématite et Pierres Diverses.* Ras Shamra-Ugarit IX. Paris: Editions Recherche sur les Civilisations.

Andreasen, Niels.-Erik A. 1983. "The Role of the Queen Mother in Isrealite Society." *Catholic Biblical Quarterly* 45:179–94.

Annus, Amar. 2001. "Ninurta and the Son of Man." In Whiting 2001, 7–17.

Arnaud, Daniel. 1987. *Recherches au Pays d' Astata. Emar.* Vol. VI.4: *Textes de la Bibliothèque. Transcriptions et Traductions.* Paris: Editions Recherche sur les Civilisations.

Aruz, Joan. 1995. "Syrian Seals and the Evidence for Cultural Interaction between the Levant and Crete." In Müller 1995, 2–21.

Bachofen, Johann J. 1941. *Mutterrecht und Urreligion. Eine Auswahl. Herausgegeben von R. Marx.* Stuttgart: Kröner.

Badawy, Alexander. 1966. *Architecture in Ancient Egypt and the Near East.* Cambridge: MIT Press.

Bernett, Monika, and Othmar Keel. 1998. *Mond, Stier und Kult am Stadttor: Die Stele von Betsaida (et-Tell).* Orbis Biblicus et Orientalis 161. Göttingen: Vandenhoeck and Ruprecht.

Betancourt, Philip P. 1990. *The Final Neolithic through Middle Minoan III Pottery.* Vol 2 of *Kommos: An Excavation of the South Coast of Crete.* Princeton: Princeton University Press.

Betancourt, Philip P. 2002. "Who Was in Charge of the Palaces?" In Driessen, Schoep, and Laffineur 2002, 207–11.

Betancourt, Philip P., and Costis Davaras, eds. 1995. *Pseira I: Minoan Buildings on the West Side of Area A.* University Museum Monograph 90. Philadelphia: University Museum of Pennsylvania.

Betancourt, Philip P., and Costis Davaras, eds. 1999. *Pseira IV: Minoan Buildings in Areas B, C, D, and F.* Philadelphia: University Museum of Pennsylvania.

Betancourt, Philip P., Vassos Karageorghis, Robert Laffineur, and Wolf-Dietrich Niemeier, eds. 1999. *Meletemata: Studies in Aegean Archaeology Presented to Malcolm H. Wiener as He Enters His 65th Year.* Aegaeum 20. 3 vols. Liège: Université de Liège.

Betts, John H. 1981. "The Seal from Shaft Grave Gamma: A 'Mycenaean Chieftain'?" *TUAS* 6:2–8.

Bietak, Manfred. 1994. "Die Wandmalereien aus Tell el Dab'a /'Ezbet Helmi: Erste Eindrücke." *Ägypten und Levante* IV:44–58.

Bietak, Manfred. 1996. *Avaris: The Capital of the Hyksos: Recent Excavations.* London: British Museum Publications Ltd.

Bietak, Manfred. 2004. "Review of Manning, W. 'A Test of Time.'" *Bibliotheca Orientalis* LXI:199–221.

Bietak, Manfred, Nanno Marinatos, and Clairy Palyvou. 2000. "The Maze Tableau from Tell el Dab'a." In Sherratt 2000: 77–90.

Bietak, Manfred, Nanno Marinatos, and Clairy Palyvou. 2007. *Taureador Scenes in Tell el-Dab'a (Avaris) and Knossos.* Vienna: Österreichische Akademie der Wissenschaften.

Bin-Nun, Shoshana R. 1975. *The Tawananna in the Hittite Kingdom.* Texte der Hethiter 5. Heidelberg: Carl Winter.

Biran, Abraham, ed. 1981. *Temples and High Places in Biblical Times. Hebrew Union College Colloquium, 14–16 March 1977.* Jerusalem: The Nelson Glück School of Biblical Archaeology.

Bittel, Kurt. 1976. *Die Hethiter: Die Kunst Anatoliens vom Ende des 3. bis zum Anfang des 1. Jahrtausends vor Christus.* München: Beck.

Bittel, Kurt, Rudolf Nauman, and Heinz Otto. 1941. *Yazilikaya: Architektur, Felsbilder, Inschriften und Kleinfunde.* Wissenschaftliche Veröffentlichung der Deutschen Orientgesellschaft 61. Leipzig: Hinrichs.

Black, Jeremy, and Anthony Green. 1992. *Gods, Demons and Symbols of Ancient Mesopotamia: An Illustrated Dictionary.* Austin: University of Texas Press.

Bleeker, Claas J. 1967. *Egyptian Festivals: Enactments of Religious Renewal.* Leiden: Brill.

Bonnet, Hans. 2000. "Amduat." In *Reallexikon der Ägyptischen Religionsgeschichte:* 17–20. Berlin and New York: W. De Gruyter.

Bosanquet, Robert C., and Richard M. Dawkins. 1923. *The Unpublished Objects from the Palaikastro Excavations, 1902–1906.* BSA Suppl. no. 1. London: Macmillan & Co.

Bossert, Helmut T. 1932. "Santas und Kupapa: Neue Beiträge zur Entzifferung der kretischen und hethitischen Bilderschrift." *Mitteilungen der Altorientalischen Gesellschaft* VI:5–88.

Bossert, Helmut T. 1937. *Altkreta: Kunst und Handwerk in Griechenland Kreta und in der Ägais von den Anfangen bis zur Eisenzeit.* Berlin: Wasmuth.

Bossert, Helmut T. 1944. *Ein Hethitisches Königssiegel: Neue Beiträge zur Geschichte und Entzifferung der Hethitischen Hieroglyphenschrift.* Istanbuler Forschungen 18. Berlin: Wasmuth.

Boulotis, Christos. 1987. "Nochmals zum Prozessionsfresko von Knossos: Palast und Darbringung von Prestige-Objekten." In Hägg and Marinatos 1987, 145–56.

Buccholz, Hans-Günter. 1959. *Zur Herkunft der kretischen Doppelaxt. Geschichte und auswartige Beziehungen eines minoischen Kultsymbols.* München: Kiefhaber & Elbl.

Buchholz, Hans-Günter. 1999. *Ugarit, Zypern und Agais: Kulturbeziehungen im zweiten Jahrtausend v. Chr.* Alter Orient und Altes Testament, Bd 261. Münster: Ugarit Verlag.

Burkert, Walter. 1975. "Resep-Figuren, Apollon von Amyklai und die 'Erfindung' des Opfers auf Cypern. Zur Religionsgeschichte der 'Dunklen Jahrhunderte.'" *Grazer Beiträge* 4:51–79.

Burkert, Walter. 1979. *Structure and History in Greek Mythology and Ritual.* Berkeley: University of California Press.

Burkert, Walter. 1985. *Greek Religion: Archaic and Classical.* Trans. J. Raffan. Oxford: Blackwell.

Burkert, Walter. 1992. *The Orientalizing Revolution: Near Eastern Influence on Greek Culture in the Early Archaic Age.* Transl. W. Burkert and M. E. Pinder. Cambridge: Harvard University Press.

Burkert, Walter. 1996. *Creation of the Sacred: Tracks of Biology in Early Religions.* Cambridge: Harvard University Press.

Burkert, Walter. 2000. "Migrating Gods and Syncretisms: Forms of Cult Transfer in the Ancient Mediterranean." In Burkert et al. 2003, 17–36.

Burkert, Walter. 2004a. *Babylon, Memphis, Persepolis: Eastern Contexts of Greek Culture.* Cambridge: Harvard University Press.

Burkert, Walter. 2004b. "Epiphanies and Signs of Power." In Shanzer and Marinatos 2004, 1–24.

Burkert, Walter, Laura Gemelli Marciano, Franzisca Egli, Lucius Hartmann, and Andreas Schatzmann, eds. 2003. *Kleine Schriften II: Orientalia.* Hypomnemata Suppl.-Reihe 2. Göttingen: Vandenhoeck and Ruprecht.

Cain, C. Dawn. 2001. "Dancing in the Dark: Deconstructing a Narrative of Epiphany on the Isopata Ring." *AJA* 105:27–49.

Cameron, Mark A. S. 1967. "Unpublished Fresco Fragments of a Chariot Composition from Knossos." *AA* 82:330–44.

Cameron, Mark A. S. 1987. "The Palatial Thematic System in the Knossos Murals." In Hägg and Marinatos 1987, 321–29.

Carter, Jane B., and Sarah P. Morris, eds. 1995. *The Ages of Homer: A Tribute to Emily Townsend Vermeule.* Austin: University of Texas Press.

Caubet, Annie. 1999. *l'Acrobat au Taureau: Les découvertes de Tell el-Dab'a et l'archéologie de la Méditerranée orientale. Actes du Colloque Organisée au musée du Louvre, 3 Decémbre 1994.* Paris: Musée du Louvre.

Chadwick, John. 1970. *The Decipherment of Linear B.* Cambridge: Cambridge University Press.

Clifford, Richard J. 1972. *The Cosmic Mountain in Canaan and the Old Testament.* Cambridge: Harvard University Press.

Cline, Eric. 1987. "Amenhotep III and the Aegean: A Reassessment of Egypto-Aegean Relations in the 14th Century BC" *Orientalia* 56:1–36.

Cline, Eric. 1995. "'My Brother, My Son': Rulership and Trade Between the Late Bronze Age Aegean, Egypt and the Near East." In Rehak 1995a, 143–50.

Cline, Eric H., and Diane Harris-Cline, eds. 1998. *The Aegean and the Orient in the Second Millennium. Proceedings of the 50th Anniversary Symposium, University of Cincinnati, 18–20 April 1997.* Aegaeum 18. Liège: Université de Liège.

Collon, Dominique. 1972. "The Smiting God: A Study of a Bronze in the Pomerance Collection in New York." *Levant* 4:111–34.

Collon, Dominique. 1982. *Catalogue of the Westen Asiatic Seals in the British Museum.* Vol. 2, Akkadian, Post Akkadian, Ur III periods. London: Trustees of the British Museum.

Collon, Dominique. 1987. *First Impressions: Cylinder Seals in the Ancient Near East.* Chicago: University of Chicago Press.

Collon, Dominique. 1994. "Bull-Leaping in Syria." *Ägypten und Levante* IV:81–88.

Cornelius, Izak. 1994. *The Iconography of the Canaanite Gods Reshef and Ba'al: Late Bronze Age and Iron Age I periods (c. 1500–1000 BCE).* Orbis Biblicus et Orientalis 140. Fribourg: Academic Press Fribourg.

Cornelius, Izak. 2004. *The Many Faces of the Goddess: The Iconography of the Syro-Palestinian Goddeses Anat, Astarte, Qedeshet, and Asherah c. 1500–1100 BCE.* Orbis Biblicus et Orientalis 204. Fribourg: Academic Press Fribourg.

Crouwel, Joost H. 1981. *Chariots and Other Means of Transport in Bronze Age Greece.* Allard Pierson Series 3. Amsterdam: Allard Pierson Museum.

Crowley, Janice L. 1995. "Images of Power in the Bronze Age Aegean." In Laffineur and Niemeier 1995, 475–91.

Cultraro, Massimo. 2000. "l'Affresco del Cantore di Pilo e l'Investitura del Potere." *Ostraka* IX:9–30.

Cultraro, Massimo. 2001. *l'Anello di Minosse: Archeologia della Regalitá Nell' Egeo Minoico.* Biblioteca di Archeologia. Milano: Longanesi & C.

Dalley, Stephanie. 1989. *Myths from Mesopotamia: Creation, the Flood and Others,* Rev ed., Oxford University Press: Oxford, 2000.

Dalley, Stephanie. 1998. *The Legacy of Mesopotamia.* Oxford: Oxford University Press.

Danthine, Hélène. 1937. *Le Palmier-dattier et les Arbres Sacrés dans l'Iconographie de l'Asie Occidentale Ancienne.* 2 vols. Paris: Republique Française.

Darcque, Pascal, and Jean-Claude Poursat, eds. 1985. *l'Iconographie Minoenne: Actes de la Table Ronde d'Athènes, 21–22 Avril 1983.* BCH Suppl. XI. Paris: Diffusion de Boccard.

Davaras, Costis. 1976. *Guide to Cretan Antiquities.* Park Ridge, N.J.: Noyes Press.

Davaras, Costis. 1986. "Proimes Minoikes Sfragides kai Sfragistiko Daktylidi apo to Spilaio Yerondomouri Lasithiou." *Archaeologike Ephemeris,* 9- 48.

Davaras, Costis. 2003. *Führer zu den Altertümen Kretas,* Athen: Eptalofos.

Davaras, Costis, and Jeffrey Soles. 1995. "A New Oriental Cylinder Seal from Mochlos." *Archaeologike Ephemeris,* 30–66.

Davis, Ellen N. 1995. "Art and Politics in the Aegean: The Missing Ruler." In Rehak 1995a, 11–22.

Davis, Simon. 1967. *The Decipherment of the Minoan Linear A and Pictographic Scripts.* Johannesburg: Witwatersand University Press.

Decker, Wolfgang. 1987. *Sport und Spiel im Alten Ägypten.* Munich: Beck.

Demargne, Pierre. 1949. "La Robe de la Déese Minoenne sur un Cachet de Mallia." *Mélanges d'archéologie et d'histoire offerts à Charles Picard. RA* 29–30:280–88.

Dickinson, Oliver T. P. K. 1994. *The Aegean Bronze Age.* Cambridge: Cambridge University Press.

Dietrich, Bernard C. 1988. "The Instrument of Sacrifice." In Hägg et al. 1988, 35–40.

Dijkstra, Meindert. 1991. "The Weather God on Two Mountains." *Ugarit Forschungen* 23:127–40.

Dimopoulou, Nota, and George Rethemiotakis. 2000. "The 'Sacred Conversation' Ring from Poros." In Müller 2000, 39–56.

Dossin, George. 1939. "Les archives économiques du palais de Mari." *Syria* 20:102–13.

Doumas, Christos, ed. 1978. *Thera and the Aegean World I: Papers Presented at the Second International Scientific Congress, Santorini, Greece, August 1978.* London: Thera and the Aegean World.

Doumas, Christos, ed. 1980. *Thera and the Aegean World II.* London: Thera and the Aegean World.

Doumas, Christos. 1992. *The Wall Paintings of Thera.* Athens: Thera Foundation & Petros M. Nomikos.

Doumas, Christos. 2000. *Museum of Prehistoric Thera.* Athens: Ministry of Culure.

Driessen, Jan, Ilse Schoep, and Robert Laffineur, eds. 2002. *Monuments of Minos: Rethinking the Minoan Palaces. Proceedings of the International Workshop "Crete of the Hundred Palaces?", Université Catholique de Louvain-la-Neuve, 14–15 December 2001.* Aegaeum 23. Liège: Université de Liège.

Durand, Jean.-Marie. 1997. "Les prophéties des textes de Mari." In *Oracles et Prophéties dans l'Antiquité. Actes du Colloque de Strasburg, 15–17 Juin 1995*, ed. J.-G. Heintz, 115–34. Paris: Diffusion de Boccard.

Evans, Arthur J. 1901. "The Mycenaean Tree and Pillar Cult and Its Mediterranean Relations." *JHS* 21:99–204.

Evans, Arthur J. 1909. *Scripta Minoa: The Written Documents of Minoan Crete, with Special Reference to the Archives of Knossos,* Vol 1. Oxford: Clarendon Press.

Evans, Arthur J. 1914. "The 'Tomb of the Double Axes' and Associated Group, and the Pillar Rooms and Ritual Vessels of the 'Little Palace' at Knossos." *Archaeologia* 65:1–94.

Evans-Pritchard, Edward Evan. 1951. *Social Anthropology.* Glencoe: Free Press.

Farnoux, Alexandre. 1995. "La fondation de la Royauté Minoenne: XXème Siècle Avant ou Après Jésus-Christ?" In Laffineur and Niemeier 1995, 323–33.

Faulkner, Raymond O. 1985. *The Ancient Egyptian Book of the Dead.* London: British Museum Press.

Fitton, J. Leslie. 1996. *The Discovery of the Greek Bronze Age.* Cambridge: Harvard University Press.

Fleming, Daniel E. 1992. *The Installation of Baal's High Priestess at Emar: A Window on Ancient Syrian Religion.* Harvard Semitic Studies 42. Harvard: Harvard Semitic Museum.

Foster, K. Pollinger, and R. Laffineur eds. 2003. *Metron, Measuring the Aegean Bronze Age.* Aegaeum 24. Liège: Universite de Liège.

Frankfort, Henri. 1948. *Kingship and the Gods: A Study of Ancient Near Eastern Religion as the Integration of Society and Nature.* Chicago: University of Chicago Press.

Frankfort, Henri. 1954. *The Art and Architecture of the Ancient Orient.* Harmondsworth: Penguin.

Frazer, James George. 1927. *Man God and Immortality: Thoughts on Human Progress, Passages Chosen from the Writings of Sir James George Frazer,* rev. ed. New York: Macmillan.

Frazer, James G. 1949. *The Golden Bough: A Study of Magic and Religion,* abridged ed. London: Macmillan.

Fulco, William J. 1976. *The Canaanite God Reshep.* American Oriental Society Essay 8. New Haven, Conn.: American Oriental Society.

Gaballa, G. A. 1976. *Narrative in Egyptian Art.* Mainz: Philipp von Zabern.

Gaerte, Wilhelm. 1922. "Die 'Horns of Consecration.'" Archiv für Religionswissenschaft 21:72–75.

Genette, Gerard. 1980. *Narrative Discourse: An Essay in Method.* Transl. J. E. Lewin. Ithaca: Cornell University Press.

Gerard-Rousseau, Monique. 1968. *Les Mentions Religieuses dans les Tablettes Mycéniennes.* Incunabula Graeca 29. Rome: Edizioni dell'Ateneo.

Gesell, Geraldine C. 1985. *Town, Palace, and House Cult in Minoan Crete.* SIMA LXVII. Göteborg: Paul Åströms.

Gimbutas, Marija. 1995. *The Language of the Goddess.* San Francisco: Harper.

Goodison, Lucy. 1989. *Death, Women and the Sun: Symbolism of Regeneration in Early Aegean Religion.* BICS Suppl. 53. London: Institute of Classical Studies.

Goodison, Lucy. 2001. "From Tholos Tomb to Throne Room: Perceptions of the Sun in Minoan Ritual." In Laffineur and Hägg 2001, 77–88.

Götze, Albrecht. 1957. *Kleinasien. Kultutrgeschichte des Alten Orients.* München: Beck.

Graf, Fritz. 2004. "What Is Ancient Mediterranean Religion?" In Johnston 2004, 3–16.

Grumach, Ernst, ed. 1958. *Minoica. Festschrift zum 80. Geburtstag von Johannes Sundwall.* Deutsche Akademie der Wissenschaften zu Berlin. Schriften der Sektion für Altertumswissenschaften 12. Berlin: Akademie Verlag.

Guichard, Michaël. 1999. "Les mentions de la Crète à Mari." In Caubet 1999, 165–77.

Gurney, Oliver R. 1952. *The Hittites.* Harmondsworth: Penguin.

Güterbock, Hans G. 1943. "Hethitische Götterdatstellungen und Götternamen." In 26 Sayili Belletin den Ayri Basim, Ankara: 297–317.

Güterbock, Hans G., and Theo P. J. van den Hout. 1991. *The Hittite Instruction for the Royal Bodyguard.* Oriental Institute of Chicago Assyriological Studies 24. Chicago: David Brown Book.

Güterbock, Hans G., and Timothy Kendall. 1995. "A Hittite Silver Vessel in the Form of a Fist." In Carter and Morris 1995, 45–60.

Haas, Volkert. 1982. *Hethitische Berggötter und Hurritische Steindämonen: Ritten, Kulte und Mythen. Eine Einführung in die Altkleinasiatischen Religiösen Vorstellungen.* Kulturgeschichte der Antiken Welt 10. München: Philipp von Zabern.

Hägg, Robin. 1986. "Die Göttliche Epiphanie im Minoischen Ritual." *AM* 101:41–62.

Hägg, Robin. 1987. "On the Reconstruction of the West Façade of the Palace of Knossos." In Hägg and Marinatos 1987, 129–34.

Hägg, Robin, ed. 1997. *The Function of the "Minoan Villa". Proceedings of the Third International Symposium at the Swedish Institute in Athens, 6–8 June 1992.* SkrAth 4°, 46. Stockholm: Paul Åströms.

Hägg, Robin, and Yvonne Lindau. 1984. "The Minoan 'Snake Frame' Reconsidered." *OpAth* 15:67–77.

Hägg, Robin, and Nanno Marinatos, eds. 1981. *Sanctuaries and Cults in the Aegean Bronze Age. Proceedings of the First International Symposium at the Swedish Institute in Athens, 12–13 May 1980.* SkrAth 4°, 28. Stockholm: Paul Åströms.

Hägg, Robin, and Nanno Marinatos, eds. 1984. *The Minoan Thalassocracy: Myth and Reality. Proceedings of the Third International Symposium at the Swedish Institute in Athens, 31 May-5 June 1982.* SkrAth 4°, 32. Stockholm: Paul Åströms.

Hägg, Robin, and Nanno Marinatos, eds. 1987. *The Function of the Minoan Palaces. Proceedings of the Fourth International Symposium at the Swedish Institute in Athens, 10–16 June 1984.* SkrAth 4°, 35. Stockholm: Paul Åströms.

Hägg, Robin, Nanno Marinatos, and Gullög C. Nordquist, eds. 1988. *Early Greek Cult Practice. Proceedings of the Fifth International Symposium at the Swedish Institute in Athens, 26–29 June 1986.* SkrAth 4°, 38. Stockholm: Paul Åströms.

Hall, Jonathan M. 2007. *A History of the Archaic Greek World.* Oxford: Blackell.

Hallager, Eric. 1985. *The Master Impression: A Clay Sealing from the Greek-Swedish Excavations at Kastelli, Khania.* SIMA LXIX. Göteborg: Paul Åströms.

Hallager, Eric. 1990. "Roundels Among Sealings in Mnoan Administration: A Comprehensive Analysis of Function." In Palaima 1990, 121–48.

Hallager, Eric. 1996. *The Minoan Roundel and Other Sealed Documents in the Neopalatial Linear A Administration.* Aegaeum 14. 2 vols. Liège: Université de Liège.

Hamilakis, Yiannis, ed. 2002. *Labyrinth Revisited: Rethinking 'Minoan' Archaeology.* Oxford: Oxbow.

Hardy, David A., Christos G. Doumas, John A. Sakellarakis, and Peter M. Warren, eds. 1990. *Thera and the Aegean World III. Proceedings of the Third International Congress, Santorini, Greece, 3–9 September 1989.* Vol. 1. London: Thera Foundation.

Harrison, Jane E. 1962. *Epilegomena and Themis: A Study of the Social Origins of Greek Religion.* New York: University Books.

Helck, Wolfgang. 1979. *Die Beziehungen Ägyptens und Vorderasiens zur Ägäis bis ins 7. Jahrhundert v. Chr.* Darmstadt: Wissenschaftliche Buchgesellschaft.

Hiller, Stefan. 2000. "Die Kretischen Schriftsysteme und die Palatiale Administration." In Siebenmorgen 2000, 121–42.

Hitchcock, Louise A. 2000. *Minoan Architecture: A Contextual Analysis.* SIMA Pocket Book 55. Jonsered: Paul Åströms.

Hitchcock, Louise A., and Paul Koudounaris. 2002. "Virtual Discourse: Arthur Evans and the Reconstructions of the Minoan Palace at Knossos." In Hamilakis 2002, 40–58.

Hoffner, Harry A., and Gary M. Beckman, eds. 1986. *Kanissuwar. A Tribute to Hans G. Güterbock on his Seventy-fifth Birthday, May 27, 1983.* Assyriological Studies No. 23. Chicago: The Oriental Institute of the University of Chicago.

Hood, Sinclair. 1971. *The Minoans: Crete in the Bronze Age.* London: Thames and Hudson.

Hood, Sinclair. 1977. "Minoan Town Shrines?" In *Greece and the Eastern Mediterranean in Ancient History and Prehistory: Studies Presented to Fritz Schachermeyr on the Occasion of his Eightieth Birthday,* ed. K. H. Kitzl, 158–72. Berlin: de Gruyter.

Hood, Sinclair. 1978. *The Arts in Prehistoric Greece.* Harmondsworth: Penguin.

Hornung, Erik. 1982. *Conceptions of God in Ancient Egypt: The One and the Many.* Transl. J. Baines. Ithaca: Cornell University Press.

Hornung, Erik. 1990a. *The Valley of the Kings: Horizon of Eternity.* Transl. D. Warburton. New York: Timken Publisher.

Hornung, Erik. 1990b. *Das Totenbuch der Ägypter.* Zürich and München: Artemis.

Horowitz, Wayne. 1998. *Mesopotamian Cosmic Geography.* Mesopotamian Civilizations 8. Winnona Lake: Eisenbrauns.

Immerwahr, Sara A. 1990. *Aegean Painting in the Bronze Age.* University Park: Pennsylvania State University Press.

Immerwahr, Sara A. 1995. "Death and the Tanagra Larnakes." In Carter and Morris 1995, 109–22.

Jakob-Rost, Liane, Evelyn Klengel-Brandt, Joachim Marzahn, and Ralf-B. Wartke. 1992. *Das Vorderasiatische Museum.* Berlin: Staatliche Museen zu Berlin und Preusischer Kulturbesitz: Philipp von Zabern.

Johnston, Sarah I., ed. 2004. *Religions of the Ancient World: A Guide.* Harvard University Press Reference Library. Cambridge: Belknap Press.

Jones, Donald W. 1999. *Peak Sanctuaries and Sacred Caves in Minoan Crete: A Comparison of Artifacts.* SIMA Pocket Book 156. Jonsered: Paul Åströms.

Jung, Helmut. 1989. "Methodisches zur Hermeneutik der minoischen und mykenischen Bilddenkmäler." In Müller 1989, 91–110.

Kanta, Athanasia. 1973. "Ysterominoiki Sarkophagos apo to Horion Maroulas Rethymnes." *Athens Annals of Archaeology* 6:315–23.

Karageorghis, Vassos, and Nikolaos Stambolidis, eds. 1998. *Eastern Mediterranean: Cyprus, Dodecanese, Crete 16th-6th cent.* BC*: Proceedings of the International Symposium, Rethymnon, 13–16 May 1997.* Athens: University of Crete, A. G. Leventis Foundation.

Karetsou, Alexandra. 1981. "The Peak Sanctuary of Mt. Juktas." In Hägg and Marinatos 1981, 137–53.

Karetsou, Alexandra, ed. 2000. *Crete and Egypt: Three Thousand Years of Cultural Links (Herakleion Archaeological Museum).* Athens: Greek Ministry of Culture.

Karo, Georg. 1930–33. *Die Schachtgräber von Mykenai.* München: Bruckmann.

Keel, Othmar. 1978. *The Symbolism of the Biblical World: Ancient Near Eastern Iconography and the Book of Psalms.* Transl. T. J. Hallett. New York: Seabury Press.

Keel, Othmar. 1992. *Das Recht der Bilder Gesehen zu Werden: Drei Fallstudien zur Methode der Interpretation Altorientalischer Bilder.* Orbis Biblicus et Orientalis 122. Fribourg: Academic Press Fribourg.

Keel, Othmar. 1994. *The Song of Songs.* Minneapolis: Augsburg Fortress.

Keel, Othmar. 1995. *Corpus der Stempelsiegel-Amulette aus Palästina/Israel von den Anfangen bis zur Perserzeit Einleitung.* Orbis Biblicus et Orientalis Series Archaeologica 10. Friburg: Academic Press Fribourg and Göttingen: Vandenhoeck and Ruprecht.

Keel, Othmar. 1998. *Goddesses and Trees, New Moon and Yahweh: Ancient Near Eastern Art and the Hebrew Bible.* Sheffield: Sheffield Academic Press.

Keel, Othmar, and Sylvia Schroer. 1985. *Studien zu den Stempelsiegeln aus Palästina/ Israel I.* Orbis Biblicus et Orientalis 67. Fribourg: Academic Press Fribourg.

Keel, Othmar, and Sylvia Schroer. 1998. "Darstellungen des Sonnenlaufs und Totenbuchvignetten auf Skarabäen." *ZÄS* 125:13–29.

Keel, Othmar, and Sylvia Schroer. 2006. *Eva-Mutter alles Lebendingen: Frauen- und Göttinenidole aus dem Alten Orien,* 2d ed. Fribourg: Academic Press Fribourg.

Keel, Othmar, and Christoph Uehlinger. 1995. *Göttinnen, Götter und Gottessymbole: Neue Erkenntnisse zur Religionsgeschichte Kanaans und Israels Aufgrund Bislang Unerschlossener Ikonographischer Quellen. Quaestiones Disputatae* 134. Fribourg, Basel, Wien: Herder.

Kenna, Victor E. G. 1971. *Catalogue of the Cypriote Seals of the Bronze Age in the British Museum.* Göteborg: Paul Åströms.

Kilian-Dirlmeier, Imma. 1987. "Das Kuppelgrab von Vapheio (Lakonien): Die Beigabenausstattung in der Steinkiste: Untersuchungen zur Sozialstruktur in späthelladischer Zeit." *Jahrbuch des Römisch-Germanischen Zentralmuseums* 34:197–212.

Kitchen, Kenneth A. 1982. *Pharaoh Triumphant. The Life and Times of Ramesses II.* Cairo: Benben.

Koehl, Robert B. 1986. "The Chieftain Cup and a Minoan Rite of Passage." *JHS* 106: 99–110.

Koehl, Robert B. 1995. "The Nature of Minoan Kingship." In Rehak 1995a, 23–36.

Koehl, Robert B. 1997. "The Villas at Ayia Triada and Nirou Chani and the Origin of the Cretan *andreion.*" In Hägg 1997, 137–49.

Koehl, Robert B. 2001. "The 'Sacred Marriage' in Minoan Religion and Ritual." In Laffineur and Hägg 2001, 237–43.

Kourou, Nota. 2001. "The Sacred Tree in Greek Art. Mycenaean Versus Near Eastern Traditions." In Ribichini et al. 2001, 31–54.

Krattenmaker, Kathleen. 1995a. "Palace, Peak and Sceptre: The Iconography of Legitimacy." In Rehak 1995a, 49–62.

Krattenmaker, Kathleen. 1995b. "Architecture in Glyptic Cult Scenes: The Minoan Examples." In Müller 1995, 117–33.

Krzyszkowska, Olga, and Lucia Nixon, eds. 1983. *Minoan Society. Proceedings of the Cambridge Colloquium 1981.* Bristol: Bristol Classical Press.

Kyriakidis, Evangelos. 2005. "Unidentified Objects on Minoan Seals." *AJA* 109:137–54.

Laffineur, Robert, ed. 1987. *Thanatos: Les coutumes funéraires en Egée à l'âge du Bronze. Actes du colloque de Liège, 21–23 Avril 1986.* Aegaeum 1. Liège: Université de Liège.

Laffineur, Robert, ed. 1989. *Transition: Le monde égéen du Bronze moyen au Bronze récent. Actes de la 2e Rencontre égéenne internationale de l'Université de Liège, 18–20 Avril 1988.* Aegaeum 3. Liège: Université de Liège.

Laffineur, Robert, and Janice Crowley, ed. 1992. *Eikon: Aegean Bronze Age Iconography: Shaping a Methodology. Proceedings of the 4th International Aegean Conference, University of Tasmania, Hobart, Australia, 6–9 April 1992.* Aegeaeum 8. Liège: Université de Liège.

Laffineur, Robert, and Robin Hägg, eds. 2001. *Potnia: Deities and Religion in the Aegean Bronze Age. Proceedings of the 8th International Aegean Conference, Göteborg University, 12–15 April 2000.* Aegeaum 22. Liège: Université de Liège.

Laffineur, Robert, and Wolf-Dietrich Niemeier, eds. 1995. *Politeia: Society and State in the Aegean Bronze Age. Proceedings of the 5th International Aegean Conference, University of Heidelberg, Archäologisches Institut, 10–13 April 1994.* Aegaeum 12. 2 vols. Liège: Université de Liège.

Lambert, Wilfred G. 1996. *Babylonian Wisdom Literature.* Winona Lake, Ind.: Eisenbrauns.

Lang, Mabel L. 1969. *The Frescoes.* Vol 3 of *The Palace of Nestor at Pylos in Western Messenia.* Princeton: Princeton University Press.

Lange, Kurt, Max Hirmer. 1956. *Aegypten: Architektur, Plastik, Malerei in Drei Jahrtausenden.* 2nd ed. München: Hirmer.

Lapatin, Kenneth. 2002. *Mysteries of the Snake Goddess: Art, Desire, and the Forging of History.* Boston: Houghton Miffin.

Laroche, Emanuel. 1960. *Les Hiéroglyphes Hittites.* Paris: CNRS.

Lebessi, Aggeliki, and Polymnia Muhly. 1990. "Aspects of Minoan Cult: Sacred Enclosures. The Evidence from the Syme Sanctuary (Crete)." *AA:* 315–336.

Lebessi, Aggeliki, Polymnia Muhly, and George Papassavas. 2004. "The Runner's Ring. A Minoan Athlete's Dedication at the Syme Sanctuary, Crete." *AM* 119:1–31.

Levi, Doro. 1925–26a. "Le cretule di Hagia Triada presso Phaistos." *ASAtene* 8–9:71–156.

Levi, Doro. 1925–26b. "Le cretule di Zakro." *ASAtene* 8–9: 157–201.

Long, Charlotte L. 1974. *The Ayia Triadha Sarcophagus: A Study of Late Minoan and Mycenaean Funerary Practices and Beliefs.* SIMA XLI. Göteborg: Paul Åströms.

Loud, Gordon. 1939. *The Megiddo Ivories.* Chicago: University of Chicago.

Lurker, Manfred. 1980. *The Gods and Symbols of Ancient Egypt.* London: Thames and Hudson.

MacGillivray, Joseph A. 2000a. "The Religious Context." In *The Palaikastro Kouros: A Minoan Chryselephantine Statuette and Its Aegean Bronze Age Context,* eds. J. A. MacGillvray, J. M. Driessen, and L. H. Sackett, 123–30. BSA Studies 6. London: British School at Athens.

MacGillivray, Joseph A. 2000b. "Labyrinths and Bull-Leapers." *Archaeology* 53: 53–56.

MacGillivray, Joseph A. 2000c. *Minotaur: Sir Arthur Evans and the Archaeology of the Minoan Myth.* London: Jonathan Cape.

Manning, Sturt W. 1999. *A Test of Time: The Volcano of Thera and the Chronology and History of the Aegean and East Mediterranean in the mid-Second Millennium B.C.* Oxford: Oxbow.

Maran, Joseph, and Eftychia Stavrianopoulou. 2007. "Potnios Aner: Reflections on the Ideology of Mycenaean Kingship." In Alram-Stern and Nightingale, 350.

Marinatos, Nanno. 1984a. "The Date-palm in Minoan Iconography and Religion." *OpAth* 15:115–22.

Marinatos, Nanno. 1984b. "Minoan Threskeiocracy on Thera." In Hägg and Marinatos 1984, 167–78.

Marinatos, Nanno. 1986. *Minoan Sacrificial Ritual: Cult Practice and Symbolism.* SkrAth 8°, IX. Stockholm: Paul Åströms.

Marinatos, Nanno. 1987. "Public Festivals in the West Courts of the Palaces." In Hägg and Marinatos 1987, 135–43.

Marinatos, Nanno. 1989. "The Tree as a Focus of Ritual Action in Minoan Glyptic Art." In Müller 1989, 127–43.

Marinatos, Nanno. 1990. "Minoan-Cycladic Syncretism." In Hardy et al. 1990, 370–77.

Marinatos, Nanno. 1993. *Minoan Religion: Ritual, Image and Symbol.* Columbia: University of South Carolina Press.

Marinatos, Nanno. 1995. "Divine Kingship in Minoan Crete." In Rehak 1995a, 37–48.

Marinatos, Nanno. 1997. "Minoan and Mycenaean Larnakes: a Comparison." In *La Crète Mycénienne: Actes de la table Ronde Internationale Organisée par l'ecole Francaise d' Athènes, 26–28 Mars 1991,* eds. J. Driessen and A. Farnoux, 281–92. BCH Suppl. 30. Paris: De Boccard.

Marinatos, Nanno. 2000. "Nature as Ideology: Landscapes on the Theran Ships." In Sherratt 2000, 907–13.

Marinatos, Nanno. 2002. "The Cosmic Journey of Odysseus." *Numen* 48: 383–416.

Marinatos, Nanno. 2004. "The Character of Minoan Epiphanies." In Shanzer and Marinatos 2004: 25–42.

Marinatos, Nanno, and Robin Hägg. 1983. "Anthropomorphic Cult Images in Minoan Crete?" In Krzyszkowska and Nixon 1983, 185–201.

Marinatos, Spyridon. 1926. "Minoiki kai Homeriki Skylla." *Archaiologikon Deltion* X:51–62.

Marinatos, Spyridon. 1939. "The Volcanic Destruction of Minoan Crete." *Antiquity* 13:425–39.

Marinatos, Spyridon. 1967. *Kleidung Haar- und Barttracht.* Archaeologia Homerica, Band 1:A, B. Göttingen: Vandenhoeck & Ruprecht.

Marinatos, Spyridon. 1976. *Excavations at Thera VII. 1973 Season.* Athens: Archaeological Society at Athens.

Marinatos, Spyridon, and Max Hirmer. 1976. *Kreta, Thera and das Mykenische Hellas.* München: Hirmer.

Markoe, Glenn. 1985. *Phoenician Bronze and Silver Bowls from Cyprus and the Mediterranean.* Classical Studies 26. Berkeley: University of California Publications.

Matthiae, Paolo. 1984. *I Tesori di Ebla,* Roma-Bari: Laterza.

Matz, Friedrich. 1958. *Göttererscheinung und Kultbild im minoischen Kreta.* Abhandlungen der Geistes und Sozialwissenschaftlichen Klasse, Akademie der Wissenschaften und der Literatur in Mainz vol. 7. Wiesbaden: Akademie der Wissenschaften und der Literatur.

Mavriyiannaki, Katerina. 1972. *Recherches sur les larnakes minoennes de la Créte Occidentale.* Incunabula Graeca 54. Roma: Edizioni dell'Ateneo.

Meissner, Bruno. 1920–1925. *Babylonien und Assyrien I–II.* Heidelberg: Carl Winters Universitätsbuchhandlung.

Mettinger, Tryggve N. D. 1995. *No Graven Image? Israelite Aniconism in Its Ancient Near Eastern Context.* Coniectanea Biblica. Old Testament Series 42. Stockholm: Almqvist & Wiksell.

Mettinger, Tryggve N. D. 2001. *The Riddle of Resurrection. Dying and Rising Gods in the Ancient Near East.* Coniectanea Biblica. Old Testament Series 50. Stockholm: Almqvist & Wiksell.

Mirie, Sieglinde. 1979. *Das Thronraumareal des Palastes von Knossos. Versuch einer Neuinterpretation seiner Entstehung und seiner Funktion.* Saarbrücker Beiträge zur Altertumswissenschaft 26. Bonn: Habelt.

Moran, William L. 1992. *The Amarna Letters.* Baltimore: Johns Hopkins University Press.

Morgan, Lyvia. 1985. "Idea, Idiom and Iconography." In Darcque and Poursat 1985, 5–19.

Morgan, Lyvia. 1988. *The Wall Paintings from Thera: A Study in Aegean Culture and Iconography.* Cambridge: Cambridge University Press.

Morgan, Lyvia, ed. 2005. *Aegean Wall Painting: A Tribute to Mark Cameron.* BSA Studies 13. London: British School at Athens.

Morris, Christine. 2001. "The Language of Gesture in Minoan Religion." In Laffineur and Hägg 2001, 245–51.

Moss, M. L. 2005. *The Minoan Pantheon: Towards an Understanding of Its Nature and Extent.* BAR International Series 343. Oxford: John and Erica Hedges Ltd.

Müller, Walter, ed. 1989. *Fragen und Probleme der Bronzezeitlichen Ägäischen Glyptik: Beiträge zum 3. Internationalen Marburger Siegel-Symposium 5–7 September 1985.* CMS Beiheft 3. Berlin: Gebr. Mann.

Müller, Walter, ed. 1995. *Sceaux Minoens et Mycéniens.* CMS Beiheft 5. Berlin: Gebr. Mann.

Müller, Walter, ed. 2000. *Minoisch-mykenische Glyptik: Stil, Ikonographie, Funktion: Ergebnisse eines Internationalen Siegelsymposiums, Marburg, 23.-25. September 1999.* CMS Beiheft 6. Berlin: Gebr. Mann.

Munn, Mark H. 2006. *The Mother of the Gods, Athens, and the Tyranny of Asia: A Study of Sovereignty in Ancient Religion.* Berkeley: University of California Press.

Nickelsburg, George W. E. 2001. *1 Enoch 1: A Commentary on the Book of 1 Enoch, Chapters 1–36; 81–108.* Minneapolis: Fortress.

Niemeier, Wolf-Dietrich. 1981. *Studien zur Minoischen und Helladischen Glyptik: Beiträge zum 2. Marburger Siegel-Symposium 26–30 September 1978.* CMS Beiheft 1. Berlin: Gebr. Mann.

Niemeier, Wolf-Dietrich. 1985. *Die Palaststilkeramik von Knossos: Stil, Chronologie und historischer Kontext.* Archäologische Forschungen des Deutschen Archäologischen Instituts 13. Berlin: Gebr. Mann.

Niemeier, Wolf-Dietrich. 1986. "Zur Deutung des Thronraumes im Palast von Knossos." *AM* 101: 63–95.

Niemeier, Wolf-Dietrich. 1987. "Das Stuckrelief des 'Prinzen mit der Federkrone' aus Knossos und Minoische Götterdarstellungen." *AM* 102: 65–98.

Niemeier, Wolf-Dietrich. 1989. "Zur Ikonographie von Gottheiten und Adoranten in den Kultszenen auf Minoischen und Mykenischen Siegeln." In Müller 1989, 163–86.

Niemeier, Wolf-Dietrich, and Barbara Niemeier. 1999. "The Minoans of Miletus." In Betancourt et al. 1999: 543–554.

Niemeier, Wolf-Dietrich, and Barbara Niemeier. 2000. "Aegean Frescoes in Syria-Palestine: Alalakh and Tel Kabri." In Sherratt 2000, 763–802.

Nilsson, Martin P. 1950. *The Minoan-Mycenaean Religion and Its Survival in Greek Religion.* 2d ed. Lund: Kungl. Humanistiska Vetenskapssamfundet.

Nissinen, Martti. 2001a. "Akkadian Rituals and Poetry of Divine Love." In Whiting 2001, 93–136.

Nissinen, Martti, ed. 2003. *Prophets and Prophecy in the Ancient Near East.* Writings from the Ancient World 12. Society of Biblical Literature. Atlanta: Brill.

Nissinen, Martti. 2004. "What Is Prophecy? An Ancient Near Eastern Perspective." In *Inspired Speech: Prophecy in the Ancient Near East. Essays in Honor of Herbert B. Huffmon,* eds. J. Kaltner and L. Stulman, 17–37. Journal for the Study of the Old Testament, Supplement Series 378. London and New York: T&T Clark.

Oates, Joan. 1986. *Babylon.* 2d ed. London: Thames and Hudson.

Olyan, Saul M. 1988. *Asherah and the Cult of Yahweh in Israel.* Society of Biblical Literature Monograph Series. Atlanta: Scholars Press.

Ornan, Tallay. 2001. "Istar as Depicted on Finds from Israel." In *Studies in the Archaeology of the Iron Age in Israel and Jordan,* eds. A. Mazar and G. Mathias, 235–56. *Journal for the Study of the Old Testament,* Supplement Series 331. Sheffield: Sheffield Academic Press.

Otto, Adelheid. 2000. *Die Entstehung und Entwicklung der Klassish-Syrischen Glyptik.* Untersuchungen zur Assyriologie und Vorderasiatische Archaeologie 8. Berlin: de Gruyter.

Otto, Brinna. 2001. "Der Altkretische Jahresgott und seine Feste." In *Kreta und Zypern: Religion und Schrift. Von der Frühgeschichte bis zum Ende der Archaischen Zeit. 26.-28.2.1999, Ohlstadt / Oberbayern - Deutschland,* eds. A. Kyriatsoulis, 27–48. Altenburg: DZA Verlag für Kultur und Wissenschaft.

Owens, Gareth A. 1996a. "Evidence for the Minoan Language: The Minoan Libation Formula." *Cretan Studies* 5:163–208.

Owens, Gareth A. 1996b. "'All Religions Are One' (William Blake 1757–1827), Astarte/Ishtar/Ishassaras/Asasarame: The Great Mother Goddess of Minoan Crete and the Eastern Mediterranean." *Cretan Studies* 5:209–18.

Palaima, Thomas G., ed. 1990. *Aegean Seals, Sealings and Administration. Proceedings of the NEH-Dickson Conference of the Program in Aegean Scripts and Prehistory of the Department of Classics, University of Texas at Austin, January 11–13, 1989.* Aegaeum 5. Liège: Université de Liège.

Palaima, Thomas G. 1995. "The Nature of the Mycenaean Wanax: Non-Indo-European Origins and Priestly Functions." In Rehak 1995a, 119–42.

Palyvou, Clairy. 2005. "Architecture in Aegean Bronze Age Art: Façades with No Interiors." In Morgan 2005, 185–98.

Pardee, Dennis. 2002. *Ritual and Cult at Ugarit.* Writings from the Ancient World 10. Society of Biblical Literature. Atlanta: Brill.

Paribeni, Roberto. 1904. "Ricerche nel Sepolcreto di Haghia Triada presso Phaestos." *Monumenti Antichi* 14:677–755.

Paribeni, Roberto. 1908. "Il sarcophago dipinto di Hagia Triada." *Monumenti Antichi* 19:5–87.

Parrot, André. 1958. *Mission archéologique de Mari.* Vol. II, *Le Palais.* Paris: Geuthner.

Peatfield, Alan A. 1983. "The Topography of Minoan Peak Sanctuaries." *BSA* 78:273–79.

Peatfield, Alan A. 1987. "Palace and Peak: The Political and Religious Relationship between Palaces and Peak Sanctuaries." In Hägg and Marinatos 1987, 89–93.

Peatfield, Alan A. 1990. "Minoan Peak Sanctuaries: History and Society." *OpAth* 18:117–32.

Peatfield, Alan A. 1992. "Rural Ritual in Bronze Age Crete: The Peak Sanctaury at Atsipadhes." *CAJ* 2:59–87.

Pecchioli Daddi, Franca. 2001. "Lotte di dèi per la supremazia celeste." In Ribichini et al. 2001, 403–11.

Pelon, Olivier. 1995. "Royauté et Iconographie Royale dans la Crète Minoenne." In Laffineur and Niemeier 1995, 309–21.

Pendlebury, John D. S. 1939. *The Archaeology of Crete: An Introduction.* London: Methuen.

Perrot, Georges, and Charles Chipiez. 1887. *Histoire del'Art dans l'Antiquité Tome IV: Judée, Sardaigne, Syrie, Cappadoce.* Paris: Librairie Hachette et Cie.

Persson, Axel W. 1942. *The Religion of Greece in Prehistoric Times.* Berkeley: University of California Press.

Pini, Ingo. 1971. "Ein Siegelabdruck im Archäologischen Museum Iraklion." In *Pepragmena tou Tritou Diethnous Cretologikou Synedriou, Rethymno, 18–23 September 1971*, 221–230. Rethymno: Dimos Rethymnis.

Pini, Ingo. 1981. "Echt oder Falsch?—Einige Fälle." In Niemeier 1981, 135–58.

Pini, Ingo. 1989. "Zur 'Richtigen' Ansicht Minoisch-Mykenisher Siegel- und Ringdarstellungen." In Müller 1989, 201–18.

Pini, Ingo. 2000. "Der Aussagewert von Bildthemen für die Chronologie der Spätbronzezeitlichen Glyptik." In Müller 2000, 239–44.

Platon, Lefteris. 2003. "To Anaglypho Rhyto tis Zakrou Kato Apo Ena Neo Semasiologiko Prisma." In *Argonautis: Fetschrift for Prof. Doumas*, eds. A. Vlachopoulos and K. Birtaha, 331–66. Athens: I Kathimerini.

Platon, Nikolaos. 1951. "To Ieron Maza kai ta Minoika Iera Koryfis." *CretChron* 5:96–160.

Platon, Nikolaos. 1954. "Ta minoika oikiaka iera." *CretChron* 8:428–83.

Platon, Nikolaos. 1958. "Inscribed Libation Vessel from a Minoan House at Prassa, Herakleion." In Grumach 1958, 305–18.

Platon, Nikolaos. 1971. *Zakros: The Discovery of a Lost Palace of Ancient Crete.* New York: Scribner.

Popham, Mervyn. 1974. "Sellopoulo Tombs 3 and 4. Two Late Minoan Graves near Knossos." *BSA* 69:195–257.

Porada, Edith. 1984. "The Cylinder Seal from Tell el Dab'a." *AJA* 88:485–88.

Pötscher, Walter. 1990. *Aspekte und Probleme der Minoischen Religion: Ein Versuch.* Religionswissenschaftliche Texte und Studien 4. Hildesheim, Zurich and New York: Olms.

Poursat, Jean-Claude. 1977. *Catalogue des Ivoires Mycèniens du Museè National d' Athènes.* Bibliotheque des ecoles Françaises d' Athènes et de Rome fasc. 230. Athènes: ecole Francaise d' Athènes.

Powell, Barry B. 1977. "The Significance of the So-Called 'Horns of Consecration.'" *Kadmos* 16:70–82.

Preziosi, Donald, and Louise A. Hitchcock. 1999. *Aegean Art and Architecture.* Oxford: Oxford University Press.

Ramsey, J. T. 2006. *A Descriptive Catalogue of Comets from 500 BC to AD 400.* Syllecta Classics XVII. Iowa: University of Iowa.

Reade, Julian. 1983. *Assyrian Sculpture.* British Museum. London: British Museum Publications.

Redford, Donald B. 1984. *Akhenaten: The Heretic King.* Princeton: Princeton University Press.

Reeves, Nicholas. 1990. *The Complete Tutankhamun: The King, the Tomb, the Royal Treasure.* London: Thames and Hudson.

Rehak, Paul. 1994. "The Aegean 'Priest' on CMS I.223." *Kadmos* 33:76–84.

Rehak, Paul, ed. 1995a. *The Role of the Ruler in the Prehistoric Aegean. Proceedings of a Panel Discussion presented at the Annual Meeting of the Archaeological Institute of America, New Orleans, Louisiana, 28 December 1992.* Aegaeum 11. Liège: Université de Liège.

Rehak, Paul. 1995b. "Enthroned Figures in Aegean Art and the Function of the Mycenaean Megaron." In Rehak 1995a, 95–118.

Rehak, Paul. 2002. "The Isopata Ring." In Müller 2000, 269–75.

Rehak, Paul, and John Younger. 2001. "Review of Aegean Prehistory VII: Neopalatial, Final Palatial, and Postpalatial Crete; Addendum 1998–1999." In *Aegean Prehistory: A Review,* ed. T. Cullen, 383–465. AJA Suppl. 1. Boston: Archaeological Institute of America.

Renfrew, Colin. 1985. *The Archaeology of Cult: The Sanctuary at Phylakopi.* BSA Suppl. 18. London: Thames & Hudson.

Rethemiotakis, George. 1979. "Larnakes kai Aggeia apo to Kavrochori Irakliou." *ArchDelt* 34, Meletai B2:228–59.

Rethemiotakis, George. 1995. "Minoiki Larnaka apo to Klima Mesaras." *Archaeologike Ephemeris,* 163–83.

Rethemiotakis, George. 1997. "A Chest-Shaped Vessel and Other LM IIIC Pottery from Kastelli Pediada." In *La Crète Mycénienne: Actes de la table Ronde Internationale Organisée par l'ecole Francaise d' Athènes, 26–28 Mars 1991,* eds. J. Driessen and A. Farnoux, 407–421. BCH Suppl. 30. Paris: De Boccard.

Rethemiotakis, George. 1999. "The Hearths of the Minoan Palace at Galatas." In Betancourt et al. 1999, 721–28.

Rethemiotakis, George. 2002. "Evidence of Social and Economic Changes at Galatas and Pediada in the New-Palace Period." In Driessen et al. 2002, 55–69.

Rethemiotakis, George. 2003. "The Sacred Mansion Ring from Poros, Herakleion." *AM* 118:1–22.

Reusch, Helga. 1958. "Zum Wandschmuck des Thronsaales in Knossos." In Grumach 1958, 334–58.

Ribichini, Sergio, Maria Rocchi, and Paolo Xella. 2001. *La Questione delle Influenze Vicino-Orientali sulla Religione Greca: Stato degli Studi e Prospettive della Ricerca.*

Atti del Colloquio Internazionale, Roma, 20–22 maggio 1999. Roma: Consiglio Nationale delle Ricerche.

Rieu, E. V., and Peter Jones, transl., with D. C. H. Rieu. 2003. *Homer's Iliad,* rev. ed., New York: Penguin Books.

Rutkowski, Bogdan. 1966. *Larnaksy Egejskie.* Instytut Historii Kultury Materialnej Polskiej Akademii Nauk. Bibliotheca antiqua; vol. 7. Warszawa: Polskiej Akademii Nauk.

Rutkowski, Bogdan. 1981. *Frühgriechische Kultdarstellungen.* AM Beiheft 8. Berlin: Gebr. Mann.

Rutkowski, Bogdan. 1986. *The Cult Places of the Aegean.* New Haven: Yale University Press.

Rutkowski, Bogdan. 1988. "Minoan Peak Sanctuaries: The Topography and Architecture." *Aegaeum* 2:71–100.

Sakellarakis, Effie, and Yannis Sakellarakis. 1984. "The Keftiu and the Minoan Thalassocracy." In Hägg and Marinatos 1984, 197–203.

Sakellarakis, John A. 1967. "Minoan Cemeteries at Arkhanes." *Archaeology* 20:276–81.

Sakellarakis, John A. 1971. "Über die Echtheit des Sogenannten Nestorringes." In *Pepragmena tou Tritou Diethnous Cretologikou Synedriou, Rethymno, 18–23 September 1971,* 303–18. Rethymno: Dimos Rethymnis.

Sakellarakis, John, and Effie Sakellarakis. 1991. *Crete: Archanes.* Athens: Ekdotiki Athinon.

Saleh, Mohamed, and Hourig Sourouzian. 1986. Die Hauptwerke im Ägyptischen Museum Kairo. Offizieller Katalog. Mainz: Philipp von Zabern.

Sapouna-Sakellaraki, Effie. 1971. *Minoikon Zoma (Minoan Zoma).* The Archaeological Society at Athens Library Series 71. Athens: The Archaeological Society at Athens.

Schroer, Sylvia. 1985. "Der Mann in Wulstsaummantel. Ein Motiv der Mittelbronzezeit IIB." In Keel and Schroer 1985.

Shanzer, Danuta, ed., and Nanno Marinatos, guest ed. 2004. *Divine Epiphanies in the Ancient World.* Illinois Classical Studies 29. Urbana: University of Illinois.

Shaw, Joseph. 1978. "Evidence for the Minoan Tripartite Shrine." *AJA* 82:429–48.

Shaw, Maria C. 1970. "Ceiling Patterns from the Tomb of Hepzefa." *AJA* 74:25–30.

Shaw, Maria C. 1986. "The Lion Gate Relief of Mycenae Reconsidered." In *Philia Epi to George E. Mylonas to Commemorate His Sixty Years as an Excavator,* 108–23. The Archaeological Society at Athens Library Series 103, vol. 1. Athens: The Archaeological Society at Athens.

Shaw, Maria C. 2004. "The 'Priest-King' Fresco from Knossos: Man, Woman, Priest, King, or Someone Else?" In *Charis: Essays in Honor of Sara A. Immerwahr,* edited by A. P. Chapin, 65–84. Hesperia Supplement 33. Princeton: American School of Classical Studies at Athens.

Sherratt, Susan, ed. 2000. *The Wall Paintings of Thera. Proceedings of the First International Symposium, Thera, Hellas, 30 August-4 September 1997.* 3 vols. Piraeus: Petros M. Nomikos and the Thera Foundation.

Siebenmorgen, Harald, ed. 2000. *Im Labyrinth des Minos: Kreta—die erste europäische*

Hochkultur. Ausstellung des Badischen Landesmuseums 27.1 bis 29.4.2001, Karlsruhe, Schloss. München: Biering & Brinkmann: Archäologische Veröffentlichungen des Badischen Landesmuseums.

Sippel, Donald V. 1986a. "The Supposed Site of the Cretan Labyrinth." *The Ancient World* 14:67–79.

Sippel, Donald V. 1986b. "Minoan Religion and the Sign of the Double Axe." *The Ancient World* 14:87–94.

Smith, Mark. 2004. "Israel Monotheism." In Johnston 2004, 402–3.

Sourvinou-Inwood, Christiane. 1971. "On the Authenticity of the Ashmolean Ring 1919.56." *Kadmos* 10:60–69.

Sourvinou-Inwood, Christiane. 1973. "On the Lost 'Boat' Ring from Mochlos." *Kadmos* 12:149–58.

Sourvinou-Inwood, Christiane. 1989. "Space in Late Minoan Religious Scenes in Glyptik: Some Remarks." In Müller 1989, 241–57.

Stadelmann, Rainer. 1967. *Syrisch-Palästinensische Gottheiten in Ägypten.* Probleme der Ägyptologie 5. Leiden: Brill.

Steel, Louise. 1994. "Representations of a Shrine on a Mycenaean Chariot Krater from Kalavassos-Ayios Dimitrios, Cyprus." *BSA* 89:201–11.

Stevenson Smith, William S. 1965. *Interconnections in the Ancient Near East: A Study of the Relationships between the Arts of Egypt, the Aegean, and Western Asia.* New Haven: Yale University Press.

Strasburger, Gisela. 1998. "Die Fahrt des Odysseus zu den Toten im Vergleich mit Älteren Jenseitsfahrten." *Antike und Abendland* 44:1–29.

Sugaya, Charles. 2000. "A Foreign Goddess in the Minoan World." In *Pepragmena tou Ogdoou Diethnous Cretologikou Synedriou, Herakleion, 9–14 September 1996,* vol. A3, 273–86. Herakleion: Society of Cretan Historical Studies.

Teissier, Beatrice. 1984. *Ancient Near Eastern Cylinder Seals from the Marcopoli Collection.* Berkeley: University of California Press.

Teissier, Beatrice. 1996. *Egyptian Topography on Syro-Palestinian Cylinder Seals of the Middle Bronze Age.* Orbis Biblicus et Orientalis Series Archaeologica 11. Fribourg: Academic Press Fribourg.

Thimme, Jürgen, Paul Aström, Giovanni Lilliu, and Joseph Wiesner. 1968. *Frühe Randkulturen des Mittelmeerraumes: Kykladen, Zypern, Malta, Altsyrien.* Kunst der Welt. Baden-Baden: Holle.

Thomas, Carl, and Michael Wedde. 2001. "Desperately Seeking Potnia." In Laffineur and Hägg 2001, 3–14.

Thomassen, Einar. 2004. "Musings on Syncretism." In *Unterwegs: Neue Pfade in der Religionswissenschaft,* Festschrift für Michael Pye zum 65. Geburtstag, edited by C. Kleine, M. Schrimpf, and K. Triplett, 137–47. München: Biblion.

Time-Life Education. 1993. *Wondrous Realms of the Aegean.* Lost Civilizations. Alexandria, Virginia: Time-Life Education.

Troy, Lana. 1986. *Patterns of Queenship in Ancient Egyptian Myth and History.* Boreas, Uppsala Studies in Ancient Mediterranean and Near Eastern Civilizations 14. Uppsala: Acta Universitatis Upsaliensis.

Turner, Victor. 1967. *The Forest of Symbols. Aspects of Ndembu Ritual.* Ithaca: Cornell University Press.

Tzedakis, Yiannis. 1971. "Larnakes Ysterominoikou Nekrotaphiou Armenon Kretes." *AAA* 4:216–22.

Uehlinger, Christoph. 1995. "Drachen und Drachenkämpfe im Alten Vorderen Orient und in der Bibel." In *Auf Drachenspuren: Ein Buch zum Drachenprojekt des Hamburgischen Museums für Völkerkunde,* edited by B. Schmelz und R. Vossen, 55–101. Bonn: Holos.

Uehlinger, Christoph, ed. 2000. *Images as Media. Sources for the Cultural History of the Ancient Near East and the Eastern Mediterranean (1st Millennium BCE). Proceedings of an International Symposium held in Fribourg, 25–29 November 1997.* Orbis Biblicus et Orientalis 175. Fribourg: Academic Press Fribourg and Göttingen: Vandenhoeck and Ruprecht.

Unger, Eckhard. 1922. *Assyrische und Babylonische Kunst.* Berlin: Bruno Cassirer.

Van den Hout, Theo P. J. 1998. *Purity of Kingship: An Edition of Cht 569 and Related Hittite Oracle Inquiries of Tuthaliya IV.* Leiden: Brill.

Van de Mieroop, Marc. 2004. *A History of the Ancient Near East.* Oxford: Blackwell.

Van de Mieroop, Marc. 2005. *King Hammurabi of Babylon.* Oxford: Blackwell.

Van Gennep, Arnold. 1960. *The Rites of Passage.* Translated from the French. 1913 by M. B. Vizedom and G. L. Caffe. London: Routledge & Keegan Paul.

Ventris, Michael, and John Chadwick. 1973. *Documents in Mycenaean Greek.* 2d ed. Cambridge: Cambridge University Press.

Vercoutter, Jean. 1911. *l'Egypte et le monde égéen préhellénique: étude critique des sources égyptiennes (du début de la XVIIIe à la fin de la XIXe dynastie.* Bibliothèque d'Étude t. 22. Cairo: Impr. de l'Institut français d'archéologie orientale.

Vermeule, Emily. 1964. *Greece in the Bronze Age.* Chicago: University of Chicago Press.

Vermeule, Emily. 1979. *Aspects of Death in Early Greek Art and Poetry.* Berkeley: University of California Press.

Vernant, Jean-Pierre. 1980. *Myth and Society in Ancient Greece.* Translated by J. Lloyd. Sussex: Harvester Press.

Wallis Budge, Ernest A. 1906. *The Egyptian Heaven and Hell.* London: Kegan Paul, Trench, Trübner & Co.

Warren, Peter M. 1986. *Minoan Religion as Ritual Action.* SIMA Pocket Book 72. Göteborg: Paul Åströms.

Warren, Peter. 1990. "Of Baetyls." *OpAth* 18:193–206.

Warren, Peter, and Vrowny Hankey. 1989. *Aegean Bronze Age Chronology.* Bristol: Bristol Classical Press.

Watrous, Vance L. 1989. "Egypt and Crete in the Early Middle Bronze Age: A Case of Trade and Cultural Diffusion." In Cline and Harris-Cline 1989, 19–28.

Watrous, Vance L. 1991. "The Origin and Iconography of the Late Minoan Painted Larnax." *Hesperia* 60:285–307.

Watrous, Vance L. 1995. "Some Observations on Minoan Peak Sanctuaries." In Laffineur and Niemeier 1995, 393–403.

Watson, Wilfred G. E., and Nicolas Wyatt, eds. 1999. *Handbook of Ugaritic Studies.* Handbook of Oriental Studies, Part One: The Near and Middle East 39. Leiden: Brill.

Wedde, Michael. 1992. "Pictorial Architecture: For a Theory-Based Analysis of Imagery." In Laffineur and Crowley 1992, 181–203.

Wedde, Michael. 1999. "Talking Hands: A Study of Minoan Mycenaean Ritual Gesture—Some Preliminary Notes." In Betancourt et al. 1999, 911–20.

Weißl, Michael. 2000. "Halbrosetten oder Federfächer? Zu Bedeutung und Funktion eines ägäischen Ornamentes." In *Österreichische Forschungen zur Ägäischen Bronzezeit 1998. Akten der Tagung am Institut für Klassische Archäologie der Universität Wien 2.-3. Mai 1998,* ed. F. Blakolmer, 89–95. Wiener Forschungen zur Archäologie 3. Wien: Phoibos.

Werner, Rudolf. 1991. *Kleine Einführung ins Hieroglyphen-Luwische.* Orbis Biblicus et Orientalis 106. Fribourg: Academic Press Fribourg.

West, Martin L. 1997. *East Face of Helicon: West Asiatic Elements in Early Poetry and Myth.* Oxford: Clarendon Press.

Wiener, Malcolm H. 1984. "Crete and the Cyclades in LM I: The tale of the Conical Cups." In Hägg and Marinatos 1984, 17–26.

Wiener, Malcolm H. 2003. "Time Out. The Current Impasse in Bronze Age Archaeological Dating." In Foster and Laffineur 2003, 363–95.

Wiese, André. 1990. *Zum Bild des Königs auf Ägyptische Siegelamuletten.* Orbis Biblicus et Orientalis 96. Fribourg: Academic Press Fribourg.

Wiesner, Joseph. 1968. "Die Kunst Altsyriens." In Thimme et al. 1968.

Wilkinson, Richard H. 1992. *Reading Egyptian Art: A Hieroglyphic Guide to Ancient Egyptian Painting and Sculpture.* London: Thames and Hudson.

Wilkinson, Richard H. 1994. *Symbol and Magic in Egyptian Art.* London: Thames and Hudson.

Winter, Urs. 1983. *Frau und Göttin. Exegetische und Ikonographische Studien zum Weiblichen Gottesbild im Alten Israel und in dessen Umwelt.* Orbis Biblicus et Orientalis 53. Göttingen: Vandenhoeck und Ruprecht.

Winter, Irene. 2000. "Le Palais Imaginaire: Scale and Meaning in the Iconography of Neo-Assyrian Cylinder Seals." In Uehlinger 2000, 51–88.

Wyatt, Nicolas. 1997. "Ilimilku's Ideological Programme: Ugaritic Royal Propaganda, and a Biblical Postscript." *Ugarit-Forschungen, Internationales Jahrbuch für die Altertumskunde Syrien-Palästinas* 29:775–96.

Wyatt, Nicolas. 1998. "Understanding Polytheism: Structure and Dynamic in a West Semitic Pantheon." *Journal of Higher Criticism* 5:24–63.

Wyatt, Nicolas. 1999. "Religion of Ugarit: An Overview." In Watson and Wyatt 1999, 529–85.

Wyatt, Nicolas. 1999–2000. "Just How 'Divine' Were the Kings of Ugarit?" In *Arbor Scientiae: Estudios del Proximo Oriente Antiguo Dedicados a Gregorio del Olmo Lete con Ocasion de su 65 Aniversario,* edited by M. Molina, I. Marquez Rowe, and J. Sanmartin. *Aula Orientalis* 17–18:133–41.

Wyatt, Nicolas. 2001. *Space and Time in the Religious Life of the Ancient Near East.* The Biblical Seminar 85. Sheffield: Sheffield Academic Press.

Wyatt, Nicolas. 2002. *Religious Texts from Ugarit: The Words of Ilimilku and His Colleagues.* The Biblical Seminar 33. 2d ed. Sheffield: Sheffield Academic Press.

Wyatt, Nicolas. 2005a. *The Mythic Mind: Essays on Cosmology and Religion in Ugaritic and Old Testament Literature.* Bible World. London: Equinox.

Wyatt, Nicolas. 2005b. "There's Such Divinity Doth Hedge a King." *Selected Essays of Nicolas Wyatt on Royal Ideology in Ugaritic and Old Testament Literature.* Society for Old Testament Study Monographs. Aldershot and Burlington: Ashgate.

Wyatt, Nicolas. 2006. "The Religious Role of the King: The Ritual Tradition." In *Ugarit at 75: Its Environs and the Bible. Mid-West Meeting of AOS/SBL/ASOR, 18–20 February 2005*, Chicago.

Younger, John G. 1988. *The Iconography of Late Minoan and Mycenaean Sealstones and Finger Rings.* Bristol: Bristol Classical Press.

Younger, John G. 1995. "The Iconography of Rulership in the Aegean: A Conspectus." In Rehak 1995a, 151–211.

Figures and Credits

Chapter 1

Fig. 1.1. Map of East Mediterranean.

Chapter 2

Fig. 2.1. Fresco fragment from Knossos. After Evans PM III, fig. 504b.
Fig. 2.2. Ring impression from Knossos. CMS II, 8, 248.
Fig. 2.3. Ivory mirror handle from Knossos. After Evans PM II, fig. 506a.
Fig. 2.4. Syrian seal. After Teissier 1996, no. 142.
Fig. 2.5. Sarcophagus of Hagia Triada. After Evans PM I, fig. 317.
Fig. 2.6. W-D. Niemeier's reconstruction of the "Prince of Lilies." After Niemeier 1987, fig. 24.
Fig. 2.7. E. Gilliéron's and A. Evans's restoration of "Prince of Lilies." After Evans PM II, pl. XIV.
Fig. 2.8. Hittite king. Drawing V. Pliatsika after Haas 1982, 80, fig. 18.
Fig. 2.9. Old Syrian seal. After Winter 1983, fig. 127.
Fig. 2.10. Hittite silver vessel in the shape of a fist. After Gütterbock and Kendall 1995, 52, fig. 3.7.
Fig. 2.11. Statuette from Qatna, Syria. Second half of the second millennium. After Winter 1983, fig. 227.
Fig. 2.12. Scarab seal from Jericho. After Schroer 1985, 79, fig. 33.
Fig. 2.13. Seals from Knossos. After Evans PM IV, 414, fig. 343.
Fig. 2.14. (a) Seal from Vapheio, Lakonia. After CMS I, 223. (b) CMS X, 268.
Fig. 2.15. "Harvesters' Vase" from Hagia Triada. After Marinatos and Hirmer 1975, pl. 105.
Fig. 2.16. (a) Seal impression from Knossos. After CMS II. 3, 13. (b) Mask/portrait from Grave V, Grave Circle A. Drawing Vasso Pliatsika after Taylour 1977, pl. 16.
Fig. 2.17. Stone seal. After CMS X, 278. In private collection, Switzerland.

Fig. 2.18. Egyptianizing seal from southern Palestine. After Keel and Uehlinger 1995, 93, fig. 96.
Fig. 2.19. Shaft Grave stele from Grave V, Mycenae. After Evans PM IV, 251, fig. 189.
Fig. 2.20. Composite drawing made of ring imprints from Hagia Triada, Sklavokampos and Akrotiri. After CMS VS. 3, 391.
Fig. 2.21. Ring impression from Knossos. After CMS II, 8, 193.
Fig. 2.22. Processional scene from Knossos. After Cameron 1967.
Fig. 2.23. (a) Corridor of the Processions fresco at Knossos. After Evans PM II, fig. 436. (b) Throne room frieze at Knossos. After Evans PM IV, fig. 894.
Fig. 2.24. Mural from Knossos. After Bossert 1937, fig. 233.
Fig. 2.25. Gold ring from Tiryns. After CMS I, 179.
Fig. 2.26. (a) Mycenaean bracelet from Shaft Grave IV, Mycenae. After Karo 1933, 76, pl. XLII, no. 263. (b) Assyrian relief from King Assurnassipal's palace, Nimrud. After Jakob-Rost et al. 1992, cat. no. 109.
Fig. 2.27. Hittite king and sun god from rock sanctuary at Yazilikaya. After Bittel 1976, pls. 249, 234.

Chapter 3

Fig. 3.1. (a–b) Two-sided seal from the palace of Knossos. After CMS II, 3. 13. (c) Seal from Crete. After CMS II. 3, 196.
Fig. 3.2. (a) "Harvesters' Vase," Hagia Triada. Courtesy N. Dimopoulou, Herakleion Museum. (b) Ring impression from Knossos. After CMS II, 7, 16. (c) Detail from the Hagia Triada sarcophagus. After Marinatos 1993, fig. 27.
Fig. 3.3. Relief from the temple of Seti I. After Keel 1978, fig. 379.
Fig. 3.4. (a) Ring from Mycenae. After CMS I, 86. (b) Ring from Mycenae. After CMS I, 108.
Fig. 3.5. Ring from Mycenae. After CMS I, 128.
Fig. 3.6. a-b. Long side of sarcophagus of Hagia Triada. After Evans PM I, fig. 317. c-d. Long sides of sarcophagus of Hagia Triada. Drawing L.Papageorgiou, after Marinatos 1993, Fig. 27.
Fig. 3.7. Cult standard of the Assyrian King Tukulti Ninurta I. Berlin Museum. After Jakob-Rost et al. 1992, 161.
Fig. 3.8 Hagia Triada Sarcophagus (details), after Marinatos 1993, fig. 27–29.
Fig. 3.9. (a and b) Hittite silver cup after Gütterbock and Kendal 1995. (c) Hagia Triada Sarcophagus, side B (detail) after Evans PM I, fig. 317.

Chapter 4

Fig. 4.1. The throne room at Knossos. After Evans PM IV, fig. 895.
Fig. 4.2. (a) Throne room at Knossos. After Evans PM IV, fig. 877. (b) Plan of Throne room at Mari. After Al-Khalesi 1978, pl. iii.
Fig. 4.3. Plan of the throne room at Knossos with route of the king. Modified plan after Evans PM IV, fig. 877 and Niemeier 1989.
Fig. 4.4. (a) Ring impression from Zakros. After CMS II, 7. (b) Seal from Knossos. After Evans PM I, fig. 312a.

Fig. 4.5. Wooden throne in the anteroom of the throne room Knossos. Photo by M. Stasinopoulos.
Fig. 4.6. Egyptian statue of pharaoh and Horus. After Keel 1978, fig. 353. Drawing Hildi Lieu-Keel.
Fig. 4.7. Palm landscape and throne at Knossos. After Evans PM IV, pl. xxxiii.
Fig. 4.8. (a) Knossos stone throne. After Evans PM IV, fig. 895 (detail). (b) Stone rhyton from the palace of Zakros (detail). After Platon 2003, 338, fig. 6.
Fig. 4.9. Mari throne room fresco. After Parrot 1958, 280, fig. 346.
Fig. 4.10. (a) Syrian seal. After Teissier 1996, no. 193. (b) Syrian cylinder seal. After Teissier 1996, fig. 189.
Fig. 4.11. Ugaritic seal. After Amiet 1992, no. 464.
Fig. 4.12. Minoan ring impression. After CMS II, 8, 192.
Fig. 4.13. Minoan/Mycenaean seal. After CMS XIII, 39.
Fig. 4.14. Minoan/Mycenaean seal from Naxos. After CMS V, 608.
Fig. 4.15. (a) Mycenaean gold ring. After CMS I, 87. (b) Egyptianizing Syrian seal. After Teissier 1996, 192.

Chapter 5

Fig. 5.1. Stone rhyton from Zakros. Drawing after Platon 2003, 338, fig. 6.
Fig. 5.2. Model of sanctuary from East Crete. Redrawn after Davaras 2003, 254, fig. 25c.
Fig. 5.3. Ring impression from Knossos. CMS II, 8, 256.
Fig. 5.4. Ring from Thebes. CMS V, 199.
Fig. 5.5. Vase from Cyprus. After Buchholz 1999, fig. 97.
Fig. 5.6. Ring from Poros. After Rethemiotakis 2003, fig. 1.
Fig. 5.7. Ring from Knossos now in Oxford. After Evans PM I, fig. 115.
Fig. 5.8. Ring from Mycenae. CMS I, 119.
Fig. 5.9. Ring from Aidonia. CMS VS. 1B, 114.
Fig. 5.10. Ring impression from a house at Chania. CMS V1A, 142.

Chapter 6

Fig. 6.1. Diorite stele of king Hammurabi. After Keel 1978, fig. 390. Drawing Hildi Keel-Leu.
Fig. 6.2. Syro-Palestinian seal. After Teissier 1996, 66, no. 79.
Fig. 6.3. (a) Berlin Ring. CMS XI, 28. (b) Oxford Ring. After Evans PM I, fig. 115.
Fig. 6.4. Ring from Messenia (southern Greece) with an epiphany scene. CMS I, 292.
Fig. 6.5. (a) Knossos ring impression. CMS II, 8, 125. (b) Syrian seal (detail). After Winter (Urs) 1983, fig. 240.
Fig. 6.6. Assyrian cylinder seal. After Winter (Irene) 2000.

Chapter 7

Fig. 7.1. Roman-Tyrian coin. After Mettinger 1992, fig. 5.6.
Fig. 7.2. (a) Ring from Sellopoulo. CMS archive. After Popham 1974, fig. 14D. (b) Ring impression from Hagia Triada. After CMS II, 6, 4.

Fig. 7.3. Incubation rituals on seal from Knossos. After Warren 1986, fig. 9.

Fig. 7.4. (a) Minoan seal. CMS XII, 264. (b) Syro-Palestinian seal. After Keel and Uehlinger 1995, fig. 233.

Fig. 7.5. Ring from Mycenae. CMS I, 126.

Fig. 7.6 (a) Ring from Archanes. CMS archive, Sakellarakis 1991. (b) Ring from Vapheio. CMS I, 219.

Fig. 7.7. (a) Ring impression from Zakros. CMS II, 7, 6. (b) Ring impression from Hagia Triada. CMS II, 6, 4.

Fig. 7.8. Seal from Zakros. CMS II, 7, 41.

Fig. 7.9. (a) Ring from cemetery of Kalyvia near Phaistos. CMS II, 3, 114. (b) Ring from cemetery of Sellopoulo. CMS archive: Popham 1974, fig. 14D.

Fig. 7.10. Gold ring from a tomb at Poros, near Knossos. After Dimopoulou and Rethemiotakis 2000, 4c.

Chapter 8

Fig. 8.1. Minoan hieroglyphs. After Evans PM I, fig. 214.

Fig. 8.2. Mount Juktas and Minoan Twin Peak mountain from palace of Knossos. After Evans PM II, 159, fig. 81.

Fig. 8.3. Stele in the Louvre. After Perrot-Chipiez IV, 1887, 392, fig. 206.

Fig. 8.4. (a) Minoan twin peak sacred mountain. After Marinatos 1993, fig. 2. (b) Egyptian sign of the mountain of the horizon. After Wilkinson 1992, 135. (c) Akkadian seal. After Keel 1978, fig. 9 (detail). (d) Twin peak mountian on Syrian seal (detail).

Fig. 8.5. Votive tablet from Psychro. After Evans PM I, 632, fig. 470.

Fig. 8.6. Seal stone from Vapheio. CMS I, 231.

Fig. 8.7. (a) Seal from Kydonia, West Crete. After CMS V, 201. (b) Drawing of Egyptian god Geb rising from a mountain. After Wilkinson 132, fig. 1. (c) Rock relief from Yazilikaya. After Haas 1982, fig. 8.

Fig. 8.8. (a) Minoan clay model from an East Cretan mountain sanctuary. After Marinatos 1993, fig. 86 based on Davaras. (b) Egyptian vignette from funerary papyrus. After Keel 1978, fig. 10.

Fig. 8.9. (a) Akkadian seal . After Keel 1978, 23, fig. 9. (b) Akkadian seal, third millennium. After Keel 1994, 244, fig. 138.

Fig. 8.10. Babylonian clay tablet now in British Museum. After Wyatt 2001, 81.

Chapter 9

Fig. 9.1 Egyptian mountain sign. After Wilkinson 1992, 135.

Fig. 9.2. (a) Minoan clay pictorial vessel (detail). After Buchholz 1999, fig. 98m. (b) Larnax from Giofyrakia (detail). After Buchholz 1998, fig. 98k.

Fig. 9.3. Sarcophagus of Seti I, Nineteenth Dynasty (detail). After Wilkinson 1992, 56.2.

Fig. 9.4. (a) Mycenaean seal from Argos. After Evans, PM I, fig. 312. (b) Egyptian scarab seal. After Keel and Schroer 1998, 13–29, pl. iii.

Fig. 9.5. (a) Minoan Seal from Mt. Juktas. After Karetsou in Hägg and Marinatos 1981, fig. 24. (b) Minoan Seal from Psychro. After CMS II, 3, 289. (c) Egyptian Painting, Tomb of Senmut (detail). After Evans PM II, fig. 338.

Fig. 9.6. Scarab seal impression from Boghazköy. After Bernett and Keel 1998, fig. 57.
Fig. 9.7. (a) Old Syrian Seal. After Bernett and Keel 1998, fig. 50. (b) Syro-Palestinian seal from Ugarit. After Bernett and Keel 1998, fig. 51.
Fig. 9.8. Detail from a ring from Vapheio. CMS I, 219.
Fig. 9.9. Seal impression from Knossos. CMS II, 8, 325.
Fig. 9.10. Primeval lotus drawing. After Wilkinson 1992, 121.
Fig. 9.11. Vase from Pseira (detail). After Betancourt and Davaras 1995, fig. 16.
Fig. 9.12. Pithos from Knossos (detail). After Evans PM IV, fig. 286.
Fig. 9.13. Double axes combined with ankh sign on Minoan vases. After Niemeier 1985, fig. 57, nos. 21–24.
Fig. 9.14. Drawing of the knot of Isis. After Wilkinson 1992, 121, V39.
Fig. 9.15. Minoan and Hittite double axes. After Bossert 1932, figs. 5–6.
Fig. 9.16. Old Syrian Seal. After Winter 1983, fig. 127.
Fig. 9.17. (a) Rhyton from Palaikastro. After Bossert 1923, pl. 166. (b) Rhyton from Palaikastro (detail). After Evans PM II, fig. 312e.
Fig. 9.18 (a) Short side of larnax (clay coffin) from Kavrochori. After Rethemiotakis 1979, 228–59. (b) Clay cylindrical vessel. After Evans PM II, fig. 390.
Fig. 9.19. (a) Lid of a cultic vase from Pseira, east Crete. After Betancourt 1995, fig. 15, BQ 15. (b) Cultic vase from Pseira, east Crete. After Nilsson 1950, fig. 96.
Fig. 9.20. Ring impression from Knossos. CMS II, 8, 125.
Fig. 9.21. Gold ring from Mycenae. CMS I, 17.
Fig. 9.22. (a) Design of the Double axe. (b) Egyptian scarab. After Wilkinson 1992, 113.

Chapter 10

Fig. 10.1. Minoan hieroglyphs. After Evans PM I, 221.
Fig. 10.2. (a) Mitanni seal. After Winter 1983, fig. 125. (b) Seal of princess Matrunna. After Teissier 1996, fig. 186.
Fig. 10.3. (a and b) Hittite hieroglyphs. After Laroche 1960, nos. 189, 190–91.
Fig. 10.4. Vase from Knossos (detail). After Evans PM II, fig. 254.
Fig. 10.5. (a) Hagia Triada sarcophagus (detail). (b) Old Syrian seal. After Teissier 1996, fig. 193 (detail).
Fig. 10.6. Minoan from Tell el Dab'a, Egypt (detail). After Bietak, Marinatos and Palyvou 2000, fig. 1.
Fig. 10.7. (a) Minoan fresco from Knossos: design on the dress of a female from Knossos. After Evans PM II, fig. 450. (b) Hittite hieroglyph. After Laroche 1960, nos. 190–91.
Fig. 10.8. (a) Hittite hieroglyph. After Laroche 1960, 133, no. 249. (b) Gold plate ornament from Shaft Grave at Mycenae. After Evans PM II, fig. 381.
Fig. 10.9. The rosette and the incurved altar design. After Evans PM II, fig. 379.
Fig. 10.10. Mycenaean Seal. CMS I, 73.
Fig. 10.11. Egyptian hieroglyph for headrest and sun support. After Wilkinson 1992, 159.
Fig. 10.12. (a) Headrest from Tutankhamun's tomb. After Wilkinson 1992, 158, fig. 2. (b) Seal from Crete. CMS II, 8, 326.
Fig. 10.13. Reconstruction of edifice depicted on ring from Poros. After Rethemiotakis 2003, fig. 5.

Chapter 11

Fig. 11.1. Larnax from Palaikastro. After Marinatos and Hirmer 1976, pl. 137.
Fig. 11.2. Larnax from Armenoi. After Tzedakis 1971, fig. 4.
Fig. 11.3. Larnax from Armenoi. After Tzedakis 1971, fig. 7.
Fig. 11.4. Larnax from Kavrochori. After Rethemiotakis 1979.
Fig. 11.5. Larnax from Pachyamnos. After Marinatos 1993, fig. 234.
Fig. 11.6. Larnax from Vassilika Anogeia. After Marinatos 1993, fig. 237.
Fig. 11.7. The axe on a larnax from Giofyrakia (detail). After Buchholz 1999, fig. 98m.
Fig. 11.8. Vignettes on funerary Egyptian papyrus of Ani. Redrawn after Faulkner 1985, 79.

Chapter 12

Fig. 12.1. (a) Tiryns ring. After CMS I, 178. (b) Mycenae. CMS I, 128.
Fig. 12.2. Ring from Mycenae, After CMS I, 101.
Fig. 12.3. Seal now in Geneva. After CMS X, 261.
Fig. 12.4. Ring from Thebes. After CMS V, 199.
Fig. 12.5. Old Syrian seal. After Keel 1998, fig. 27.
Fig. 12.6. Syrian cylinder seal found in Cyprus. After Winter 1983, 452, fig. 489.
Fig. 12.7. Syrian seal found in Cyprus. Storm god and enthroned goddess. After Winter 1983, 449, fig. 484.
Fig. 12.8. Relief from Iron Age Malatya in Anatolia. After Winter 1983, 63, fig. 6.
Fig. 12.9. Hittite relief from Yazilikaya. Readrawn after Bittel et al. 1941, fig. 29.
Fig. 12.10. Ring from Mochlos, Crete. After CMS II. 3, 252.
Fig. 12.11. Ring from Tiryns. CMS I, 179.
Fig. 12.12. (a and b) Mould from Siteia, East Crete. After Zervos 1956, pls. 745–46.
Fig. 12.13. Short sides of the Hagia Triada sarcophagus. After Marinatos 1993, fig. 31. Photo courtesy A. Franz.
Fig. 12.14. Divinities with plumed head-dresses in a griffin drawn chariot. CMS V1B, 137.

Chapter 13

Fig. 13.1. Ring impression from Knossos. After Evans PM III, fig. 325.
Fig. 13.2. Seal from mainland. After Nilsson 1950, fig. 168.
Fig. 13.3. (a) Ring Impression from Hagia Triada. CMS II. 6. 36. (b) Hittite God Sharuma from rock Relief, Yazilikaya. After Bittel et al. 1941, 87, fig. 29. (c) Minoan statuette. After Evans PM II, fig. 132. (d) God Reshep. Syrian statuette. After Cornelius 1994, fig. 27a.
Fig. 13.4. (a) Minoan god. Ring from Palaikastro (detail) after A. MacGillivray. (b) Syrian seal from Tell el Dab'a, Egypt. After Bietak 1994, fig. 19.
Fig. 13.5. (a) Ring impression from Hagia Triada. CMS II. 6, 15. (b) Syro-Palestinian Egyptianizing seal. After Keel and Uehlinger 1995, 93, fig. 97b. (c) Egyptian relief of Ramses II at Abu Simbel. After Keel 1978, fig. 404.

Fig. 13.6. (a) Ring impression from Chania. CMS VS.1S, 133. (b) Ring from Athens. CMS V, 173. (c) Ivory piece from Megiddo. After Loud 1939, pl. 4.
Fig. 13.7. Ring from Kato Syme. After Lebessi et al. 2004, pl. 1.
Fig. 13.8. Seal now in the Fogg Art Museum. After CMS XIII, 39.
Fig. 13.9. Ring impression from Knossos. CMS II, 8, 234. Slightly restored by N. Marinatos.
Fig. 13.10. Egyptian Papyrus. After Keel 1978, fig. 55.
Fig. 13.11. (a) Syrian seal. After Keel 1992, fig. 233. (b) Syrian seal. After Keel 1992, fig. 237. (c) Assyrian seal. After Keel 1992, fig. 245.
Fig. 13.12. Ring now in Berlin. CMS XI, 29.
Fig. 13.13. Ring from Knossos now in Ashmolean, Oxford
Fig. 13.14. (a) Ring impression from Zakros. CMS II. 7, 3. (b) Reconstruction of Ring impression from Zakros by N. Marinatos and A. Wiegand.

Chapter 14

Fig. 14.1. Ivory lid from Ugarit. After Cornelius 2004, pl. 2.7.
Fig. 14.2. (a) Rock relief. After Bossert 1932, fig. 25a. (b) Split rosette. After Evans PM II, fig. 379.

Chapter 15

Fig. 15.1. (a) Clay vessel (detail). After Buchholz 1999, fig. 98 M. (b) Seal from Argos. After Evans PM I, fig. 312. (c) Detail of vase from Pseira. After Marinatos and Hirmer 1976, pl. 81. (d) Ceiling from Malkata, Egypt. After Karetsou 2000, pl. 289a.

Index

Abraham, 72
Abu Simbel, temple of, 175
Abydos, 42
Achilles, armor of, 181
Adad, 182
Adonis, 88, 167, 220n3
Ahab, 47, 95, 97
Aidonia ring, 73, 74
Akkad, 79, 205n70
Akkadian: language, 4, 10, 73, 93, 217n11; seals, 107–12, 115
Akrotiri ring imprint, 26, 201n42
Aleppo, 187
Alexiou, Stylianos, 73, 218n3, 220n1
Amarna, 5, 8, 48, 184, 198n20
Amasis, 5, 198n21
Amenhotep III, pharaoh, 5, 8, 188, 195
Amenophis III, pharaoh, 3, 197n9
Amon, 187, 223n7, 223n10
Amphiaraus, 93
Anat, 35, 166, 171, 191, 218n2
Anatolia: ankh sign, 122; double axe, 214n2; god and king images, 19, 30–31, 84, 140; holy stones, 87, 95; mountain peak image, 107; and Near East *koine,* 1, 7, 72, 139, 193; ox head image, 119; solar worship, 47, 65, 157–58, 166; split rosette, 132–33, 189; Storm God, 171; tiara, 168
Ani papyrus, 149
ankh, 19, 81, 122–23, 129, 189
Annunitum, temple of, 93
Anu, 158, 179
Anzu, 158, 183
Aphrodite, 191
Apollo, 95, 99, 171, 191, 220n1
Apophis, 179–80
Archanes ring, 96, 212n41
Ares, 191
Argos (gem from), 117, 195
Arinna: goddess of, 47, 49, 65, 157, 223n11; gods of, 187
Armenoi larnakes, 144–46
Arsu wa Sanuma, 34
Artemis, 191, 220n8
Asa, king, 47
A-sa-sa-ra, 165, 188
Asherah, 47, 63–64, 95–96, 188, 209n32
Ashkelon, 184
Ashmolean ring, 96, 181–82
Ashurbanibal, king, 42, 215n35, 217n12
Assur, 85
Assurnassipal, king, 29
Assur-uballit, king, 8
Assyria: cult standard base from, 42–43; and goddess, 152; seals from, 85, 179; texts from, 111, 159, 183
Astarte, 151, 166, 218n2
atef crown, 16

Athena, 75, 99, 220n8
Athens ring, 174, 176
Athirat: and El, 159–60; and fecundity, 223n70; high priestess of, 47; offerings to, 35; seated figure of, 188, 219n21; and Shapshu, 65, 166; Ugaritic *Atrt,* 165
Athtar, 160, 207n8
Athtart, 69
Atrt. See Athirat
Attary, 35

Baal: and Asherah, 96; and Athtar, 207n8; offerings to, 35, 72; prophets of, 95; *proskynesis* of, 184; as Storm God, 171–72, 179, 182; as warrior, 191, 221n6. See also *Baal Cycle*
Baal Cycle, 94, 124, 159, 183
Babylon: city of El, 75; cosmic map from, 112–13, 142, 144; goddess Ishtar of, 151; god Ninurta of, 171; god Shamash of, 65, 111, 124, 160; king of, 8; stele of Hammurabi, 79–80. *See also* Anzu; *Enuma Elish*; Hammurabi; Mami
Bachofen, Johann J., 218nn5–6
baetyl, 86–88, 91, 210n5, 211n15
Baka trees, 92, 94
Bakekhons, 202n2
Bathsheba, 47
Belet-ili, 158–59, 213n27
Berlin ring, 181
Betancourt, Philip, 13, 214n25, 215n2, 215n50
Beth-El, 87, 91
Boghazköy seal impression, 117–18
Book of the Dead, 110, 120–21, 124, 150
Bossert, Helmut Theodor, 1, 123, 135, 189–90, 223n15
boukephalion, 105, 116, 119–20
Boulis, 184
bow, 168, 172, 179, 181, 222n58
Burkert, Walter, 7, 186, 220n1
Burr-Buriash, king, 8

Cain, Dawn, 170
Cameron, Mark, 58
Canaan: cosmic mountain in, 213n25; god Baal of, 171; god El of, 172; iconography of deities of, 173, 220n7; ivory from Megiddo, 174, 176; naked goddess of, 188–89; sacred tree, 72
Carmel, Mount, 95
Chadwick, John, 7
Chania ring impression, 75, 167–68, 174, 176
chaos, 124, 158–59, 172, 177, 221n20
chariot: collection of scenes, 201n43; date of, 201n40; goddesses riding, 163–65; king riding, 14, 24–26, 34, 174, 198n11; transport to netherworld, 146
Charybdis, 179
Chronicles, 8, 34, 57, 72, 84
Circe, 143
city of god, 73, 75–76, 168
coffins. *See* larnakes
Collon, Dominique, 30, 213n23, 219n14
cosmic axis, 67, 108, 136, 138, 147
cosmic center, 67, 75–76, 106, 194, 213n20
cosmic frontier, 103–13, 146, 217n16
cosmic map, 108; from Babylon, 112–13, 142, 144
cosmic mountain, 69, 77, 103–13, 115–16, 142
cosmic pillar, 67, 113, 136–39, 208n14
cosmic river, 112, 144
cosmic tree, 108–9
cosmic triangle, 107
cosmos: center of, 67, 76, 124, 127, 194; ideograms of, 107, 131, 136, 138, 164; journey around, 111, 143–44; king and, 5; map of, 113; protector of, 172–73
Crete: destruction of, 5–6; larnakes from, 141, 144, 146–48, 150; mould from, 162; Near East influences on, 151; and Near East *koine,* 1–2, 7, 39, 120, 134, 139, 193–96; ring impression from, 62; rings from, 8–9, 97, 152, 173, 178, 181; royalty, 16, 21, 32, 34; ruler deification on, 140; ruler of, 12–13, 31; sanctuaries in, 72; seals from, 33, 138; seated goddess, 155, 157; temples, 66–69, 75–77; and Ugarit, 172, 179; vessels from, 126–27; written sources from, 10, 190. *See also baetyl*; chariot; double

axe; epiphany; Evans, Sir Arthur; incurved altar; Kaphtor; Keftiu; Mari; New Palace period; Old Palace period; *pax minoica*; prophecy; *proskynesis*; sacrality; sacred horns; solar deity; split rosette
Croesus, king, 5, 198n21
Crowley, Janice, 202n54
cryptography, 7
Cultraro, Massimo, 13
cult standard, 41–43, 61, 63, 132–34
cuneiform, 4, 10
Cybele, 151, 210n18
cylinder seals, 9, 21, 84–85, 110–11, 155–56
Cypro-Minoan, 10
Cyprus, 4–5, 69–70, 155–56, 193, 212n4

Dagan, 34, 57, 93
David, 92, 94
Deborah, 94
Delphi, 49, 93, 95
Demeter, 166, 186, 191, 223n7
Deuteronomy, 72
Dimopoulou, Nota, 167, 212n46, 218–19n13
distance perspective, 78
Divine palace, 67–73, 136, 154
Dodone, 95
double axe: 114–30; as aniconic emblem, 55–56; as cult symbol, 47–48; decipherment of, 10; and dragonfly, 99; as goddess' emblem, 161–63, 177, 181, 194–95; on Hagia Triada sarcophagus, 41–42; on larnakes, 141, 143, 145–46, 149–50; and lily, 18; and rosette, 133–34, 138–39; and twin peaks, 108, 113; at Yazilikaya, 157
Doumas, Christos, 199n46
duality: in double axe, 114, 130, 194; Minoan pictograms and, 139, 150, 166
Durand, Jean-Marie, 102; with, 212n49

earthquakes, 5–6
Ebla, 20
ecstasy, 86–102, 120; Friedrich Matz's theory, 10, 79, 81, 205n8
ecstatic worship. *See* ecstasy
Egypt: afterlife beliefs, 140–43, 148–50; and bull, 116–18; chronology, 3–5; cult narratives, 42, 44; and flagpole, 73; god and king, 57–58, 79; and gold, 8; hieroglyphs, 103, 106–7, 122–23, 137–39; and Keftiu, 2, 197n3; and lotus, 120–21; and Near East *koine*, 1, 7, 134, 186–89, 193–96; priests, 32–33, 36–37, 202n2; queen of, 46–48; rising god, 109; royal iconography, 14, 16, 22, 24, 198n11; storm god, 171–75, 177, 179–80, 185; sun goddess, 160, 166; sun's journey, 124–25, 129–30; sun symbol, 60–62, 65, 115, 132; temples, 66; and vassalage, 6
Eighteenth Dynasty, 4, 24, 48, 185, 198n11
El, 159, 183
Elhul, 80
Elijah, 95–97, 184
Elysium (Elysion), 142, 144
Enoch, 58, 112, 213n30
Enuma Elish, 179, 222n40
epiphany: 78–85, 194; definition of, 10, 205n8; of goddess, 97–99; location of, 72–73, 75, 86–89, 91; social setting, 53; of Storm God, 181; of sunlight, 65
Ereshkigal, 166, 222n40
Ethiopia, 2
Euphrates, 50, 92
Evans, Sir Arthur, 193–96; afterlife scenes, 140, 144; *baetyl*, 210n5; clenched fist interpretation, 210n17; cosmic ideograms, 131; Cybele, 210n18; destruction of Knossos, 5–6, 198n27; double axe, 114, 116, 120–22, 162; duality of goddess, 165; Greek myth lens, 7; Hagia Triada sarcophagus, 204n50; Harvester's Vase, 21, 37; incurved altar, 136; Knossos fresco reconstruction, 16–18; Knossos ring impression, 177; lustral basin, 205n3; male god, 167; mother goddess, 151, 153, 155, 205n69; Mother of the Mountains, 83; omega object, 222n43; *papa re*, 12–14, 32, 184, 200n3; *Pax Minoica*, 3–4, 199n32; prophecy, 86–88, 97, 208n30; rayed disc, 215n1; rosette, 27, 216n17; sacred horns, 103–6, 113; Temple Tomb, 46; throne, 50, 52–56

Exodus, 84, 105
Ezekiel, 73, 191, 212n45

Frankfort, Henri, 57
Frazer, Sir James, 86, 88, 167, 169, 193
fringed mantle, 19, 21, 25, 36–37

Gaerte,Wilhelm, 106
Galatas, palace of, 34
Garden of Eden, 142–43
Geb, 109
gebira, 47
Genesis, 72–73, 90, 143, 147
Genette, Gerard, 170
Gideon, 73, 87
Gilgamesh, 89–90, 111–12, 124, 142–44, 147–48
Gilliéron, Emile, 16–18, 58
Giofyrakia larnax, 115, 149
Godley, A. D., 184
gold lance, 54
Goodison, Lucy, 65, 108, 165–66, 205n67, 207n49
Gospel of Philip, 129
Graf, Fritz, 186
griffin: god or king with, 21, 23; god with, 25–26; with incurved altar, 136–37; on Knossos throne room, 52, 55, 58, 60; on larnakes, 141, 143, 149; with solar goddess, 152, 163, 165; on Syrian seals, 61–63, 65, 132
Grosskönige, 4

Hägg, Robin, 205n8
Hagia Triada: ring impressions, 89, 97–98, 170, 173, 175, 206n22; sarcophagus, 16–17, 39, 41, 43–48, 133–34, 161, 163–66. *See also* Harvester's Vase
halentuwa house, 36
half rosette. *See* rosette
Hallager, Erik, 167, 199n47
Hammurabi, 79–80, 92, 209n4
Hankey, Vroney, 3
Haran, Menahem, 72
Harvester's Vase, 21–22, 36–37
Hathor, female cow, 116; house of Horus, 47, 54, 160, 166; partial representation, 81, 189
Hatshepsut, queen, 6, 118, 193
Hatti, 187
Hattushili, 46–47, 204n58
Heb-Sed festival, 177
Hekateus, map of, 144
Hepat, 65, 157–58, 169
Hermes, 176, 223n2
Herodotus, 93, 144, 184, 187, 198
Hesiod, 94, 144
hide skirt, 36–38, 41–45
high priestess, 10, 16, 42, 65, 193, 211n38; of Asherah, 95–96; in Near East, 47
Hittite: ankh, 123; bulls, 214n19; hieroglyphs, 52, 103, holy stones, 87; king, 4, 18–19, 3, 200n23; king and sun god, 30; ox, 117–18; palace, 69; rosette, 133–36, 189, 216n14, 216n21; Sharuma, 168, 170; shield deity, 222n62; silver cup, 45; Storm God, 171, 190; sun deity, 65, 124, 157–58, 223n11; texts, 30, 35–36, 38–39, 43–44, 46–48; throne, 53–55, 57; treaty, 187–88
Homer, 94, 179
Horemheb, king, 57
horizon: double axe, 127–30, 139, 149, 162; lions, 138, 213n23; lotus, 120; mountain peaks, 145, 106–7, 110; split rosette, 189; sun's journey, 124–25; on Thebes ring, 69, 153
horn-crown, 30–31, 79
horns of consecration, 103–16
Hornung, Eric, 129, 220n8
Horus, 57–58, 65, 116, 160, 179–80. *See also* Hathor, female cow
house of god, 66–77; Beth-el, 87, 91; epiphany scene, 81–83; on Hagia Triada Sarcophagus, 41, 44; split rosette, 136, 138
Hurrian, 5, 157, 171
huwasi, 87
Hyksos dynasties, 3–4

ideogram, 103–7, 115, 122, 131–39, 212n14
Igigi, 159, 183
Iliad, 95, 99–100, 181, 188

Ilimilku, 172
Illuyanka(s), 171
Ilu, 34, 220n42
incense altar, 87, 105
incurved altar, 63, 136–39, 166, 194
insignia dignitatis, 9, 14, 19–20, 29, 84
Ishtar: on Akkadian seals, 111; on Cyprian seal, 155; and Ereshkigal, 166; fertility goddess, 151; Mari mural, 60, 69; Mari texts, 95; on Syrian seal, 85
Isis, 54, 65, 122, 160, 166, 186
Isopata, 46, 126, 140
Israel, 65, 72–73, 97, 157, 197n3. *See also* Asherah

Jacob, 89–91
Jahweh, 47, 63, 72, 84, 210n22. *See also* Yahweh
Jeremiah, 166
Jericho, 19–20
Jezebel, 47, 95–96
Joshua, 87
Judah seal, 91
Judges, 73, 87, 94
Juktas, Mount, 103–4, 113, 118
Jung, Helmut, 210n5

kalmush, 54
Kaphtor, 1, 197nn2–3, 197n5, 215n3
Kaptaru. *See* Kaphtor
Karetsou, Alexandra, 113
Kato Syme ring, 177–78
Kavrochori (larnax from), 126, 146–47
Keel, Othmar: *boukephalion,* 116; king and cult, 22; king and god, 57; lunar disc, 14n14; palm and sun, 216n15; pictorial dictionary, 187; triumphant gods, 173–74
Keftiu, 1–2, 4–5, 117–18, 193, 197nn2–3
Keret, king, 55, 160
kheper, 129
Khepri, 124
Kimmary, 34
Kings, 47, 93–97, 184
Kizuwadna, 187
Knossos: chariot scenes, 24–26; destruction of, 3–7, 140, 150, 199n32; dolphins, 201n24; double axe, 213n2; double axe tomb, 126; mountain peaks, 67, 69, 103–4; pithos from, 122; Prince of Lilies fresco, 14–18; regime of, 13, 199n32; ring impressions from, 37, 62, 70, 83, 127–28, 168–69, 177, 180; rings from, 73–74, 82, 180–82; rosette, 27–28, 131–35, 190; seals from, 20, 22–23, 33, 89–91, 119–20; Temple Tomb, 46; throne room, 50–52, 54–56, 59–60, 64–65, 143. *See also* Crete; Juktas, Mount
knot of Isis, 122
Kotaru, 34
Kothar-and-hasis, 1, 160–61, 179
Kristensen, W. B., 106
Kydonia seal, 109

labrys, 213n2
larnakes, 115, 126, 129, 140–50. *See also* Hagia Triada: sarcophagus
Leto, 191, 207n47
Levant, and Near East *koine,* 1, 7, 95, 122, 193; rosette, 132–34, 139; solar bird, 61–62; Storm God, 157, 171; sun goddess, 166; vassalage, 198n20
Leviathan, 179
lictus, 19
Lihzina, 187
Linear A, 13, 103, 165, 213n2, 220n43
Linear B, 6, 32, 34, 165, 213n2, 218n3
Litanu, 179
lotus, 62, 120–22, 129, 149
lustral basin, 57, 205n3
Luwian. *See* Hittite
Luxor, 42, 208n24

Maachah, 47
MacGillivray, Alexander, 106, 167, 213–14n2
Malatya relief, 157–58, 190
Mami, 158–59
Mamre, 72
Marduk, 79, 171, 179, 222n40
Mari: palace, 50–52, 60, 84; prophetic texts, 92–95, 97, 101, 182; temple throne, 57

Marinatos, Spyridon, 177, 198n27, 201n31, 201n38, 220n43
marratu, 112
Mashu, Mount, 112, 142
matriarchy, 151, 157, 218nn5–6
Matrunna, princess, seal of, 132
Matz, Friedrich, 10, 53, 78–79, 81, 204n50, 209–10n15
Medinet Habu, 42, 203n26
Megiddo ivory, 174, 176
Mesopotamia: cosmology, 112, 142, 150; cultic nudity, 38; fringed mantle, 19, 21; goddesses, 151, 166; and Near East *koine,* 7, 107; *proskynesis,* 183; Storm God and dragon, 171, 179, 222n46; sun and palm, 62; temples, 66; throne room, 50
Messenia ring, 83
Mettinger, Tryggve, 87, 211n17, 220n3
Minet el Beida ivory, 188–89
Minoan-Mycenaean, 6, 9
Minos, 1, 12–13, 32, 52–53
Mitanni, 4, 8, 24, 188, 193; seal, 132
Mochlos ring, 160–61
monotheism, 151
moon: on Akkadian stele, 79; in Egyptian mythology, 116; on Hittite seal, 118; ideogram, 31, 160; on Mycenaean ring, 127–29, 153, 155; on Poros ring, 218–19n13; on Psychro tablet, 108; on Syrian seals, 61; on Syrian stele, 80; on Tiryns ring, 28, 61
Moran, William, 4, 188
Moses, 13, 84
Mot, 171, 183
Mother Goddess, 151, 158, 161, 167, 191
Mother of Gods, 159, 166, 191
Mother of the Mountains, 83
mountain. *See* cosmic mountain
muhhum, 93
mukar, 54

Nabonidus, king, 80
nagu, 112
Naram Sin, king, 79, 205
navy, 4–5, 52
Naxos seal, 63–64
Nerik, 157
New Palace period: archaeological evidence, 34, 60; chronology, 3, 219n14; rings from, 184, 221n31; split rosette, 135; vases from, 216n10
Niemeier, Wolf-Dietrich: fresco restoration, 17; Knossos ring epiphany, 209–10n15; Minoan chronology, 219n14; *pithos* on ring, 211n17; rosette, 215n2, 216n10; throne room architecture, 53
Nikkal, sanctuary of, 69
Nilsson, Martin P.: on altars, 212n10; Athens ring interpretation, 176; dancer on rings, 11n39; double axe, 114, 116, 162; epiphany scenes, 78, 88, 99; fertility goddess, 166; Great Goddess, 218n11; Hagia Triada sarcophagus, 46, 204n50; Harvester's Vase, 201n31; hunting god, 167–68; incurved altar, 136; Knossos ring interpretation, 209n15; larnakes, 140; Mycenae ring interpretation, 153; primitive religion, 151; sacral horns, 106, 108, 110; shrine typology, 76; tree cult, 102
Nimrud, 29
Nineteenth Dynasty, 24, 42, 110, 116, 173
Nineveh, 42, 75, 97, 101, 158
Ninurta, 42–43, 159, 171, 221n22, 221n25
Niqmaddu III-IV, king, 172
Nissinen, Martti, 93, 97, 101

oak tree, 72, 94–95, 99
Ocean, 112, 144
Odysseus, 143, 181, 211n30
Odyssey, 94–95, 143–44, 181, 217n16
Old Palace period, 3, 60, 69, 103–4
omega crown, 177–78, 222n43
omphalos, 95
opet feast, 22, 204n41
oval axe, 20
ox head, 116–21, 145, 181, 195

Pachyammos larnax, 147–48
palm, 55–65; and afterlife, 141, 143, 146–48; Asherah with, 47; and axe, 133–34; Cyprus seal, 155; Judah seal, 91; Leto with, 91; between mountain peaks, 109; Peloponnese ring, 165; Thera mural, 23

paradise, 57, 141, 143–44, 147, 149
Pardee, Dennis, 35, 203n18, 220n42
papa re, 12–13
Pax Minoica, 3, 199n32
Pelon, Olivier, 13
Penelope, 95, 144, 211n30
Persephone, 166
Persia, 5, 105, 184, 198
Persson, Axel W., 88, 176, 211n17
Pe(tt)iyarik, 187
Phaecia, 2, 217n16
Phaistos disc, 215n1–2
pharaoh: and boukephalion, 119; and chariot, 24–25; cultic robes, 36–37; at Heb-Sed festival, 177, 203n26; and Horus, 58; and Isis, 54, 65; at *opet* feast, 22; priest, 202n2; Syro-Palestinian seal, 175; vassalage, 4, 8, 198n20
Philistines, 92, 197n3
plumed crown, 14–18; Archanes ring, 96–97; Ashmolean ring, 181; figures lacking, 84; Hagia Triada sarcophagus, 41–42, 163; Naxos seal, 63; Peloponnese ring, 165; Thera mural, 23
Poros ring, 69, 100–101, 139, 153, 167–68, 218n13
po-t-ni-ja/po-ti-ni-ja, 47, 166
Poursat, Jean-Claude, 200n16
Powell, Barry, 106
primeval lotus. *See* lotus
Prince of Lilies fresco, 14–15, 17–18
prophecy, 86–102, 194; on Berlin ring, 181; in Hebrew bible, 47, 84, 112, 184; on Kato Syme ring, 177
proskynesis, 182–85
Proteus, 144
Pseira vessels, 121, 127, 195
Psychro: seal, 118; tablet, 108
Puduhepa, queen, 157
Pylos, 27, 34, 206n18
Pythia, 93

Qatna figure, 19–20, 201n24

Ramses II, pharaoh, 33, 175, 187, 201n37, 223n9
rbt, 47, 159, 166
Re, 62, 65, 187–88, 223n11
regeneration: Arthur Evans and, 151; double axe and, 121–23, 134, 149–50; on Hagia Triada sarcophagus, 204n50; lotus and, 120; solar deity and, 65; sun disc and, 129; underwater and, 147
Reshep, 35, 169–71, 191, 221n16
Rethemiotakis, George, 139, 212n46, 217n4, 218–19n13
Reusch, Helga, 52–54, 58, 60, 135, 202n46
Rhea, 151, 191
Rieu, E. V., 144
rosette, 131–39, 194–95; on axe, 121–22, 129; on Chania ring, 76; flowery meadow interpretation, 204n49; on Hittite silver cup, 45; invention of, 189; on Knossos ring, 73; on Knossos ring impression, 127–28; in Knossos throne room, 2; at Mycenae, 202n47; with palm, 60; on Poros ring, 69; as royal emblem, 27–29; on Senmut tomb mural, 117; and solar goddess, 161–66; on Syrian seals, 81; on Thebes ring, 68
rpum, 46

sacerdotalism, 6, 32
sacrality, 35–37, 39, 43–44, 48, 54
sacred horns. *See* horns of consecration
sacred mansion, 139
sacred tree: of Asherah, 47; cult standard, 62–63; on Hagia Triada sarcophagus, 46; and house of god, 72–73, 83, 87; on Syro-Palestinian seal, 91, 93
Samuel, 92, 94, 97
Sapunu, Mount, 34
Saul, 97
scale dress, 21–22, 36–37
scarab seals, 19–20, 24, 117, 129–30, 197n9, 214n12
Schroer, Sylvia, 19, 201n24
Scylla, 179
Sellopoulo ring, 89, 99–100
Senacherib, king, 85
Senmut, tomb of, 4, 117–18
Serapis, 186
Seth, 116, 171–72, 179–80, 187–88

Seti I, pharaoh, 38, 117, 201
Shaft Graves, 22, 24–25, 29, 136
Shamash: on Akkadian seals, 109–11, 115; in Babylonian hymns, 124; on Hammurabi stele, 79–80; as male diety, 65; rosette, 134; on sacred rock, 73, 213n23; solar bark, 160; throne offering, 57
Shantash, 171
Shapsh(u): and Kaphtor, 1–2; and royal ideology, 65, 69; and underworld, 124, 160, 165–66, 171, 220n42
Sharuma, 157, 169–70
Shaushga, 188
Shaw, Maria, 18, 137, 207n7, 208n9, 208n20
Shirmegi, Mount, 145
Sidouri, 124
Sin, 80
sistrum, 21
Siteia mould, 162–63
Sklavokampos, 26, 198n27, 201n42
solar disc. *See* sun disc
solar goddess, 151–66, 194; Near East equivalences, 47–49, 188, 191; omega crown, 177–78; in palace 62, 65, 72; queen and, 97; sacred tree and, 91; split rosette, 136; and Storm God, 167, 181, 185
Solomon, 8, 34, 47, 57, 84
sphinx, 14–17, 42, 64, 200n16
split rosette. *See* rosette
Storm God, 167–85; festival of, 36, 38, 43–46, 53–55; on Malatya relief, 157–58, 190; and mother goddess, 166, 191, 194; on Syrian seal, 155–56
sun disc, 194–95; and double axe, 125, 129; and Hathor, 47, 116; and lions, 138; on Malatya relief, 158; on Megiddo ivory, 176; and mountain peaks, 107; and ox head, 117–20; on Palaikastro larnax, 144; on Persian stele, 105; and rosette, 132–34; in seascape, 124–25; and solar goddess, 161–62; on Syrian seals, 16, 61–62; on Thebes ring, 153; on Tiryns ring, 28
sun goddess. *See* solar goddess
symbol. *See* ideogram
syncretism, 186
Syria: ankh, 123; Egyptianizing seals, 14, 16; headdress, 30; Kaphtor and, 197n2; king and goddess, 81; mantle with seam, 19–21, 84; and Minoan god, 168–71, 173; mountain peaks, 107; Nabonidus stele, 80; and Near East *koine,* 1, 5, 122; ox head, 119; palm, 60–65; rosette, 132, 134; seated goddess, 155–57, 188; sphinx, 200n16; Storm God, 179–80

Tamuz, 88, 167
Tarrumannuma, 69
tawannana, 46–47, 49
Teissier, Beatrice, 62, 134, 216n7
Tell el Dab'a, 6, 13, 135, 173–74, 193
temple tomb, 46, 140
Terqa, 93
Teshub, 171
Thebes, 34, 93; ring, 68, 70, 153–54, 161
Thera: independence of, 199n46; mural, 23, 177; volcano of, 5, 198n27, 219n14
Thomassen, Einar, 186
throne room, 50–65, 202n46; griffin in, 52, 58, 60–63, 143; at Pylos, 34; split rosette in, 27, 52, 131, 135
Thucydides, 52
Tiryns ring, 27–28, 69, 99, 152, 161–62
tree sanctuary, 72–73, 87
Trgz, Mount, 145
tripartite: gate, 67, 77; shrine, 208n13
Tudhaliya IV, king, 48, 87, 219n20
Tukulti Ninurta I, king, 42–43
Tushratta, 8, 188
Tutankhamun, 38, 120, 138, 201n41
Tuthmosis III, 4, 6, 118, 193, 198n30
Tylor, Edward, 86
Tyre, 8

Uehlinger, Christoph, 173
Ugarit: Athirat, 159–61, 219n21; bow contest, 222n58; deified king, 46; house of god, 69; mantles, 201n24; matrilineality, 218n6; Minet el Beida ivory, 187–89; mountain peaks, 145; and Near East *koine,* 2, 4; purification ritual, 55, 57; queen, 47; sacrificial

texts, 32–35, 39, 44, 48, 72; seals from, 62, 119; stone and tree, 94–95; Storm God, 171–72, 179, 182–83; sun goddess, 65, 124, 165–66; texts surviving from, 10; throne, 206n28, 207n8
underworld: chapel to, 205n3; double axe in, 124–26, 129; gate to, 110–13, 145, 150; Storm God, 171; sun in, 46, 48, 163–66, 189, 194
Utnapishtim, 111, 142, 144, 147, 217n16

Van de Mieroop, Marc, 4, 8, 190, 209n5, 211n20
Van den Hout, Theo, 36
Van Gennep, Arnold, 36, 203n27
Vapheio: cups, 42; oval axes, 20; ring, 96, 119–20; seals, 21, 108–9
vassalage, 4–6, 8, 13, 184, 198n20
Vassilika Anogeia larnax, 147–48
volcano. *See* Thera

wanax, 34
Warren, Peter, 3, 210n5, 211n15
Watrous, Vance, 76, 106, 209n43, 214n7, 217n4
waz, 120–21
weapon(s), 172, 179–82; cult of, 222n62; on Hagia Triada ring, 221n34; in Hittite text, 4; on Knossos ring impression, 177; on Palaikastro ring, 173; on Syrian seal, 155
weres, 137
West, Martin L., 5
Wilkinson, Richard, 116, 138
Winter, Irene, 85
Winter, Urs, 200n23, 201n24, 219n16
Wyatt, Nicolas: *Baal Cycle* poet, 172; Babylonian map, 112; deity classification, 185, 223n70; on historiography, 9; king and weapons, 182; matrilineality, 218n6; queen's role, 47, 157, 160; sacrality, 35–36, 203n18, 206n19

Yahweh, 34, 172, 179
Yam, 159–60, 173, 179
Yazilikaya reliefs: artistic exaggeration, 188, 219n16; bulls, 214n19; god and king, 30; goddess and son, 157–58, 169–70; mountain god, 109

Zakros: pottery dating, 198n27; rhyton, 58–59, 66–68; ring impressions, 56, 97–99, 182–85
Zeus, 99–100, 113, 171–72
Zimrilim, king: Kaphtor and, 215n3; palace 51, 69; prophetic texts, 92, 95; and Storm God, 182; throne, 57

NANNO MARINATOS is professor of classics at the University of Illinois, Chicago. She is daughter of the archaeologist Spyridon Marinatos and, like her father, has worked for a very long time on the subject of Minoan culture. Her special field is history of ideas in Minoan and Greek religion. Her books include *Minoan Religion: Ritual, Image, and Symbol*; *Minoan Sacrificial Ritual*; *Greek Sanctuaries* (co-edited with R. Hägg); and *The Goddess and the Warrior.* Her latest book (co-authored with M. Bietak and C. Palyvou) is *Taureador Scenes in Tell el-Dab'a (Avaris) and Knossos.*

The University of Illinois Press
is a founding member of the
Association of American University Presses.

University of Illinois Press
1325 South Oak Street
Champaign, IL 61820-6903
www.press.uillinois.edu